KT-415-351

Microsoft®
Word 2000
At a
Glance

Microsoft Press

Microsoft Word 2000 At a Glance

PUBLISHED BY
Microsoft Press
A Division of Microsoft Corporation
One Microsoft Way
Redmond, Washington 98052-6399

Library of Congress Cataloging-in-Publication Data
Joyce, Jerry, 1950–

    Microsoft Word 2000 At a Glance / Jerry Joyce and Marianne Moon.
      p.   cm.
    Includes index.
    ISBN 1-57231-940-2
    1. Microsoft Word.   2. Word processing. I. Moon, Marianne. II. Title.
    Z52.5.M52J69   1999
    652.5'5369--dc21   98-48187
                                             CIP

Printed and bound in the United States of America.

1 2 3 4 5 6 7 8 9 WCWC 4 3 2 1 0 9

Distributed in Canada by ITP Nelson, a division of Thomson Canada Limited.

A CIP catalogue record for this book is available from the British Library.

Microsoft Press books are available through booksellers and distributors worldwide. For further information about international editions, contact your local Microsoft Corporation office, or contact Microsoft Press International directly at fax (425) 936-7329. Visit our Web site at mspress.microsoft.com.

Acquisitions Editors: Kim Fryer, Susanne M. Forderer   **Technical Editor:** Moon Joyce Resources
Project Editor: Jenny Moss Benson   **Manuscript Editor:** Marianne Moon

Dedicated with love to Zuzu Abeni Krause.
Welcome to the family...welcome to the world.

Contents

Start Word when Windows starts.

See page 8.

Print your document.
See page 24.

New2000

Favorite fruit:
- Apples
- Oranges
- Bananas
- Cherries
- Grapes

Create a custom
bulleted list.
See page 39.

*"What do
those squiggles
mean?"*

Ther are alternitives.
There are alternatives.

See pages 47–48.

Create a memo.
See page 62.

6 Creating a Long Document — 85

"What are styles?"

See page 77.

Print an envelope.
See page 82.

Find items in documents.
See pages 96–97.

Create a table of contents.
See page 108.

"How do I insert accented characters?"

See page 120.

Figure 1. Resident of the study area

Create a caption.
See page 129.

"How does the Clipboard work?"

See page 141.

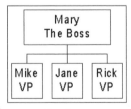

Mary
The Boss

| Mike VP | Jane VP | Rick VP |

Create an organization chart.
See page 149.

Add borders and
shading to tables.
See page 162.

9   Putting Pictures into Your Document   173

10   Desktop Publishing   187

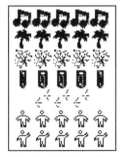

Add a picture
from a scanner.
See page 176.

Create artistic borders.
See page 200.

Create drawings
with AutoShapes.
See page 202.

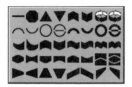

Turn text into art.
See page 218.

*"How do I create
hyperlinks?"*

See pages 230–234.

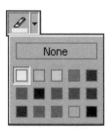

Highlight text in color.
See page 238.

"Can I compare documents on the screen?"

See page 250.

Create a Web page.
See page 258.

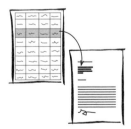

Create form letters.
See page 274.

Insert personalized
messages into merged
documents.
See page 294.

Choose an
Office Assistant.
See page 309.

Acknowledgments

This book is the result of the combined efforts of a team of people whose work we trust and admire and whose friendship we value highly. Kari Fera, our talented typographer, meticulously laid out the complex design; no detail was too small to escape her eagle-eyed scrutiny. Herb Payton refined and produced the interior graphics and then cheerfully reworked them as the inevitable interface changes occurred. Sue Bishop and Judith Joyce provided the hand-drawn art for us, and we're happy to have their distinctive sketches in our book. We've worked with Alice Copp Smith on many other books. Alice does so much more than proofread: her gentle and witty chiding on countless yellow sticky notes makes us groan but always teaches us to write better. We thank them all for their exceptional work and their good-humored patience under unpredictable deadlines.

At Microsoft Press, first and foremost we thank Lucinda Rowley for making it possible for us to write this book and our previous books in the *At a Glance* series. Many thanks also to Jenny Moss Benson, Kim Fryer, Kristen Weatherby, Susanne Forderer, Kevin Coomes, Mary DeJong, Jim Kramer, and Bill Teel, all of whom provided help and valuable advice along the way.

On the home front, Roberta Moon-Krause, Rick Krause, and Zuzu Abeni Krause allowed their puppies, Baiser and Pierre, to roam freely on our virtual and literal desktops, and to grace some of our pages with their furry little images.

About This Book

Microsoft Word 2000 At a Glance is for anyone who wants to get the most from Microsoft Word with the least amount of time and effort. Do you write one letter a week or hundreds? Are your documents simply a few lines of text or are they complex productions with graphics and tables, put together by several authors? Whether your documents are printed, shared on a network, e-mailed, or published as Web pages on the Internet or on a company intranet, you'll find this book to be a straightforward, easy-to-read reference tool. With the premise that Word should work for you, not you for it, this book's purpose is to help you get your work done quickly and efficiently so that you can get away from the computer and live your life.

No Computerese!

Let's face it—when there's a task you don't know how to do but you need to get it done in a hurry, or when you're stuck in the middle of a task and can't figure out what to do next, there's nothing more frustrating than having to read page after page of technical background material. You want the information you need—nothing more, nothing less—and you want it now! *And* it should be easy to find and understand.

That's what this book is all about. It's written in plain English—no technical jargon and no computerese. No single task in the book takes more than two pages. Just browse through a relevant section or look up a task in the index or the table of contents, turn to the page, and there's the information, laid out step by step and accompanied by illustrations that add visual clarity. You don't get bogged down by the whys and wherefores: just follow the steps, look at the illustrations, and get your work done with a minimum of hassle.

Occasionally, when the procedure you're working on has a "See Also" in the left column, you might need to turn to another page for some related information. That's because there's a lot of overlap among tasks, and we didn't want to keep repeating ourselves. We've also added some useful tips here and there, and thrown in a "Try This" once in a while, but by and large we've tried to remain true to the heart and soul of the book, which is that the information you need should be available to you at a glance.

Useful Tasks...

Whether you use Word 2000 for work, school, personal correspondence, or some of each, we've tried to pack this book with procedures for everything we could think of that you might want to do, from the simplest tasks to some of the more esoteric ones. The book also describes some tasks that you might not have realized you wanted to accomplish or that you didn't know you could do in Word. Try them out, and you'll probably find ways to have Word do even more of your work for you.

...And the Easiest Way To Do Them

Another thing we've tried to do in *Microsoft Word 2000 At A Glance* is find and describe the easiest way to accomplish a task. Word often provides a multitude of methods to achieve a single end result—which can be daunting or delightful, depending on the way you like to work. If you tend to stick with one favorite and familiar approach, we think the methods described in this book are the way to go. If you like trying out alternative techniques, go ahead! The intuitiveness of Word invites exploration, and you're likely to discover ways of doing things that you think are easier or that you like better than ours. If you do, that's great! It's exactly what the designers of Word had in mind when they provided so many alternatives.

A Quick Overview

This book isn't meant to be read in any particular order. It's designed so that you can jump in, get the information you need, and then close the book and keep it near your computer until the next time you need to know how to get something done. But that doesn't mean we scattered the information about with wild abandon. If you were to read the book from front to back, you'd find a logical progression from the basic tasks to the more advanced ones. Here's a quick overview.

First, we're assuming that Word is already installed on your computer as part of Microsoft Office 2000. If it's not, the Windows Installer makes installation so simple that you won't need our help anyway. So, unlike many computer books, this one doesn't start out with installation instructions and a list of system requirements. However, if you want to install additional Word or Office components or remove the ones you never use, turn to "Adding or Removing Components" on page 306 for the information you need. (If Word is installed on its own without the other Office 2000 programs, you can still use everything in this book except the instructions for those tasks that incorporate material from other Office components.)

Sections 2 through 4 of the book cover some of the basic tasks you can use to produce professional-looking documents: starting, saving, reopening, and closing a Word document; entering, editing, and formatting text; using special formatting for certain types of paragraphs; using Word's proofreading tools and dictionaries to check your spelling and grammar and improve your hyphenation and word usage (even if you're working in more than one language); and setting up your page layout.

Sections 5 through 9 describe tasks that are bit more technical but are really useful: using Word's templates and wizards to create letters, memos, and other frequently used documents; using the power of styles for speed and consistency; working with tables, running heads, footnotes, and lists; incorporating material from other programs; combining several documents into one; and inserting pictures, clip art, and other graphics elements into your documents. If you think these tasks sound complex, rest assured that they're not; Word makes them so easy that you'll sail right through them.

Section 10 is all about desktop publishing: you'll feel your creative juices flowing as you use the simple techniques we describe to create artistic borders, backgrounds, watermarks, drop caps, pull quotes, captions, margin notes, and drawings; flow text into columns or around objects; and transform ordinary text into eye-popping art with WordArt.

Sections 11 and 12 are all about collaborating with your coworkers and reaching out beyond your computer: communicating electronically using e-mail, and sharing documents by circulating them on line for comments from your colleagues; using *hyperlinks*, or jumps, in your documents to access other documents or Web pages; adding special effects such as sound, video, and animated text for online viewing; and expanding your horizons by creating and publishing your own Web pages on the Internet or on your company's intranet.

Section 13 shows you how to use Word's power to automate many of your everyday tasks: let Word keep track of document information for you; use Word's mail merge feature to create mass mailings; learn some simple ways to make fields work for you; and set Word's Auto-Format and AutoCorrect features so that they do your bidding.

Last but not least, Section 14 lets you take control of Word by customizing almost everything: create your own commands, customize menus, add tools to toolbars, and so on. You'll also learn how to speed up Word if it's running too slowly, and how to use diagnostic programs to fix any bad behavior.

What's New?

Microsoft Word 2000 has quite a few new features, as well as many older features that have been substantially improved. If you're familiar with an earlier version of Word, the first big change you'll notice in Word 2000 is that each document is contained in its own window rather than in separate panes inside a single window. As you explore Word further, you'll realize that it's even smarter than it used to be. It will not only point out your spelling errors and suggest any correct alternative spellings but—without consulting you—it will insert the proper spelling of any unambiguous words directly from a dictionary. With the necessary Office tools installed on your computer, you can work with different languages in your documents; Word will detect which language is being used and will use the appropriate proofing tools and dictionaries for that language. It's always been easy to customize Word, but now Word can automatically customize itself, adapting its menus and toolbars based on the way you use Word and on the tools and commands you use most frequently.

Word 2000 is also a much more powerful program for working on line and on the Internet. Now you can create a document with *frames,* which make it possible for you to display more than one document in an online page. Far from being only a starting point in creating a Web page, Word 2000 now provides tools that let you create impressive Web pages and post them directly to your Web server.

There are many other improvements and new features in Word 2000. We've identified both the new and the improved features with this **New**2000 icon. You'll see the icon as you scan the table of contents at the beginning of the book and also in the section contents on the opening page of each section.

A Final Word (or Two)

We had three goals in writing this book:

◆ Whatever you *want* to do, we want the book to help you get it done.

◆ We want the book to help you discover how to do things you *didn't* know you wanted to do.

◆ And, finally, if we've achieved the first two goals, we'll be well on the way to the third, which is for our book to help you *enjoy* doing your work with Word. We think that's the best gift we could give you to thank you for buying our book.

We hope you'll have as much fun using *Microsoft Word 2000 At a Glance* as we've had writing it. The best way to learn is by *doing,* and that's how we hope you'll use this book.

Jump right in!

2

Jump Right In

You can use Microsoft Word as a word processor or as a multifaceted *thought processor*. Word was designed to be either or both, and you can choose how you want to use its multitude of tools and features. You can stick with the basics or you can jump right in and go exploring—opening menus and drop-down lists, clicking buttons, turning options on and off to see what happens, and so on. You'll learn a lot about Word and the way it works by simply trying to accomplish a task.

This section covers many of the basic skills that you'll use every day. If you're not familiar with Word, step through these first few tasks and see how easily you can produce really professional-looking documents. Once you realize how intuitive Word is, you'll find it easy and rewarding to explore and try things out—in other words, to learn by doing.

If you try one of the more advanced tasks and you get stuck in some way, you'll find the answers to most of your questions in other sections of this book, or in Word's Help system. Even if you never try any advanced tasks and never read the rest of this book, you'll have learned the basics, and Word as a "smart typewriter" will make your life that much easier. But Word really shines as a thought processor. Try it. And read this book!

Microsoft Word at a Glance

Microsoft Word has many faces and can be customized in countless ways. Shown below is an unmodified, generic view of Word. We've identified many of the screen elements for you on this page and on the facing page. It's a good idea to explore Word's interface as you look at these two pages. For example, open all the menus

and familiarize yourself with the names of the commands. If you're not sure what the buttons on the toolbars are used for, point to one of them and, in a moment or two, you'll see a *ScreenTip* that tells you the button's name and usually gives you a pretty good idea of the tool's function.

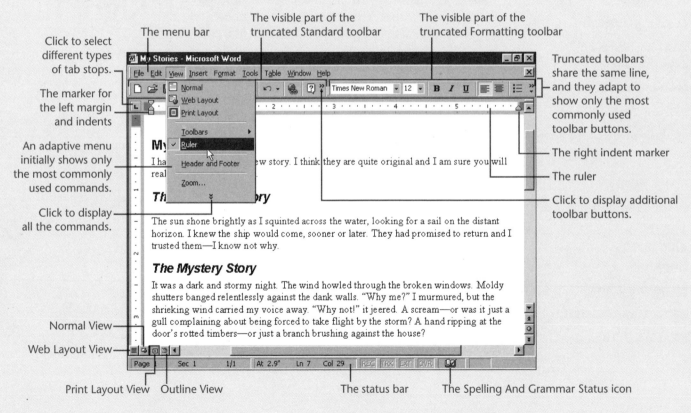

Click to select different types of tab stops.

The menu bar

The visible part of the truncated Standard toolbar

The visible part of the truncated Formatting toolbar

The marker for the left margin and indents

Truncated toolbars share the same line, and they adapt to show only the most commonly used toolbar buttons.

An adaptive menu initially shows only the most commonly used commands.

The right indent marker

The ruler

Click to display all the commands.

Click to display additional toolbar buttons.

Normal View

Web Layout View

Print Layout View   Outline View

The status bar

The Spelling And Grammar Status icon

The picture below shows the Word interface after it's been customized. You can see more toolbars, including a floating toolbar, and many toolbar buttons that were hidden in the picture on the facing page. You'll find all you ever wanted to know about toolbars in "Using Toolbars" on page 16, "Word's Most Useful Toolbars" on pages 18–19, and "Word's Dynamic Menus and Toolbars" on page 42. The pictures on these two pages show only some of the *many* ways you can view Word's interface. Turn to "So Many Ways to View It" on page 64 to see some of Word's other faces.

2

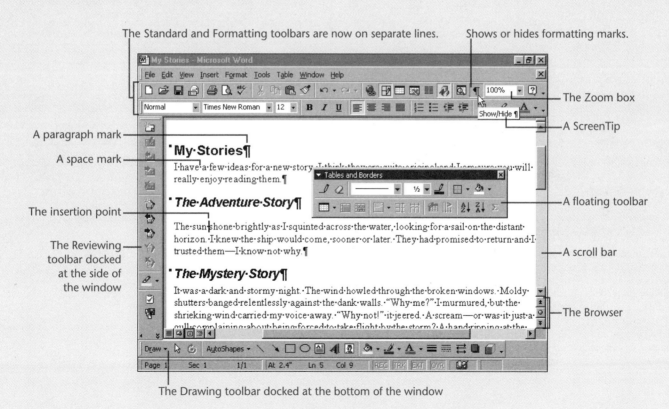

The Standard and Formatting toolbars are now on separate lines.

Shows or hides formatting marks.

The Zoom box

A ScreenTip

A paragraph mark

A space mark

The insertion point

The Reviewing toolbar docked at the side of the window

A floating toolbar

A scroll bar

The Browser

The Drawing toolbar docked at the bottom of the window

Creating a Document

The way you start Word depends on how it was installed. Like most Microsoft Windows programs, Word can be started in several different ways. If Word was installed as part of Microsoft Office 2000, you can start it from the Start menu, from the Office shortcut bar, or, if you're a bit adventurous, from the Office folder or from the Run command on the Start menu. Without Office, you might have fewer choices but you still have plenty of options. Word is ready— are you?

Start Word, and Enter Some Text

1 Start a new blank document.

   ◆ If Word isn't already running, click the Start button, point to Programs, and choose Microsoft Word.

   ◆ If Word is already running, click the New Blank Document button on the Standard toolbar.

2 Type your text. It appears on your screen at the left of the blinking insertion point.

3 When you reach the end of a line, continue typing. Word automatically moves, or *wraps,* your words onto the next line.

4 Press Enter only when you want to start a new paragraph.

Press Enter to start a new paragraph.

Word automatically wraps your text onto a new line.

The Show/Hide ¶ button

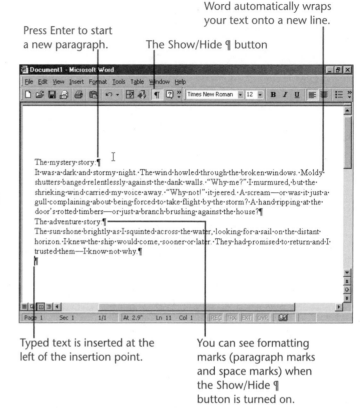

Typed text is inserted at the left of the insertion point.

You can see formatting marks (paragraph marks and space marks) when the Show/Hide ¶ button is turned on.

New document, new window. *When you open a new document, Word opens a new Word window for the document. To switch between open documents, click the name of the document you want on the Windows taskbar.*

No Office Assistant? *If the Office Assistant isn't installed or isn't turned on, and you attempt to close a document that contains unsaved changes, Word will display a dialog box asking you whether you want to save the changes.*

Save now, save often. *After you've named your document, click the Save button or press the key combination Ctrl+S periodically as you work. Word will save the document and all your changes under that document name, and the Save As dialog box won't keep popping up. It's so quick and easy that you can do it every few minutes, and you'll never have to worry about losing your work if the computer is accidentally shut off or if there's a power failure.*

Save the Document

1. Click the Save button on the Standard toolbar.

2. If necessary, navigate to the folder in which you want to store the document.

3. Type a name for the document in the File Name box if you don't want the name that Word proposes. Filenames can be as long as 250 characters and can include spaces, but you can't use the \ / * ? < > and | characters.

4. Click the Save button.

5. Work on the document, saving your work frequently.

6. When you've finished working on the document, click the Close button.

7. If there are unsaved changes in the document, click Yes or No when Word asks you whether you want to save the changes.

Click to navigate to these special locations…

…or navigate to any location.

Working with an Existing Document

Unless you always create short documents—letters, memos, and so on—you'll often need to continue working on a document that you started but didn't complete in an earlier session. You simply open the saved document, add more text, and then save and close the document again.

SEE ALSO

For information about selecting, deleting, replacing, and moving text, see "Editing Text" on page 12.

TIP

Quick opener. *If the document you want to open is one you used recently, it might be listed at the bottom of the File menu. If it is, click the document's name to open it.*

Open a Document

1. Click the Open button.

2. If necessary, navigate to find the folder that contains the document you want.

3. Select the document.

4. Click Open.

5. Add new text or edit the existing text.

6. Click the Save button on the Standard toolbar to save your changes.

Click to navigate to these special locations...

...or navigate to any location.

Click to change your view of the document and the information that's displayed.

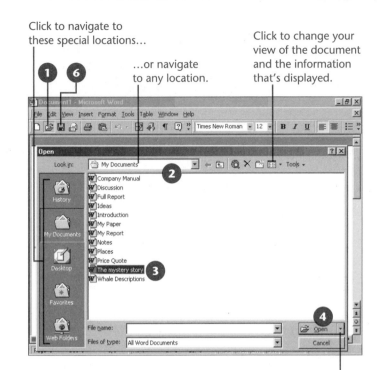

Click to open as a Read-Only document or as a copy.

Undoing Mistakes

If this cry sounds familiar—"Oh no, I didn't mean to do that!"—you can quickly undo the kinds of mistakes you make when you're working fast and you accidentally delete, replace, or move something.

TIP

Redo an Undo. *When you've undone one or more mistakes and then decided they weren't mistakes at all, you can restore them with the Redo button. It works exactly like the Undo button—just think of it as the Undo Undo button.*

SEE ALSO

For information about using toolbar buttons that aren't displayed, see "Using Toolbars" on page 16.

Undo One Mistake

 As soon as you realize the mistake, click the Undo button to restore the document to its original state.

Undo Several Mistakes

When you know that you've made several mistakes, you can

◆ Keep clicking the Undo button until you've returned the document to its original state.

◆ Click the down arrow at the right of the Undo button to see a list of actions that you can undo.

Text was accidentally deleted from here.

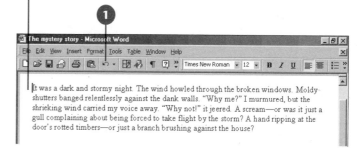

The deleted text is restored.

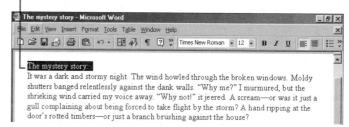

Click to see a list of Undo actions.

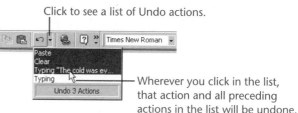

Wherever you click in the list, that action and all preceding actions in the list will be undone.

Editing Text

Whether you're creating a business letter, a financial report, or the Great American Novel, it's a sure bet that you're going to need to go back into your document and do some editing. Word provides a great variety of ways to edit. To edit existing content, you simply select it and make your changes.

TIP

Use Overtype. *To replace text without first selecting it, you can use Overtype mode. To turn it on, double-click the OVR button on the status bar. Double-click OVR again to turn off Overtype mode.*

SEE ALSO

For more information about different ways to select text, see "So Many Ways to Do It" on pages 14–15.

Select Text

1 Click at the beginning of the text to be selected.

2 Drag the mouse over all the text to be selected, and then release the mouse button.

The mystery story:
It was a dark and stormy night. The wind howled through the broken windows. Moldy shutters banged relentlessly against the dank walls. "Why me?" I murmured, but the shrieking wind carried my voice away. "Why not!" it jeered. A scream—or was it just a gull complaining about being forced to take flight by the storm? A hand ripping at the door's rotted timbers—or just a branch brushing against the house?

Delete Text

1 Press the Delete key.

The selected text has been deleted.

The mystery story:
It was a dark and stormy night. Moldy shutters banged relentlessly against the dank walls. "Why me?" I murmured, but the shrieking wind carried my voice away. "Why not!" it jeered. A scream—or was it just a gull complaining about being forced to take flight by the storm? A hand ripping at the door's rotted timbers—or just a branch brushing against the house?

Replace Text

1 Select the text to be replaced.

2 Type the new text.

The mystery story:
It was a dark and stormy night. Moldy shutters banged relentlessly against the dank walls. "Why me?" I murmured, but the shrieking wind carried my voice away. "Why not!" it jeered. A scream—or was it just a gull complaining about being forced to take flight by the storm? A hand ripping at the door's rotted timbers—or just a branch brushing against the house?

The mystery story:
It was a dark and stormy night. Ghostly shadows danced against the dank walls. "Why me?" I murmured, but the shrieking wind carried my voice away. "Why not!" it jeered. A scream—or was it just a gull complaining about being forced to take flight by the storm? A hand ripping at the door's rotted timbers—or just a branch brushing against the house?

Moving or Copying Text

Word uses a feature of Windows—the *Clipboard*—as a temporary holding area for text that you want to move or copy to another part of your document, to another document in the same program, or to a document in another program. You simply park your text on the Clipboard and then, when you're ready, you retrieve it and "paste" it into its new location. And once the text is stored on the Clipboard, you can paste it into any document as many times as you want.

SEE ALSO

For information about the many different ways to copy and move text, see "So Many Ways to Do It" on pages 14–15 and "Copying Information from Multiple Sources" on page 141.

Drag Text a Short Distance

1. Select the text to be moved.

2. Point to the selection and drag the text. (You'll see what looks like a little package attached to the pointer.)

3. Drop it at the new location.

Cut (or Copy) and Paste Text

1. Select the text to be moved or copied.

2. Click the Cut button or the Copy button.

3. Click at the location where you want to insert the text.

4. Click the Paste button.

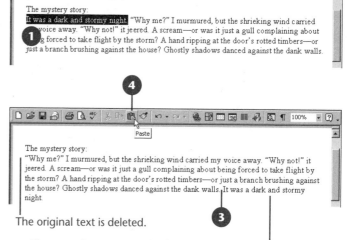

The Copy button

Cut

Paste

The original text is deleted.

The pasted text appears in the new location. (If you copied the text, the original text stays where it was and the copy appears in the new location.)

So Many Ways to Do It

Word offers you a variety of ways to do most things. You might, for example, be able to use a button, a menu item, a key combination, or a mouse-click to accomplish the same result. Why are there so many choices? Well, one reason is that we all work differently. Given several choices, we usually do some experimenting, find the way that works best for us and that we're most comfortable with, and then stick with it. Another reason is that certain methods work best in certain situations.

Two procedures that you'll be using frequently—selecting text and moving or copying text—can be accomplished using quite a few different methods, some of which might cause you some difficulty if you use them in the wrong situation. The tips we offer here will help you choose which method to use in which circumstances.

Try these common methods of selecting text and see which works best for you. Of course, there are other ways to select text, and, depending on whether and how you've customized Word, some selection methods might work a bit differently. For information about customizing Word, see Section 14, "Customizing Word," starting on page 305.

TEXT-SELECTION METHODS	
To do this	**Use this method**
Select characters in a word	Drag over the characters.
Select a word	Double-click the word.
Select several words	Drag over the words.
Select a sentence	Hold down the Ctrl key and click anywhere in the sentence.
Select a line of text	Move the pointer to the far left of the window and click when you see a right-pointing arrow.
Select a paragraph	Move the pointer to the far left of the window and double-click when you see a right-pointing arrow.
Select a long passage	Click at the beginning of the passage, double-click EXT on the status bar, click at the end of the passage, and double-click EXT on the status bar.
Select the entire document	Choose Select All from the Edit menu.

After you've selected the text, your next step might be to move it or copy it. Again, some methods are better than others, depending on the situation.

The process of moving or copying contents uses different tools, depending on what you want to do. When you use the F2 and Shift+F2 keys, the selected material is stored in Word's short-term memory, where it is remembered only until you paste it into another location or execute any other Word activity.

The Cut and Copy buttons on the Standard toolbar store the selected material on the very single-minded Windows Clipboard, from where you can retrieve the information once or numerous times. The information you've stored on the Windows Clipboard stays there until you replace it with another item or shut down Windows. The Windows Clipboard is more than just a holding area, though—it's also a pathway through which you can transfer your cut or copied information to other documents or programs. Although the *Windows* Clipboard stores only one item at a time, the *Office* Clipboard stores up to 12 items, which you can retrieve one at a time or all at once. For more information about the Office Clipboard, see "Copying Information from Multiple Sources" on page 141.

If all of this seems like an overwhelming number of ways to accomplish the same tasks, get ready for a shock—there are even more ways. If you really want to explore the full range of different ways to do these tasks, take a stroll through Word's Help and try out some of the other methods.

COPY OR MOVE METHODS	
To do this	**Use this method**
Move a short distance	Drag the selection to the new location.
Copy a short distance	Hold down the Ctrl key, drag the selection to the new location, and release the Ctrl key.
Move a long distance or to a different document or program	Click the Cut button, click at the new location, and click the Paste button. OR press Ctrl+X, click at the new location, and press Ctrl+V.
Copy a long distance or to a different document or program	Click the Copy button, click at the new location, and click the Paste button. OR press Ctrl+C, click at the new location, and press Ctrl+V.
Copy several items and insert all in one place	Click the Copy button, select the next item, click the Copy button again, and repeat to copy up to 12 items. Click at the new location and click the Paste All button on the Clipboard toolbar.
Move a long or short distance, preserving the Clipboard contents	Press the F2 key, click at the new location, and press Enter.
Copy a long or short distance, preserving the Clipboard contents	Press Shift+F2, click at the new location, and press Enter.

Using Toolbars

Word's toolbars are powerful assistants. Each toolbar (and there are *many* of them) contains the most common tools you'll need for a specific task. To save space and avoid clutter, Word sometimes hides some of the tools—generally those you use least—but you can easily display the hidden tools when you need them. Word normally displays the Standard and Formatting toolbars together on one line underneath the menu bar, but you can change the display of toolbars. Word will remember which ones you use and will display them each time you start the program.

SEE ALSO

For information about arranging toolbars on the screen and displaying all the buttons on a toolbar, see "Managing Toolbars" on page 310.

Display a Toolbar

1. Right-click anywhere in any toolbar or in the menu bar.

2. From the shortcut menu that appears, choose the toolbar to be displayed.

Click a checked toolbar to hide it.

Click an unchecked toolbar to display it.

Standard
Formatting
AutoText
Clipboard
Control Toolbox
Database
Drawing
Forms
Frames
Picture
Reviewing
Tables and Borders
Visual Basic
Web
Web Tools
WordArt

Customize...

Use a Toolbar Button

1. Point to a toolbar button.

2. If you're not sure whether this is the tool you need, hold the mouse steady until a ScreenTip (the name of the item you're pointing to) appears.

3. Click the button if the tool is the one you want, or point to another button.

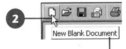

New Blank Document

A ScreenTip identifies the tool.

Escape! *To close a drop-down list or a drop-down button without choosing an item, press the Esc key. Press the Esc key a second time to cancel the selection of the list or button.*

Cool combo. *There is a variant of the drop-down list— it's called a combo box. In this form, the list might not include all the possible choices. If you see what you want in the list, you can choose it; if not, you can type your choice in the box. The Font Size list is an example of a combo box—it doesn't show a 95-point font size, but if you select some text and type 95 in the box, you'll get 95-point type (provided the font you're using supports that size).*

Drag the title bar. *Whenever a drop-down button has a little bar at the top of the list, you can drag the bar away from its button to change the list into a stand-alone toolbar.*

Use a Drop-Down List

1. Click the down arrow at the right of the list box to open the list.

2. Click the item you want from the list.

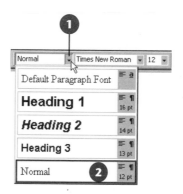

Use a Drop-Down Button

1. Click the down arrow at the right of the button.

2. Click the setting you want. The setting is used, and the button changes to that setting.

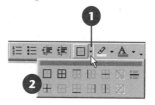

Show Hidden Buttons

1. Click the down arrow at the end of the toolbar.

2. Click the tool you want to use.

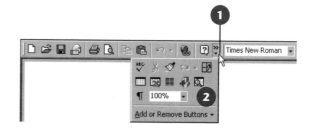

Word's Most Useful Toolbars

Word's most useful and most widely used toolbars are the Formatting and Standard toolbars. In most cases, the picture on the tool's button or the word in the list gives you an idea of what the tool does. If not, just point to the tool you're not sure of and in a second or two you'll see an identifying ScreenTip. Once you're familiar with the Standard and Formatting toolbars, you're just a mouse-click or two away from executing most of Word's actions.

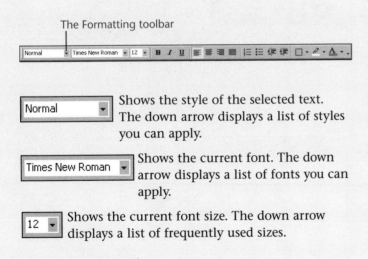

The Formatting toolbar

Normal Shows the style of the selected text. The down arrow displays a list of styles you can apply.

Times New Roman Shows the current font. The down arrow displays a list of fonts you can apply.

12 Shows the current font size. The down arrow displays a list of frequently used sizes.

B Turns boldface character emphasis on or off.

I Turns italic character emphasis on or off.

U Turns character underlining on or off.

Left-aligns the current paragraph.

Center-aligns the current paragraph.

Right-aligns the current paragraph.

Justifies the current paragraph.

Adds or removes automatic list numbering.

Adds or removes automatic list bullets.

Removes one increment of indenting from the current paragraph.

Adds one increment of indenting to the current paragraph.

Adds or removes borders. The down arrow displays a menu of different types of borders you can apply.

Turns line highlighting on or off. The down arrow displays a menu of colors you can apply.

Changes text color. The down arrow displays a menu of colors you can apply.

The Standard toolbar

Opens a new blank document.

Opens an existing document.

Saves the document.

Starts e-mail in Word.

Prints the document using default settings.

Displays the document in Print Preview.

Checks the selection or the document for errors in spelling or grammar.

Cuts the selection to the Windows and Office Clipboards and deletes it from the document.

Copies the selection to the Windows and Office Clipboards.

Pastes (inserts) the contents of the Windows Clipboard at the location you specify.

Copies formatting from the selection and applies the formatting to different material.

Undoes the last action. The down arrow displays a series of actions that can be undone.

Redoes the last action that was undone using the Undo button. The down arrow displays a series of actions that can be restored.

Inserts a jump (hyperlink) to a document or to another location.

Displays or hides the Tables And Borders toolbar.

Inserts a Word table. Drag in the drop-down menu to specify the number of rows and columns.

Inserts an Excel worksheet. Drag in the drop-down menu to specify the number of rows and columns.

Changes the number of columns in your text. Drag in the drop-down menu to specify the number of columns.

Displays or hides the Drawing toolbar.

Displays or hides the Document Map.

Displays or hides the nonprinting formatting marks in your document, including paragraph marks.

Changes the onscreen magnification of your document.

Displays the Office Assistant for on-the-spot help with any document.

Adding Character Emphasis

Sometimes you'll want to make a word or phrase stand out, by making it bold or italic or by adding underlining. With Word, you can apply this direct formatting when you're typing the text, or later as you edit it. Don't go overboard, though—too many different kinds of emphasis are more distracting than they are helpful.

Add Emphasis as You Type

1. Type your normal text as usual.

2. Click an emphasis button.

3. Type your emphasized text.

4. Click the emphasis button again to turn off the emphasis.

Add Emphasis as You Edit

1. Select the text you want to emphasize.

2. Click an emphasis button.

3. Click another emphasis button if you want to use additional emphasis.

Click to turn on italics. *I*   *I* 4 Click to turn off italics.

2

1 It was dark. The wind *howled* through the window.

3

1 It was dark. The wind *howled* through the window.

2

Underline—use sparingly to avoid their being mistaken for hyperlinks.

Italic—use to add emphasis to words or phrases in body text.

Bold—use to add emphasis, especially to headings.

TIP

Copycat. *Format Painter also copies and applies font and font-size information.*

TIP

Smart Painter. *You don't need to select a whole phrase, or even a whole word, when you're using Format Painter; selecting just one character gives Format Painter enough information to do its job.*

TIP

Use the keyboard. *To quickly apply or remove emphasis using the keyboard, press Ctrl+B for bold, Ctrl+I for italic, and Ctrl+U for underline.*

SEE ALSO

For information about using and displaying hidden toolbar buttons, see "Using Toolbars" on page 16.

For information about using character styles, see "Creating an Inline Heading" on page 194.

For information about setting font characteristics in the Font dialog box, see "Making Text Stand Out" on page 236.

Copy the Emphasis

1. Select the text that has the emphasis you want to copy.

2. Click the Format Painter button.

3. Drag the special Format Painter mouse pointer over the text you want to copy the emphasis to, and then release the mouse button.

Remove the Emphasis

1. Select the text.

2. Click to turn off any of the pressed emphasis buttons.

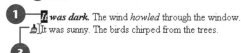

It was dark. The wind *howled* through the window.
It was sunny. The birds chirped from the trees.

Pressed buttons show what emphasis is applied to the selected text.

It was dark. The wind *howled* through the window.
It was sunny. The birds chirped from the trees.

Changing Fonts

The shapes of the characters you type—and, indeed, the look of your entire document—are determined by the font you're using. Fonts (also called *typefaces*) come in a variety of shapes and forms, and some even give you pictures, rather than letters and numbers, as you type. Some fonts come with Windows, some with your printer, and many more with Word. You might also have fonts that came with other programs you've installed, and—if you want or need even more variety—you can download or purchase additional fonts or font packages.

SEE ALSO

For information about copying font characteristics, see "Copy the Emphasis" on page 21.

Change the Font as You Type

1. Type the text you want in the current font.

2. Choose a different font from the Font drop-down list.

3. Choose a different font size from the Font Size drop-down list.

4. Type some text in the new font and size.

5. Change back to the original font and size.

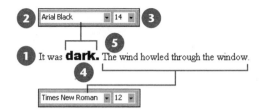

Change the Font as You Edit

1. Select the text you want to change.

2. Choose a different font from the Font drop-down list.

3. Choose a different font size from the Font Size drop-down list.

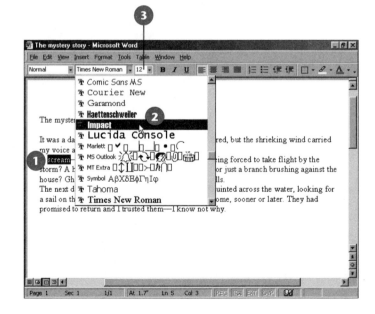

Using Standard Styles

Word provides a large selection of predefined paragraph formats, or *styles,* which you can use to create well-designed documents with consistent formatting. Many of Word's features—templates and automatic formatting are just two examples—use styles extensively. Styles are some of Word's most powerful tools, and to know them is to love them.

SEE ALSO

For information about designing your own paragraph styles, see "Creating Styles from Scratch" on page 74.

For information about making changes to existing styles, see "Modifying an Existing Style" on page 76.

Apply a Heading Style

1. Click in the paragraph you want to format. Make sure that you don't have any text selected.

2. Open the Style drop-down list box.

3. Select the heading style you want.

The names of the styles are shown in their fonts and font sizes.

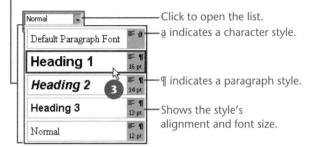

Click to open the list.

<u>a</u> indicates a character style.

¶ indicates a paragraph style.

Shows the style's alignment and font size.

Apply a Standard Style

1. Click in the paragraph or select the paragraph(s) you want to format. If you have selected any text, make sure the *entire* paragraph is selected.

2. Do either of the following:

   ◆ Open the Style drop-down list to select a style that's already being used in the document.

   ◆ Hold down the Shift key and open the Style drop-down list to see a list of all the available styles.

3. Select the style you want. (Keep scrolling—it can be a long list!)

Shows an example of the font and size for each style.

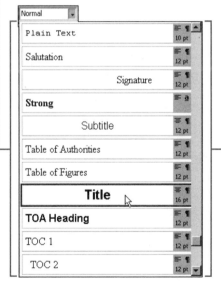

Indicates the paragraph alignment and font size.

2

Printing a Document

E-mail and Web documents are bringing the paperless office closer to reality, but the most common way to distribute a finished document is still to print it. Printing is mostly a job for Windows—Word prepares your document and then hands it off to Windows.

TIP

Printing pronto. *If you don't need to change any settings in the Print dialog box, you can quickly print a document by clicking the Print button on the Standard toolbar.*

SEE ALSO

For information about printing multiple pages on a single sheet of paper, see "Printing Two Pages on One Sheet" on page 221 and "Printing Thumbnails" on page 222.

Print a Document

1. Choose Print from the File menu.

2. Change the settings if necessary.

3. Click the Options button if you want to change which items in the document are to be printed, and click OK.

4. Click OK.

Select a printer from the list.

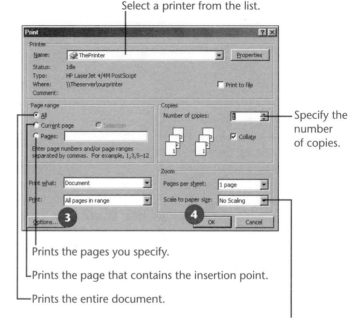

Specify the number of copies.

Prints the pages you specify.

Prints the page that contains the insertion point.

Prints the entire document.

Select a scaling size to print on paper that's a different size from the paper the document was originally set up for.

3

Improving the Look of Your Document

Different jobs require specialized tools and something to keep them in. In the days when doctors made house calls, they kept their pills and potions in big black bags. Carpenters and electricians keep their tools within easy reach on belts or aprons that they wear as they work. Microsoft Word, too, has the right tools for the task you're working on, all neatly arranged on *toolbars*. When you're not using a particular toolbar, you can put it away and use the tools from another toolbar. Word's tools are in the form of buttons and lists, and you can use them to accomplish a multitude of tasks.

You can use Word's tools to undo mistakes, change text alignment, create headings, change the style of one paragraph or many, add borders, and create a numbered or bulleted list as you're typing or convert text you've already typed into either kind of list. Give Word the word, and it does all sorts of helpful things behind the scenes as you're typing—corrects transposed letters, adds a capital letter to the first word in a sentence if you didn't do it, turns *tuesday* into *Tuesday* and *1st* into *1st*, and tells you when you've misspelled a word or used poor grammar. Word can do all this and more.

It's fun to experiment with different looks for your documents, and it's easy to keep trying new looks until you find the one you like.

Starting Anywhere on the Page

If you don't like the linear rules imposed by most word-processing programs—that is, starting the first line of text at the top left corner of the page, with subsequent paragraphs immediately below the first one—you no longer have to observe them. With Word's Click And Type feature, a double-click is all it takes to get you started at any position on the page *and* let you set the paragraph alignment at the same time. Word takes care of inserting all the necessary blank paragraph marks and tabs for you.

Choose a Starting Point

1. In Web Layout view or Print Layout view, move the mouse pointer to the location where you want to start your text. The mouse pointer changes into an alignment cursor.

2. Move the mouse pointer horizontally to select a paragraph alignment:

   ◆ Slightly in from the left side of the page for a left-aligned paragraph with a standard first-line indent

   ◆ To the center of the page for a center-aligned paragraph

   ◆ To the far right of the page for a right-aligned paragraph

   ◆ To the right side of a picture or other object for a paragraph whose text wraps around the picture or object

   ◆ To anywhere else for a left-aligned paragraph with the first line indented to the location of the mouse pointer

3. Double-click to set your starting point.

4. Type your text.

Turn on if you want to see formatting marks (paragraph marks, spacing marks, tabs, and so on).

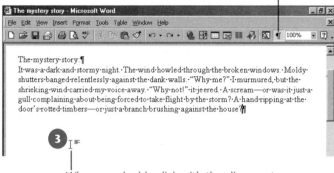

When you double-click with the alignment cursor...

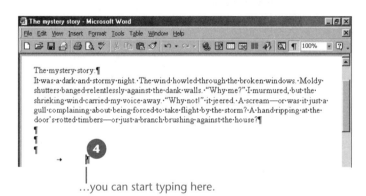

...you can start typing here.

Behind-the-Scenes Magic

You're typing as fast as you can, trying to meet one of those impossible deadlines. You type *teh* (your usual mistake when you're in a hurry) and, suddenly, it changes into *the*. Then, as if by magic, your straight quotation marks turn into nice curly ones, just like the ones typographers use. And as you type, a red squiggle appears under a misspelled word. A green squiggle appears under a couple of other words. What's going on?

These mysterious and delightful transformations are just a few examples of four features that Word can run behind the scenes while you're working: AutoCorrect, AutoFormat, and the Grammar and Spelling Checkers. As helpful as these features are, you can customize them so that they serve your purposes even better. Later we'll discuss some ways to do that, along with details of other timesaving features such as AutoText and AutoFormat tables. But right now, let's look at some of the automatic corrections Word can make for you.

Examples of AutoCorrect

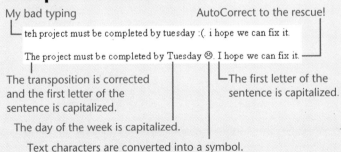

Examples of AutoFormat

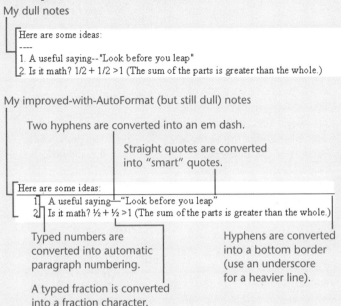

Examples of the Grammar Checker

My poor grammar

Is this not never a question?

Is this never a question?——My corrected grammar

Examples of the Spelling Checker

My poor spelling

Ther are alternivites to most situations.

There are alternatives to most situations.——My corrected spelling

Customizing Paragraphs

You create a new paragraph *and* apply formatting to the entire paragraph every time you press the Enter key— even if you don't add any text. The formatting information is stored in the paragraph mark—a usually invisible formatting mark at the end of the paragraph. By displaying paragraph marks, you can ensure that any formatting changes will apply to the entire paragraph. When you can see the paragraph mark, it's also less likely that you'll accidentally delete it and lose its formatting.

TIP

Where did that style come from? *If the paragraph format changes when you press Enter to start a new paragraph, you've encountered a sequence of paragraph styles in which a different style has been specified to follow the current paragraph style.*

Format as You Type

1. If paragraph marks are not displayed, click the Show/Hide ¶ button.

2. Press Enter to start a new paragraph.

3. Select the paragraph mark.

4. Use the buttons and lists on the toolbars to change the formatting.

5. Press the Home key to unselect (deselect) the paragraph mark.

6. Type your text.

7. Press Enter to start a new paragraph.

8. Do either of the following:

    ◆ Enter your text using the formatting you specified in the previous paragraph.

    ◆ Press Ctrl+Q to return the current paragraph to the original formatting and remove the formatting you added.

Paragraph indents

Numbered and bulleted paragraphs

Turn on…

Paragraph alignments

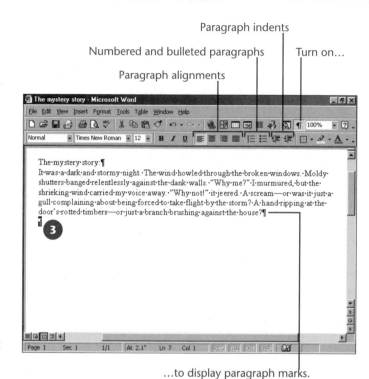

…to display paragraph marks.

TIP

Don't miss the mark! *You don't need to select the entire paragraph to apply paragraph formatting, but to apply any font settings to the entire paragraph you must include the paragraph mark in the selection. The easiest and safest method is to select the entire paragraph.*

SEE ALSO

For information about displaying toolbars and accessing hidden buttons, see "Using Toolbars" on page 16.

For information about saving special formatting as a style for later use, see "Creating Styles from Scratch" on page 74.

For information about working with a sequence of styles, see "Creating a Sequence of Styles" on page 78.

TIP

What's the key? *To see the key combinations that specify the same formatting as clicking the buttons, choose Customize from the Tools menu, and, on the Options tab, turn on the Show Shortcut Keys In ScreenTips check box. Click Close. Then point to a button and note the ScreenTip information.*

Format Existing Paragraphs

1 Select the entire paragraph or all the paragraphs that will have the same formatting.

2 Use the buttons and lists on the toolbars to change the formatting.

3 Press the Right arrow key to unselect (deselect) the paragraphs.

Combine Paragraphs

1 Move the insertion point to the end of the paragraph you want to combine with the next paragraph.

2 Press the Delete key.

3 Press the Spacebar to add a space.

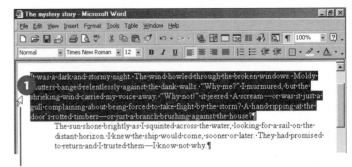

Double-click to select the entire paragraph. Double-click (without releasing the mouse button) and drag down to select multiple paragraphs.

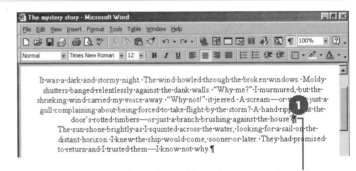

Deleting the paragraph mark combines the paragraphs and strips the paragraph formatting from the second paragraph. The combined paragraph uses the first paragraph's formatting.

Indenting Paragraphs

A paragraph is often indented to distinguish it from other paragraphs. There are four types of indent: left, right, first-line, and hanging. Left and right indents can be used together to create a *nested* paragraph for quotations or similar material. A first-line indent is used to distinguish a new paragraph from the previous one. A hanging indent indents every line of a paragraph except the first one.

Indent a Paragraph

1. If the ruler isn't displayed, choose Ruler from the View menu.

2. If the paragraph marks aren't displayed, click the Show/Hide ¶ button.

3. Click anywhere in the paragraph to be indented, or select the paragraph(s) you want to indent.

4. Click the Increase Indent button to increase the indent, or click the Decrease Indent button to move back to the previous indent.

The marker on the ruler shows the indent.

The Decrease Indent button

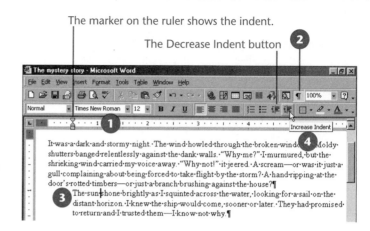

Nest a Paragraph

1. Drag the Left Indent marker to the location where you want the left indent.

2. Drag the Right Indent marker to the location where you want the right indent.

The Left Indent marker   The Right Indent marker

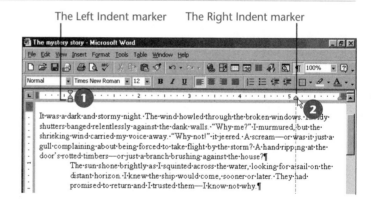

SEE ALSO

For information about creating and changing tab stops, see "Creating Tab Stops" on page 34.

TIP

Measured indents. *To specify exact measurements for indents, choose Paragraph from the Format menu, and specify the indents on the Indents And Spacing tab of the Paragraph dialog box.*

TIP

To indent or not to indent. *You'll notice that in most publications whose paragraphs have first-line indents, the first paragraph under a heading doesn't usually have an indent. That's because its placement indicates clearly that it's a new paragraph.*

TIP

The right marker. *If you're not sure which marker on the ruler is which, point to a marker and wait for the ScreenTip to identify it.*

Indent the First Line

1. Click in the paragraph that you want to have a first-line indent.

2. Drag the First Line Indent marker to the location where you want the first-line indent.

Create a Hanging Indent

1. Click in the paragraph that you want to have a hanging indent.

2. Drag the Hanging Indent marker to the location where you want all lines except the first to align.

Dragging the First Line Indent marker…

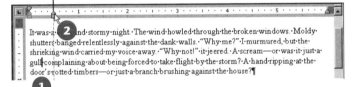

…indents only the first line.

Dragging the Hanging Indent marker…

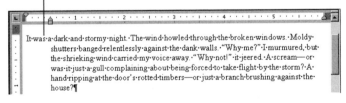

…indents all lines except the first.

Specifying Paragraph Alignment

Paragraph alignment controls how the lines of text in a paragraph are arranged. Each alignment has typical uses:

Left is the most commonly used and is the easiest to read.

Centered is used for short blocks of text, such as titles or invitations.

Right is used in limited instances—for captions that fall on the left side of an illustration, for example, or in some tables.

Justified is usually used in publications with columnar layouts—newspapers and magazines, for example.

TIP

Speedy alignment. *To quickly apply alignment from the keyboard, press Ctrl+L for left alignment, Ctrl+E for centered alignment, Ctrl+R for right alignment, or Ctrl+J for justified alignment.*

Choose an Alignment

1. Select a paragraph (or several paragraphs that are to have the same alignment).

2. Click an alignment button:
   - ◆ Align Left to start each line flush against the left margin
   - ◆ Center to center each line between the left and right margins
   - ◆ Align Right to end each line flush against the right margin
   - ◆ Justify to position the start and end of each line flush against the left and right margins

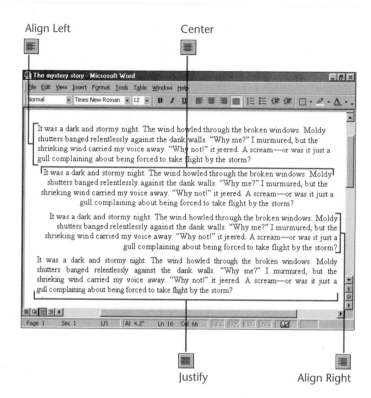

Align Left   Center

Justify   Align Right

Changing the Spacing Between Lines

The spacing between lines is the same throughout a paragraph. You can increase the spacing between the lines, and you can add extra space above or below a paragraph.

SEE ALSO

For more information about adding space before or after a paragraph, see "Creating Styles from Scratch" on page 74.

TRY THIS

I'll have a draft. *A draft copy of a document is usually double-spaced to allow room for editing or comments. To create a draft copy, save your document, press Ctrl+A to select the entire document, and then press Ctrl+2 to double-space the lines. Save the draft document using a different name, and then print the document.*

Change the Spacing

1. Click in a paragraph (or select several paragraphs that are to have the same line spacing).

2. Use the following key combinations to adjust the line spacing:

   ◆ Ctrl+0 (zero) for adding or removing a blank line before a paragraph

   ◆ Ctrl+1 for single-spaced lines

   ◆ Ctrl+5 for 1½-spaced lines

   ◆ Ctrl+2 for double-spaced lines

Press Ctrl+0 (zero) to add a blank line before the paragraph.

A paragraph with standard (default) line spacing

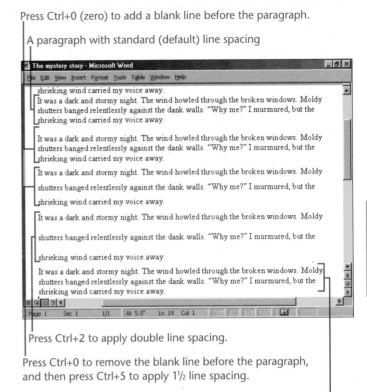

Press Ctrl+2 to apply double line spacing.

Press Ctrl+0 to remove the blank line before the paragraph, and then press Ctrl+5 to apply 1½ line spacing.

Press Ctrl+1 to apply single line spacing.

Creating Tab Stops

Tab stops, which are part of a paragraph's formatting, define the distance the insertion point moves each time you press the Tab key. Tab stops also affect the location of indents when you use the Indent buttons. If you don't create your own tab stops, Word automatically sets a tab stop every 0.5 inch. Word's tab stops aren't displayed on the ruler, but the ones you create yourself are displayed, with a different symbol for each kind of tab stop.

TIP

Lead the way. *To include tab leaders with the tab stop, choose Tabs from the Format menu, and specify the style of leader for each tab stop.*

Set Tab Stops

1. If the ruler isn't displayed, choose Ruler from the View menu.

2. Click in the paragraph, or select the paragraphs for which you want to set tab stops.

3. Click the box at the left end of the ruler to change the kind of tab stop. Keep clicking until you see the tab stop you want.

4. Click in the ruler where you want the tab stop.

5. Repeat steps 3 and 4 until all tab stops are set.

6. If necessary, change a tab stop by dragging its marker to a new location. Drag the marker off the ruler to remove that tab stop.

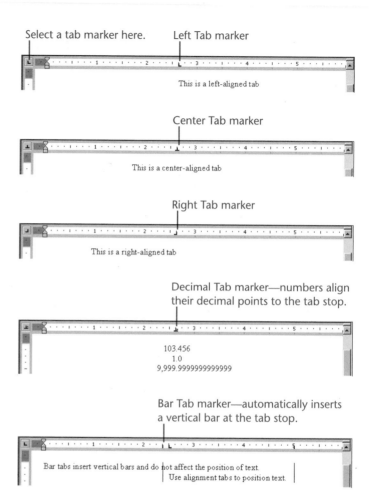

Select a tab marker here.   Left Tab marker

This is a left-aligned tab

Center Tab marker

This is a center-aligned tab

Right Tab marker

This is a right-aligned tab

Decimal Tab marker—numbers align their decimal points to the tab stop.

103.456
1.0
9,999.9999999999999

Bar Tab marker—automatically inserts a vertical bar at the tab stop.

Bar tabs insert vertical bars and do not affect the position of text.
Use alignment tabs to position text.

Copying Formatting

If you've created a character format or a paragraph format that you particularly like, you can copy all the formatting to another location in your document.

TIP

Save the formatting. *To use a specialized format in multiple locations in this or another document, you can have Word save the formatting as a character style or paragraph style.*

SEE ALSO

For information about defining your own paragraph and character styles, see "Creating Styles from Scratch" on page 74 and "Creating an Inline Heading" on page 194.

TIP

Multiple copies. *To copy formatting to multiple locations, double-click the Format Painter button. Click to turn it off when you've finished.*

Copy a Character Format

1. Select the text whose formatting you want to copy. The formatting of only the first character will be copied.

2. Click the Format Painter button.

3. Drag over the text to apply the formatting, and then release the button.

Copy a Paragraph Format

1. If paragraph marks aren't displayed, click the Show/Hide ¶ button.

2. Select the paragraph mark at the end of the paragraph whose format you want to copy.

3. Click the Format Painter button.

4. Drag over the paragraph mark (or over entire paragraphs) to apply the formatting, and then release the button.

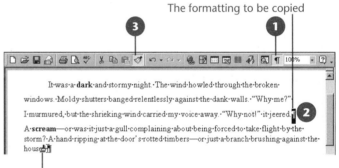

The formatting to be copied

Drag over the text to apply the formatting.

The formatting to be copied

Drag over the paragraph mark to apply the formatting.

Creating a Numbered List

A numbered list is a great way to present information when the sequence or the numbering of items is important. Word provides two easy ways to create a numbered list: by automatically creating one for you as you type, or by letting you convert a series of paragraphs into a numbered list.

Create a Numbered List

1. Type the number one (1), a period, a space, and the text of the first list item. Press Enter.

2. Type the rest of the list, pressing Enter at the end of each list item. Word automatically numbers each item for you.

3. After the last list item, press Enter again (before typing any more text) to turn off automatic numbering.

When you press Enter, Word indents the paragraph with a hanging indent, and converts the typed number into automatic numbering and the space into a tab stop.

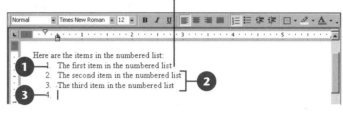

Convert Paragraphs into a Numbered List

1. Select the paragraphs that you want to convert into a numbered list.

2. Click the Numbering button.

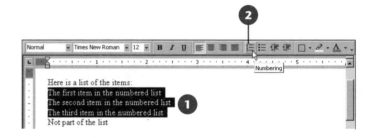

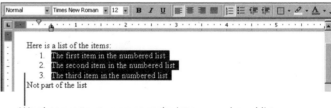

Word converts your paragraphs into a numbered list.

Creating a Custom Numbered List

If Word's standard numbered list doesn't meet your needs, you can customize your list by selecting a different numbering format or by changing the font, the position of the indent, and even the starting number.

Favorite fruit:
1 — Apples
2 — Oranges
3 — Bananas
4 — Cherries
5 — Grapes

SEE ALSO

For information about creating multiple-level numbered or bulleted lists, see "Creating a Multilevel Bulleted List" on page 152.

Select a Format

1. Choose Bullets And Numbering from the Format menu.

2. On the Numbered tab, click the format you want to use.

3. Click Customize.

4. Change the settings to customize the format.

5. Click OK.

6. Click OK.

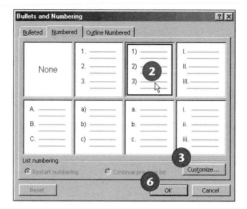

Add separator characters between the number and the text.

Change the starting number.

Click to change the font.

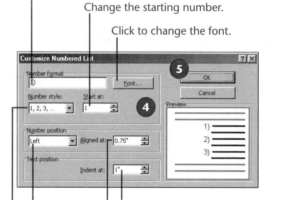

Change the paragraph's left indent.

Change the number alignment.

Change the paragraph's hanging indent.

Change the numbering style.

Creating a Bulleted List

A bulleted list is the logical alternative to a numbered list when the sequence of items is not important. It's also a great way to draw attention to a group of items for quick reference or to condense items in a wordy document or presentation into a manageable length.

Create a Bulleted List

1. Type an asterisk (*) and a space, and the text of the first list item. Press Enter.

2. Type the rest of the list, pressing Enter at the end of each list item.

3. After the last list item, press Enter again (before typing any more text) to turn off the automatic bullets.

When you press Enter, Word indents the paragraph with a hanging indent, and converts the asterisk into a bullet and the space into a tab stop.

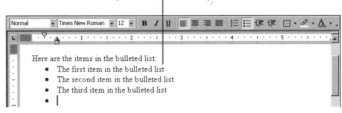

Convert Paragraphs into a Bulleted List

1. Select the paragraphs that you want to convert into a bulleted list.

2. Click the Bullets button.

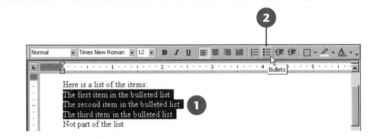

Word converts your paragraphs into a bulleted list.

Creating a Custom Bulleted List

If you'd like to make your bulleted list a little more interesting than Word's standard bulleted list, you can jazz up your list by selecting a different bullet or by changing the size or position of the bullets.

Favorite fruit:
- Apples
- Oranges
- Bananas
- Cherries
- Grapes

SEE ALSO

For information about creating multiple-level numbered or bulleted lists, see "Creating a Multilevel Bulleted List" on page 152.

Select a Format

1. Choose Bullets And Numbering from the Format menu.

2. On the Bulleted tab, click the format you want to use.

3. Click Customize to define a font-based bullet.

4. Specify the bullet position (paragraph hanging indent) and the text position (paragraph left indent).

5. Click OK.

6. Click OK.

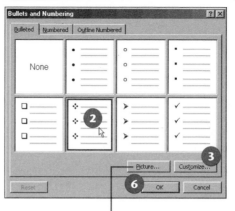

Click to use a picture as a bullet in an online document or a Web page.

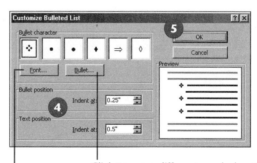

Click to use a different symbol as the bullet.

Click to change the font of the bullet.

Adding a Border to a Paragraph

A nice way to draw attention to a paragraph is to give it a border. The type of border you use can define the tone of your message and can help direct your reader's attention to a particular area of your text. A box around a paragraph makes its content stand out from the rest of the text; a bottom border underneath a heading sets the heading off from the following text. Word gives you a wide variety of quickly applied borders. If you don't like the effect of the one you chose, it's easy to remove it and try another one.

TIP

Close to the border.
Clicking the Borders button applies the border that was most recently selected from the Borders list.

Add a Border

1. Click in the paragraph that is to have the border. (To insert a Horizontal Line border underneath a paragraph, click at the end of the paragraph.)

2. Click the down arrow at the right of the Borders button.

3. Click the border you want to apply.

4. Repeat steps 2 and 3 if you want to add other borders to the paragraph.

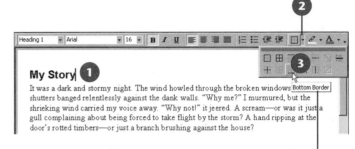

The ScreenTip describes the selected border.

Remove a Border

1. Click in the paragraph that has the border you want to remove.

2. Click the down arrow at the right of the Borders button.

3. Click the border you want to turn off.

Turn off a single border...

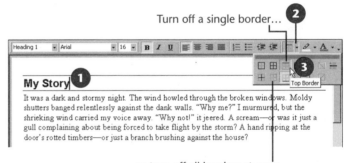

...or turn off all borders at once.

Creating a Custom Paragraph Border

If none of Word's standard borders is what you're looking for, you can customize your border by selecting a different border design, changing the size and color of the lines, and varying the distance between the border and the text.

SEE ALSO

For information about creating a border for an entire page, see "Placing a Line Border Around a Page" on page 199.

For information about adding borders to pictures and other objects, see "Placing a Border Around an Object" on page 201.

For information about adding a border to selected text, see "Making Text Stand Out" on page 236.

Define the Format

1. Click in the paragraph that is to have the border.

2. Choose Borders And Shading from the Format menu.

3. On the Borders tab, click the basic setting you want to use. To add a mix of different border styles around the paragraph, click the Custom button.

4. Select a border style.

5. Select a border color.

6. Select the width (thickness) of the border lines.

7. Click to delete a border that you don't want or to restore a border that you removed. If you're using the Custom setting, repeat steps 4 through 6, and click in the diagram to apply a different style border to each side of the paragraph.

8. Click OK.

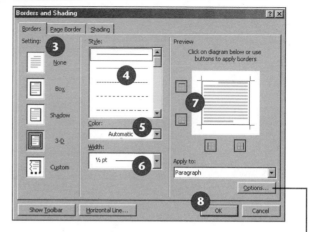

Click to change the distance between the border and the text.

3

Word's Dynamic Menus and Toolbars

Word adapts itself based on what you've tended to do in the past. If you're using Word's default setup, you can see this customization in Word's dynamic, or *adaptive*, menus and toolbars.

Your Personal Menu
Word initially displays only the most frequently used commands on its menus. If a menu item isn't displayed, wait a few seconds until the menu expands automatically and shows you all the available commands. When you choose a less frequently used command, Word adds it to the unexpanded menu so that it's immediately available in the future.

Your Personal Toolbar
Toolbars are indispensable for speeding up your work, but they occupy a lot of space on your screen, and you often have to scan a plethora of buttons to find the one you need. Word reduces these problems by placing two or more toolbars on one line and limiting which buttons are displayed. Although this takes up less space, it means that you can't see all the toolbar buttons at a glance. Here's where Word's adaptive nature comes into play once again. When you use a button that's hidden, Word places it on the visible portion of the toolbar for your future use and hides one of the buttons you don't normally use. How clever!

An unexpanded menu   An expanded menu

An unexpanded menu adapted to your usage

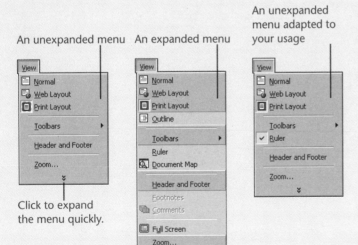

Click to expand the menu quickly.

The Standard toolbar sharing the available space on one line with...

...the Formatting toolbar. Only the most recently used tools are displayed.

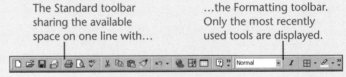

If you don't like having Word adapt to you—maybe you prefer seeing all your options all the time or perhaps you feel that your computer already knows too much about you—you can turn off *all* the adaptive features, change the way the menus and toolbars are displayed, and even customize the contents of the menus and toolbars. For more information, see Section 14, "Customizing Word," starting on page 305.

Setting Up the Page Dimensions

By default, Word creates printed documents with Portrait (longer than wide) *page orientation,* with 1-inch top and bottom margins and 1.25-inch side margins. You can change the paper size or the page orientation, and you can change some or all of the margins to fit the needs of your document and its design.

SEE ALSO

For information about creating different settings for margins and orientation in one document, see "Using Different Layouts in One Document" on page 104.

Change the Page Size or Orientation

1. Choose Page Setup from the File menu.

2. Click the Paper Size tab if it's not already selected.

3. If you're using a different paper size, select the size from the list, or specify the dimensions.

4. Click the Landscape option button if you want the page orientation to be wider than long.

5. Click OK to close the dialog box.

The preview shows the paper's orientation.

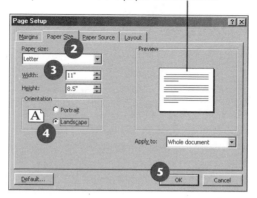

Change the Margins

1. Choose Page Setup from the File menu.

2. Click the Margins tab if it's not already selected.

3. Change the value for the Top, Bottom, Left, or Right margin.

4. Click OK to close the dialog box.

The preview shows the margin settings.

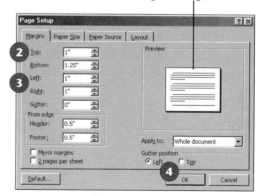

Formatting Unformatted Documents

Electronic mail, text from the Internet, text documents, or Word documents can look unattractive with little or no formatting. Word can apply automatic formatting to these documents for you, freeing you from the drudgery of applying formatting on a paragraph-by-paragraph basis, deleting extra paragraph marks, and so on. The results are usually very professional looking, and all you'll need to do is a quick review to catch anything Word missed. It's a real time-saver.

TIP

Try again. *If the formatting wasn't even close to what you wanted, click the Undo button to remove the formatting. Then try it again, but click the Options button and remove some of the formatting options.*

Format the Document

1. Choose AutoFormat from the Format menu.

2. Select a formatting option:
   - ◆ AutoFormat Now conducts full formatting and makes changes to the entire document.
   - ◆ AutoFormat And Review Each Change conducts full formatting and then gives you the opportunity to accept or reject all changes or to review individual changes.

3. Select a document type.

4. Click OK.

5. Review your document, and save it as a Word document.

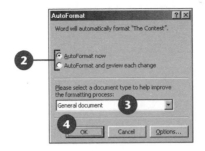

AutoFormat converts an unformatted text document...

The Contest

We received several different stories. Here's the first paragraph of our favorite one.

The sun shone brightly as I squinted across the water, looking for a sail on the distant horizon. I knew the ship would come, sooner or later. They had promised to return and I trusted them—I know not why.

Reviews

Dearing School of Fine Art:
    "Greatest works I've seen in a long time!"

...into a fully formatted Word document.

The Contest
We received several different stories. Here's the first paragraph of our favorite one.

The sun shone brightly as I squinted across the water, looking for a sail on the distant horizon. I knew the ship would come, sooner or later. They had promised to return and I trusted them—I know not why.

Reviews
Dearing School of Fine Art:
    "Greatest works I've seen in a long time!"

4

Proofreading Your Document

It's often the small, almost imperceptible details that make the difference between a document that's... well, mediocre, and one that glows with professional shine. Microsoft Word provides a variety of tools to help you make your publication inviting to look at and easy to read. When you use Word's proofing tools, you can be confident that your document doesn't contain misspelled words or grammatical errors. When your tired brain can't come up with that elusive perfect word, you can trust Word's synonym finder or the Thesaurus to find it for you. If you use specialized or difficult-to-type words in your work—legal, medical, or scientific terms, for example—you can create a customized dictionary containing those words, and Word will correct them automatically if you mistype them. If you use foreign words or phrases in your writing, Word's multilingual abilities will ensure that you don't make any embarrassing *faux pas*, whether the language you're using is Tatar or Uzbek.

Of course, spelling and grammar aren't the only things to consider when you create a publication. The appearance of your layout is every bit as important as your document's contents. Here again, Word provides all the tools you need to check and refine the look of your publication, whether you're creating a printed piece or a Web page.

Turning On the Proofing Tools

Word provides tools that you can use to check and correct your spelling and grammar. Turn on the tools, and Word will examine your writing, point out errors or problems, offer suggestions and explanations, and help you create a document that's free of embarrassing mistakes. What a great idea!

SEE ALSO

For examples of the results you'll get when you use Word's proofing tools, see "Behind-the-Scenes Magic" on page 27.

TIP

AutoCorrect. *The AutoCorrect feature corrects only obvious and unambiguous errors—*recieve *becomes* receive, yuo *becomes* you, *and so on. Where there are several possible spellings, Word suggests alternatives.*

Turn On Spelling and Grammar Checking

1. Choose Options from the Tools menu, and click the Spelling & Grammar tab.

2. Turn on the Check Spelling As You Type check box, and any other spelling options you want to use.

3. Turn on the Check Grammar As You Type check box, and any other grammar options you want to use.

4. Click OK.

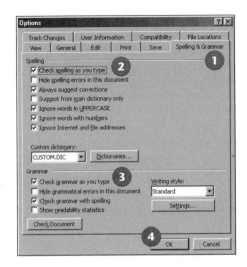

Turn on Automatic Spelling Correction

1. Choose AutoCorrect from the Tools menu.

2. On the AutoCorrect tab, turn on the Replace Text As You Type check box.

3. Turn on the Automatically Use Suggestions From The Spelling Checker check box.

4. Click OK.

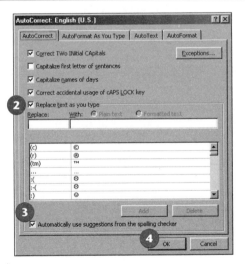

Correcting Your Spelling

As you type your text, Word follows along and checks your spelling. When Word encounters a misspelled word or a word it doesn't recognize, it places a red squiggly line under that word. Word also puts that helpful red squiggle under the kind of non-spelling error that's easy to miss even when you proof your document carefully—duplicated words (such as *the the*) and words that aren't separated by a space.

SEE ALSO

For information about spelling and grammar checking for different languages, and about disabling proofing in sections of a document, see "Proofing Different Languages" on page 50.

For information about having Word automatically correct spelling errors, see "Turn on Automatic Spelling Correction" on the facing page and "Controlling Automatic Changes" on page 302.

Correct the Spelling

① Point to a word that's marked as incorrect, and right-click.

② Click an appropriate correction.

③ Repeat steps 1 and 2 to correct all marked spelling errors in your document. To quickly find the next spelling or grammar error, double-click the Spelling And Grammar Status icon on the status bar.

④ Use the Undo button on the Standard toolbar to reverse an unintentional spelling change.

A red squiggly underline indicates a misspelled word.

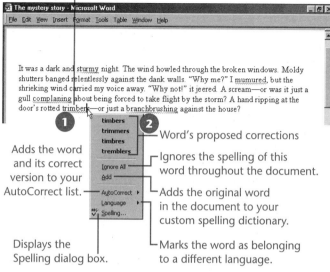

Word's proposed corrections

Adds the word and its correct version to your AutoCorrect list.

Ignores the spelling of this word throughout the document.

Adds the original word in the document to your custom spelling dictionary.

Displays the Spelling dialog box.

Marks the word as belonging to a different language.

Correcting Your Grammar

We all know that nothing can take the place of human proofreaders and editors, but if you're not fortunate enough to have a wordsmith or a grammarian at your disposal, Word's grammar-checking feature is the next best thing. Not only will it help you polish your writing, but it can be tailored to specific *types* of writing so that it will react differently depending on whether you're writing a casual letter or a scientific report. You set the rules.

SEE ALSO

For information about and examples of Word's grammar-checking feature, see "Behind-the-Scenes Magic" on page 27.

Correct the Grammar

1. Point to a word, phrase, or sentence or to punctuation that's marked as incorrect (underlined with a green squiggle), and right-click.

2. Click an appropriate correction.

3. Repeat steps 1 and 2 to correct all marked grammatical errors in your document. Use the Undo button on the Standard toolbar to reverse an unintentional grammar change.

A green squiggly underline indicates a grammatical error.

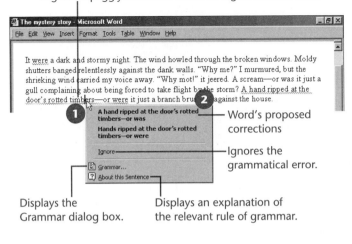

Word's proposed corrections

Ignores the grammatical error.

Displays the Grammar dialog box.

Displays an explanation of the relevant rule of grammar.

Change the Rules

1. Choose Options from the Tools menu, and click the Spelling & Grammar tab.

2. Select the writing style that best represents your own.

3. Click OK.

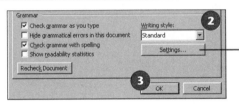

Click if you want to modify the rules of grammar for the selected style.

Correcting Your Spelling Dictionary

When Word tells you that a word is misspelled, and you then correct it and add it to the list of correctly spelled words, that word is stored in your personal dictionary. Word uses both its standard dictionary and your personal dictionary for correct spellings. Of course, if you've inadvertently added any *incorrectly* spelled words to your personal dictionary, Word won't identify those words as misspellings. However, you can easily edit the contents of your personal dictionary to correct such errors. (Note that you can't edit Word's standard dictionary.)

SEE ALSO

For information about creating dictionaries for specialized words, see "Adding or Creating a Custom Dictionary" on page 52.

Edit a Dictionary

1. Choose Options from the Tools menu, and click the Dictionaries button on the Spelling & Grammar tab.

2. Select the dictionary to be edited if it's not already selected.

3. Click the Edit button.

4. If prompted, confirm that it's okay to turn off spelling checking.

5. Correct any misspellings. Make sure there is only one word per line.

6. Click the Save button.

7. Close the document.

8. Choose Options from the Tools menu, and turn the spelling-checking option back on.

Proofing Different Languages

Word speaks many languages. Using the Microsoft Office language tools, Word can automatically identify which paragraphs are in which language. With the proper dictionaries and the spelling and grammar checkers installed, Word can check a multilingual document, using the correct proofing tools for each language. If your document contains only a few scattered words in a different language, you can identify those words as being in a different language so that they'll be checked correctly. If the proofing tools for a particular language aren't installed, Word will skip the text in that language to avoid adding unnecessary spelling and grammar squiggles to the document. And, if all else fails, you can designate sections of your document to have no proofing at all.

Turn On Office Language Detection

1 Close Word and any other Office programs that are open.

2 On the Windows Start menu, point your way through Programs and Office Tools, and choose Microsoft Office Language Settings from the submenu.

3 On the Enabled Languages tab, turn on the check boxes for the languages you want Word to detect.

4 Click OK. Office and Word will remember the enabled languages for all your Word sessions.

5 Start Word, and open your document.

6 Point to Language on the Tools menu, and choose Set Language from the submenu. Turn on the Detect Language Automatically check box if it's not already turned on, and click OK.

7 Type a paragraph in any enabled language. Word will recognize the language when you press Enter.

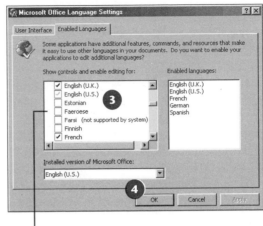

When you enable a language here...

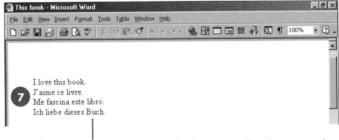

...Word can detect the language of each paragraph.

Specify the Language of Selected Text

1. Select the text.

2. Point to Language on the Tools menu, and choose Set Language from the submenu.

3. Select the language of the selected text.

4. Click OK.

Selected text will be assigned...

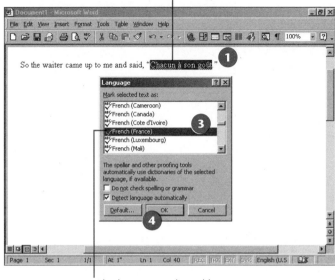

...the language selected here.

Turn Off Proofing

1. Select the text that you *don't* want to be proofed.

2. Point to Language on the Tools menu, and choose Set Language from the submenu.

3. Turn on the Do Not Check Spelling Or Grammar check box.

4. Click OK.

Selected text won't be checked for spelling or grammar errors.

Spelling icons

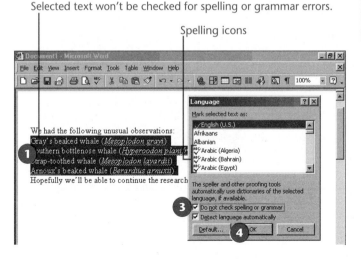

Adding or Creating a Custom Dictionary

Word automatically creates a custom dictionary to store all the entries you create when you choose the Add command from the Spelling shortcut menu. You can add other customized dictionaries that contain specialized words (technical or legal terms, for example, or foreign words) to Word's spelling checker, either by creating a new dictionary or by adding to an existing one. When you use a customized dictionary that contains those words, your spelling checker recognizes them and doesn't flag them as being incorrect.

SEE ALSO

For information about correcting your spelling dictionary see "Correcting Your Spelling Dictionary" on page 49.

Add or Create a New Dictionary

1. Choose Options from the Tools menu, and click the Dictionaries button on the Spelling & Grammar tab.

2. Click the New button or the Add button.
   - ◆ With Add clicked, locate and select an existing dictionary, and click OK.
   - ◆ With New clicked, name a new dictionary, and click Save.

3. Select a language for the dictionary.

4. Click OK.

5. Select the dictionary to which you want to add words using the Add command on the Spelling shortcut menu.

6. Click OK.

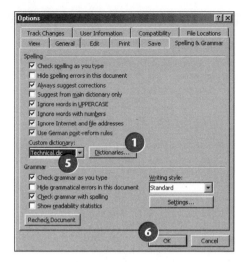

Select None if you want the selected dictionary to be used for all text.

Check only the dictionaries you want the spelling checker to use. The more dictionaries you check, the slower the spelling checker will be.

Creates a new dictionary.

Adds an existing dictionary.

Finding Alternative Wording

If you find that you're using the same word repeatedly in one sentence or paragraph (or even too many times in one document), or if a word you've used doesn't express your meaning precisely enough or provide the impact you want, Word can come to your rescue. It will automatically provide you with a wide choice of similar words. If you're still not quite satisfied, you can use the Thesaurus to browse through a list of related words until you find exactly what you're looking for.

Select an Alternative Word

1. Right-click the word you want to replace.

2. Point to Synonyms on the shortcut menu.

3. Choose an alternative word.

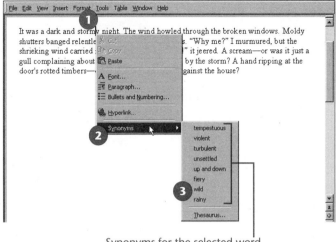

Synonyms for the selected word

Find Related Words

1. Right-click the word you want to replace, and choose Thesaurus from the shortcut menu.

2. Click one of the listed meanings of the word.

3. Click a synonym.

4. If the synonym doesn't seem appropriate, click Look Up, and repeat steps 2 and 3.

5. When you're satisfied with the synonym, click Replace.

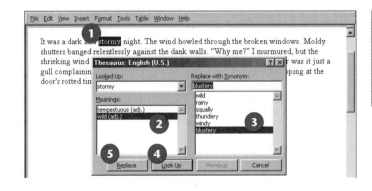

Improving Your Layout with Hyphenation

Sometimes the right edges of left-aligned paragraphs look ragged and uneven. Justified paragraphs can contain big white spaces between words, especially in columnar text. You can easily repair these common problems with automatic hyphenation. Word does the work for you by inserting *optional hyphens* where they're needed. An optional hyphen shows up only when a whole word won't fit on a line, so if a hyphenated word moves from the end of a line because of changes in your text, the optional hyphen will disappear.

SEE ALSO

For information about other ways to change line breaks (or word, column, or page breaks), see "Fine-Tuning Your Document" on page 56.

Set Automatic Hyphenation

1. Point to Language on the Tools menu, and choose Hyphenation from the submenu.

2. Turn on the Automatically Hyphenate Document check box.

3. Specify the maximum distance between the end of the last word and the edge of the column.

4. Specify whether you want to limit the number of consecutive line-end hyphens.

5. Click OK.

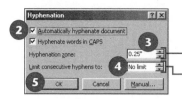

Use larger values for fewer hyphens and a ragged edge; use smaller values for more hyphens and a smoother edge.

Two or more consecutive hyphens are generally considered to be an unacceptable "stack."

The ragged right edges of an unhyphenated document…

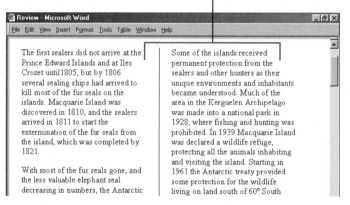

…become much smoother and easier on the eye when you apply automatic hyphenation.

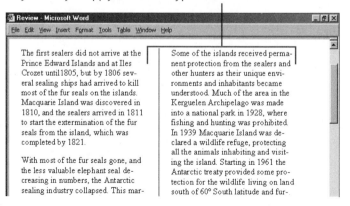

Automatic is good... *If you don't like the results of Word's automatic hyphenation, open the Hyphenation dialog box and turn off the Automatically Hyphenate Document check box to return the document to its original unhyphenated condition.*

...but manual gives you more control. *To modify the results of automatic hyphenation, try manual hyphenation. The Manual Hyphenation feature lets you stop at each hyphenated word and decide whether to change or eliminate the hyphenation.*

Look it up! *Hyphenation can be different for the same word, depending on how the word is used. For example, compare "She re-cords music..." and "She set a world rec-ord." Remember, your dictionary is your best friend here!*

Hyphenate Manually

1. Point to Language on the Tools menu, and choose Hyphenation from the submenu.

2. Specify the maximum distance between the end of the last word and the edge of the column.

3. Specify whether you want to limit the number of consecutive line-end hyphens.

4. Click the Manual button.

5. When Word proposes hyphenating a word, do any of the following:

   ◆ Click Yes to accept the proposed hyphenation.

   ◆ Click elsewhere in the word to hyphenate it differently, and then click Yes.

   ◆ Click No to skip the current word and locate the next candidate for hyphenation.

   ◆ Click Cancel to end manual hyphenation.

Acceptable locations for hyphenating the word

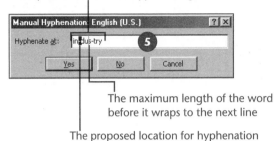

The maximum length of the word before it wraps to the next line

The proposed location for hyphenation

4

Fine-Tuning Your Document

After composing your document, you can adjust the text flow—especially when a paragraph "breaks" across pages—to improve the look of the document. Word does much of this automatically, but you can make a few adjustments yourself.

TIP

Family ties. *There are many definitions of the sad terms "widow" and "orphan" in the publishing world. In Word's world, widows and orphans are single lines that get separated from the paragraph where they belong and become marooned alone at the top (orphan) or bottom (widow) of a page. They are considered aesthetically undesirable in both worlds.*

TIP

All change. *To change widow and orphan control throughout a document, change the setting for the paragraph format in the style definition.*

Control Widows and Orphans

1. Switch to Print Layout view if you're not already in that view.

2. Select the paragraph or paragraphs to which you want to make changes.

3. Choose Paragraph from the Format menu.

4. Click the Line And Page Breaks tab.

5. Turn the Widow/Orphan Control check box on or off.

6. Click OK.

With Widow/Orphan Control turned off, the text extends to the bottom margin of the page, whether or not it creates a widow or an orphan.

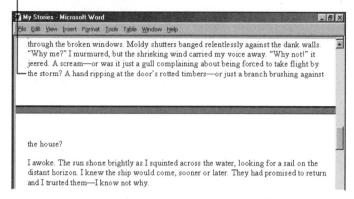

With Widow/Orphan Control turned on, the page breaks before the text reaches the bottom margin...

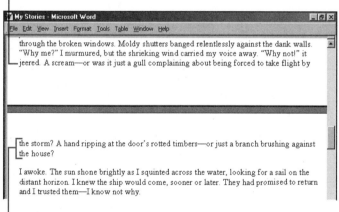

...so that there will always be at least two lines of a paragraph at the top or bottom of a page.

TIP

It's broken! *"Breaking" manually means that when you don't like the place where Word automatically ended, or broke, a line (or a word, a column, or a page, for that matter), you can change the break yourself.*

SEE ALSO

For information about turning automatic hyphenation on or off, see "Improving Your Layout with Hyphenation" on page 54.

For information about setting and changing the formatting of a style, see "Creating Styles from Scratch" on page 74 and "Organizing with Styles" on page 86.

TIP

The last task. *Always apply manual page breaks as the very last adjustment you make to a document before printing it. Editing a document after you've applied page breaks can result in an unacceptably short page or an extra blank page. However, if you do need to edit the document after page breaking, use Print Preview to examine the page breaks.*

Break Lines

1. Switch to Print Layout view if you're not already in that view.

2. Turn off automatic hyphenation if it's turned on.

3. Adjust the Zoom setting on the Standard toolbar so that you can see the entire length of the lines of text.

4. Adjust the way the lines break by pressing

   ◆ Ctrl+Hyphen (-) to create an optional hyphen—that is, a hyphen that will appear only when the whole word won't fit on the line.

   ◆ Ctrl+Shift+Hyphen (-) to create a nonbreaking hyphen that will keep a hyphenated word (or a telephone number) on the same line.

   ◆ Ctrl+Shift+Spacebar to create a nonbreaking *space* that will keep two words that shouldn't be separated on the same line.

   ◆ Shift+Enter to create a manual line break.

The story before fine-tuning

I awoke. The sun shone brightly. I squinted across the water, looking for a sail on the distant horizon. I knew the ship would come, sooner or later. They had promised to return and I trusted them—I know not why.

All I had for company was a broken radio, a waffle iron, and my 3-D glasses. The land provided for all my needs, but none of my wants.

The sand stood in sweeping mounds as if to mock me. As I fell upon a dune, the sand poured through my fingers like the sands of an hourglass. I knew, however, my wait would not be measured in hours.

The sand grew in front of me, a 25 cm. testament to the time I have lost and will never regain.

— Insert a line break.

— Replace this hyphen with a nonbreaking hyphen.

Insert an — optional hyphen.

— Replace this space with a nonbreaking space.

The result after a little tweaking

I awoke. The sun shone brightly. I squinted across the water, looking for a sail on the distant horizon. I knew the ship would come, sooner or later. They had promised to return and I trusted them—I know not why.

All I had for company was a broken radio, a waffle iron, and my 3-D glasses. The land provided for all my needs, but none of my wants.

The sand stood in sweeping mounds as if to mock me. As I fell upon a dune, the sand poured through my fingers like the sands of an hourglass. I knew, however, my wait would not be measured in hours.

The sand grew in front of me, a 25 cm. testament to the time I have lost and will never regain.

— Ideally, paragraph edges should have the shape of a backward letter "C."

4

Checking the Layout

No document is complete until you've reviewed its layout. Before you print the document, check all the details on your screen to see how the finished piece will look when it's printed. Then you can make any changes to perfect the layout.

TIP

Use TrueType fonts. *To get the best onscreen representation of your printed document, use TrueType fonts. Other fonts don't always display an accurate screen representation of their printed form, so your printed document might show different line spacing and line breaks from those you see on screen. A TrueType font has a "TT" symbol next to its name in the Font drop-down list.*

SEE ALSO

For information about checking the layout of a Web page, see "Formatting a Web Page" on page 261.

Check the Layout

① Click the Print Preview button on the Standard toolbar.

② Do any of the following to review your document:

- ◆ Click the Multiple Pages button to see several pages at once.
- ◆ Click the One Page button to see a single page.
- ◆ With the Magnifier button turned on, click in the document to zoom in on the page. Click in the document again to zoom out.
- ◆ Turn off the Magnifier button and click in the document to edit it. Use the ruler to adjust margins and paragraph indents.
- ◆ If a few words or lines of your document spill over onto an extra page, click the Shrink To Fit button to scale, or "shrink," the text to eliminate the extra page.

③ Click Close to return to your document, and make any necessary edits.

Drag to select the number of pages displayed.

The Magnifier button

The One Page button

The Multiple Pages button

Click to show the ruler.

The Shrink To Fit button

Click to show a preview using Full Screen view.

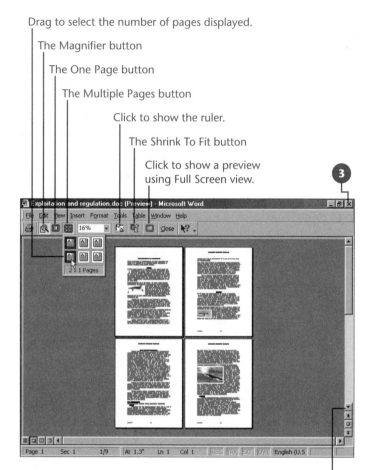

Click to see the next page or pages.

Creating Frequently Used Documents

E ven if you don't have the time, the inclination, or the experience to design the business documents you use every day in your work, you can still produce professional-looking, well-designed letters, memos, faxes, and reports, using three powerful tools that Microsoft Word provides: *styles, templates,* and *wizards*.

In this section, you'll see how invaluable these tools are for creating, designing, and maintaining consistency throughout the documents you use every day. Depending upon your desired end result and how little or how much involvement you want in the design, you can use the predesigned elements, or you can create your own styles and templates or modify existing ones so that they're tailored more precisely to your needs.

If your computer is part of a network, everyone in your workgroup can share the same set of templates so that the group's business documents have a consistent style and format.

Whether you're creating a long, detailed report or business proposal or simply modifying your company's letter template to accommodate a printed letterhead, you'll wonder how you ever managed to get your work completed without styles, templates, and wizards. For a detailed discussion of these useful tools, see "Styles, Templates, and Wizards" on page 77.

Creating a Letter

The easiest way to create a letter is to use Word's Letter Wizard. You make a few choices and you fill in a few blanks, and Word creates a letter format that's ready and waiting for you to insert your message.

SEE ALSO

For information about creating your own templates, see "Customizing a Template" on page 68 and "Creating a Template from a Document" on page 70.

For information about the Office Assistant, see "Controlling the Office Assistant" on page 309.

TRY THIS

You *can* find good help!
If the Office Assistant is installed, put it to work for you. Start a blank document, type Dear John: *(or any name you want) and press Enter. Click the option to get help, and there's the Letter Wizard waiting for you.*

Start the Letter

1 Start a new document. If you want to use your own template, start the document based on your template.

2 Choose Letter Wizard from the Tools menu.

3 Complete the items on each tab of the wizard.

◆ On the Letter Format tab, define the basic layout by choosing a page design and a letter style.

◆ On the Recipient Info tab, specify the recipient's name and address and an appropriate salutation style.

◆ On the Other Elements tab, select any additional elements you want to include, and enter the required specific information for each element.

◆ On the Sender Info tab, verify your return address, and select the letter's closing elements.

4 Click OK.

Page design: Professional Letter

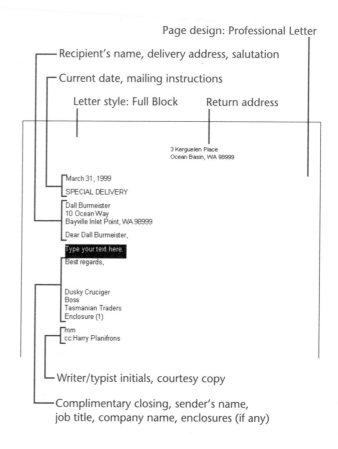

Recipient's name, delivery address, salutation

Current date, mailing instructions

Letter style: Full Block   Return address

3 Kerguelen Place
Ocean Basin, WA 98999

March 31, 1999
SPECIAL DELIVERY

Dall Burmeister
10 Ocean Way
Bayville Inlet Point, WA 98999

Dear Dall Burmeister,

Type your text here.

Best regards,

Dusky Cruciger
Boss
Tasmanian Traders
Enclosure (1)

mm
cc:Harry Planifrons

Writer/typist initials, courtesy copy

Complimentary closing, sender's name, job title, company name, enclosures (if any)

Complete the Letter

1 Replace the placeholder text with your own words.

2 Review any items that were completed by the wizard, and edit them as desired. To make several changes to items that were completed by the wizard, rerun the wizard from the Tools menu and make your changes. The changes you make in the wizard will appear in your document.

3 Save the letter.

Right-click an item completed by the wizard to see alternative choices.

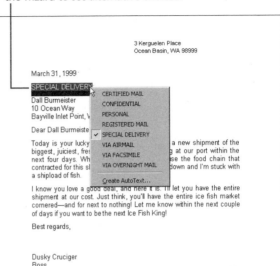

Creating a Memo

An elegantly designed, professional-looking memo creates a good impression and can help convey your message. With the design already created for you, you can concentrate on the content. Word's Memo Wizard lets you customize every memo you create. The wizard remembers your last settings too, so to create your next memo you need to make only a few changes.

Start the Memo Wizard

1 Choose New from the File menu.

2 Click the Memos tab.

3 Double-click the Memo Wizard to start it.

4 Click Next to enter the wizard.

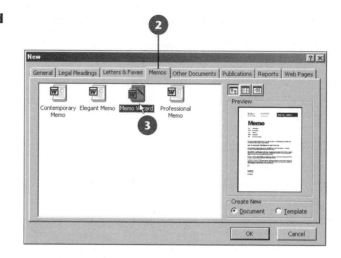

TIP

Long memo. *If your memo is longer than one page, you can use the wizard to set up running heads so that items such as the topic, the date, or the page number appear on each page.*

TIP

Jump in. *You can click a topic at the left side of any of the wizard's screens to jump to that part of the wizard.*

SEE ALSO

For information about modifying the fields completed by the wizard, see "Creating a Letter" on page 60.

For information about creating a memo from a template without using the wizard, see "Creating a Document from Any Template or Wizard" on page 66.

For information about creating a running head, see "Creating a Running Head" on page 91.

Complete the Memo

1. Work your way through the wizard, choosing the settings you want. Click Next to move to the next screen of choices; click Back to return to a previous section to change or complete a field. When you've made all your settings, click Finish.

2. Type your content to complete the memo.

3. Review the document.

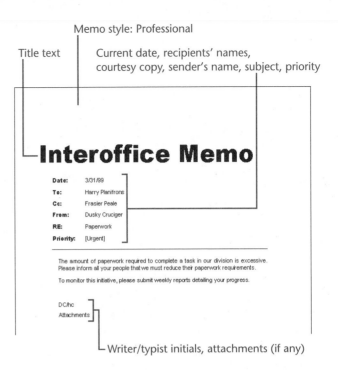

Memo style: Professional

Title text   Current date, recipients' names, courtesy copy, sender's name, subject, priority

Writer/typist initials, attachments (if any)

So Many Ways to View It

Word gives you several ways to view your document as you work on it, and you'll find that your efficiency increases and your work becomes easier when you use the correct view for the task at hand. You can use the View menu or the four view buttons at the bottom left of the window to change your view.

Normal View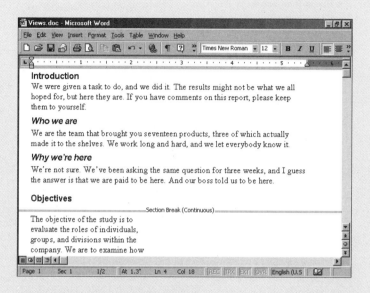

Normal view is designed for speed of entry and editing. It's based on the commercial publishing technique of creating *galleys*. You place the text and other elements in one long, continuous column that flows from one page to the next, and you deal with the placement of elements after you've ironed out any content problems.

Web Layout View

Web Layout view is exclusively for working with online documents. All the elements are in place, just as they are in Print Layout view, but the font size, line length, and page length all change to improve the onscreen readability of the document. Web Layout view is "tree-saver view"—use it when you want to read, but not print, an online document.

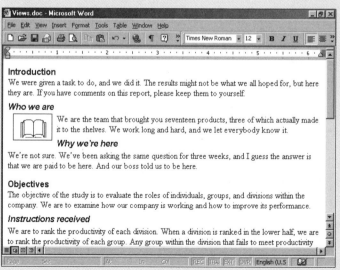

Print Layout View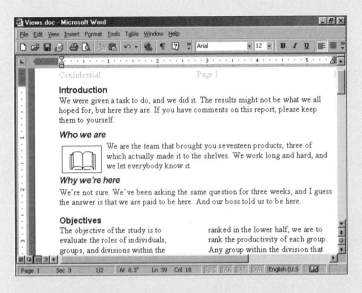

The standard working view, Print Layout view, shows you how your document will look when it's printed—the placement of pictures, the arrangement of the columns, the distance of the text from the edge of the page, and so on. You can use the Zoom drop-down list on the Standard toolbar to change the magnification of the page and how much of it you can see and work with on the screen.

Outline View

If you use an outline to create your work, you know how valuable it is for organizing information. Outline view displays your document as an outline, with the paragraph formatting defining the levels of the outline. By default, Word's standard heading styles—Heading 1 is level one, Heading 2 is level two, and so on—and other paragraph styles, such as Normal, are treated as regular text. You can use Outline view to organize your topics before you start writing, or you can use it to reorganize an existing document.

There's More...

Although these four views are the ones you'll probably use the most frequently, there are other views and options that are useful in various circumstances: Print Preview, Web Page Preview, Full Screen view, Document Map, draft font, picture placeholders, and more. You'll find information about these items in the tasks and procedures where their use is the most relevant.

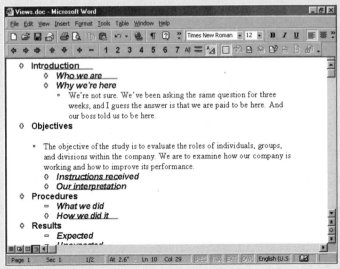

Creating a Document from Any Template or Wizard

A *template* provides the basis for a document: the layout and styles, and even the toolbars and AutoText. A *wizard* guides you through the creation of a specific type of document, including selecting the template for the document and completing some of the content. Word provides you with many templates and wizards, and you can download others from the Internet, use templates created by the company you work for, or create your own templates.

TIP

Read the instructions.
Many templates have instructions in the placeholder text. Once you're familiar with the template, you might want to modify it to eliminate the placeholder text.

Start a New Document

1. Choose New from the File menu.

2. Click the tab that contains the template or wizard you want to use.

3. Click the icon for the template or wizard to see a preview of its general layout.

4. Repeat steps 2 and 3 to locate the template or wizard you want to use.

5. With the template or wizard selected, click OK.

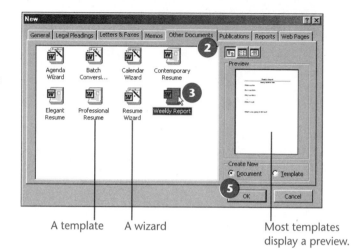

A template   A wizard   Most templates display a preview.

Use Web page templates to create Web pages.

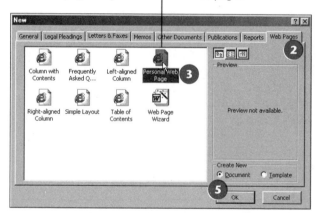

SEE ALSO

For information about modifying an existing template, see "Customizing a Template" on page 68.

For information about creating your own template from an existing document, see "Creating a Template from a Document" on page 70.

For information about workgroup templates, see "Sharing Templates" on page 72.

For information about connecting to the Microsoft Office Web site to download additional templates, see "Getting More Stuff" on page 322.

TRY THIS

Styles at a glance. *In Normal View, choose Options from the Tools menu, enter 0.7" in the Style Area Width box on the View tab, and click OK. You'll see the names of each paragraph style in your document next to the paragraph.*

Complete the Document

1. If you're using a wizard, step through it and provide the required information to complete the wizard.

2. Turn on the Show/Hide ¶ button on the Standard toolbar if it's not already turned on.

3. Edit the document to complete it.

4. Save, print, and distribute the completed document.

Don't delete paragraph marks. If you do, you'll lose the formatting.

The grayed text is the running head in the document header.

The text and formatting come from the template.

The date is inserted by a field that automatically enters the current date.

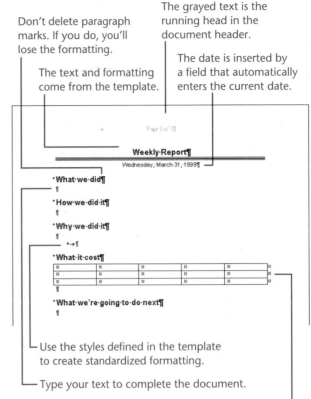

Use the styles defined in the template to create standardized formatting.

Type your text to complete the document.

Use special elements, or delete them if you don't need them.

5

Customizing a Template

Although a template is not dynamic in the same way that a wizard is dynamic, neither is a template a completely static tool. If your needs change or if you want to tweak a design, you can make substantial changes to a template. To do this, you create a new template from the existing template.

TIP

Making changes to Normal. *Most paragraph styles are based on the Normal style, so when you make changes to the Normal style, the changes also take place in the other styles.*

TIP

Modify a template. *To modify your own template without creating a new one, locate the template in the New dialog box, right-click it, and choose Open. After you've modified the template, save and close it.*

Clone a Template

1. Choose New from the File menu.

2. Select the template that you want to modify.

3. Click Template in the Create New section.

4. Click OK.

5. Click the Save button on the Standard toolbar, type a unique and descriptive filename for the template, and click Save. The template will be saved in your personal templates folder.

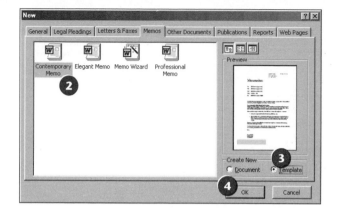

Memorandum

To:	[Click here and type name]
CC:	[Click here and type name]
From:	[Click here and type name]
Date:	3/31/99
Re:	[Click here and type subject]

How to Use This Memo Template

Select text you would like to replace, and type your memo. Use styles such as Heading 1-3 and Body Text in the Style control on the Formatting toolbar.

To delete the background elements—such as the circle, rectangles, or return address frames, click on the boundary border to highlight the "handles," and press Delete. To replace the picture in this template with a different one, first click on the picture. Then, on the Insert menu, point to Picture, and click From File. Locate the folder that contains the picture you want to insert, then double-click the picture.

To save changes to this template for future use, choose Save As from the File menu. In the Save As Type box, choose Document Template. Next time you want to use it, choose New from the File menu, and then double-click your template.

The original template contains placeholder text and graphics.

SEE ALSO

For information about starting a document based on a template, see "Creating a Document from Any Template or Wizard" on page 66.

For information about displaying templates on different tabs of the New dialog box, see "Sharing Templates" on page 72.

For information about using styles in your documents, see "Creating Styles from Scratch" on page 74.

For information about working with background graphics in a template, see "Creating a Watermark" on page 208.

TIP

No preview? *If your template doesn't display a preview in the New dialog box, open the template, choose Properties from the File menu, turn on the Save Preview Picture check box on the Summary tab, click OK, and then save and close the template.*

Modify a Template

1. Modify the template:

   ◆ Replace the placeholder text with any text that will be common to all documents based on your new template.

   ◆ Add any new text or other page elements.

   ◆ Redefine or create your own paragraph styles and character styles. Be sure to save the styles with the template.

2. Save and close the template.

3. Create a document based on the new template to confirm that the template is correct.

Replace placeholders with text that will be the same in every document.

Leave placeholders for text that will be different in every document.

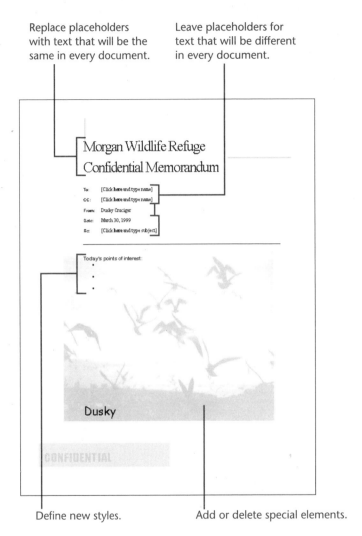

Define new styles.

Add or delete special elements.

5

Creating a Template from a Document

You can easily convert an existing document into a template, and you can use that template to create documents with the same basic layout and design. And if some or all of the same content is repeated in all documents of this type, you can include that content in the template so that you don't have to type it every time you create a document based on this template.

TIP

Templates folders. *Word stores its own templates in one folder and your templates in another folder. The location of your templates depends on the way your computer was set up and whether it has different profiles for individual users.*

Convert a Document into a Template

1. Open the document that you want to use as the basis for your template.

2. Choose Save As from the File menu.

3. Type a unique and descriptive filename.

4. Select Document Template. Word automatically switches to your templates folder. If you want to store the template in a subfolder or workgroup folder, navigate to that folder.

5. Save the template.

Open the list to see the full path to your templates folder.

SEE ALSO

For information about fields that insert and update information automatically, see "Inserting Changing Information" on page 296.

For information about locations for storing your templates, see "Organizing Your Templates" on page 308.

TIP

New dialog box tabs. *To set a template to appear on a specific tab in the New dialog box, create subfolders in your templates folder and classify your templates by moving them into the appropriate folders. Any template in the default templates folder will appear on the General tab of the New dialog box; a template in a subfolder will appear on a tab of the New dialog box, labeled with the subfolder's name.*

Customize the Content

1. Turn on the Show/Hide ¶ button on the Standard toolbar if it's not already turned on.

2. Edit the document so that it contains only the material you want to appear in every document you'll create from this template.

3. Click the Save button on the Standard toolbar.

4. Close the document when you've finished.

5. Create a document based on the new template to confirm that the template is correct.

Delete text that won't appear in every document.

Use AutoText in running heads to insert information that updates automatically.

Use a date that updates automatically.

Leave paragraph marks as placeholders.

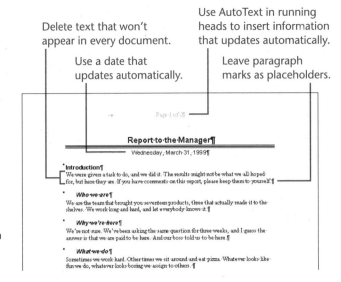

This text appears in every document.

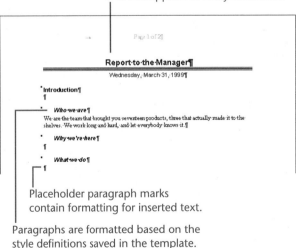

Placeholder paragraph marks contain formatting for inserted text.

Paragraphs are formatted based on the style definitions saved in the template.

5

Sharing Templates

If your computer is part of a network and everyone in your workgroup works on the same types of documents, you can all use the same templates so that all the documents produced in the group have the same general appearance. And if a template needs to be updated, only the shared template needs to be replaced.

Set Up the Templates

1 Create a templates folder on a computer that's accessible to everyone in your workgroup.

2 Create folders in the templates folder to classify the template types.

3 Place the templates to be shared in the folders.

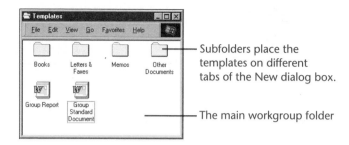

Subfolders place the templates on different tabs of the New dialog box.

The main workgroup folder

Connect to the Templates

1 On your own computer, choose Options from the Tools menu, and click the File Locations tab.

2 Double-click Workgroup Templates.

3 In the Modify Location dialog box that appears, locate the templates folder.

4 Click OK.

5 Click OK in the Options dialog box.

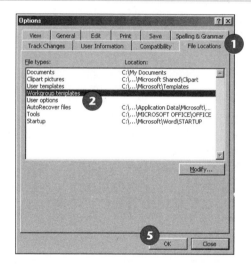

Copying Between Templates

If you have a template that contains styles, custom toolbars, macros, or AutoText, and you'd like to use those elements in another template, you can copy them quickly and easily using the Organizer.

TRY THIS

Find that template! *If you can't remember where your templates are stored, let Word tell you. Choose New from the File menu, and right-click the template. Choose Properties from the shortcut menu, and, on the General tab, note the full path to the template.*

TIP

Multiple-select. *You can select several items at one time in the list you're copying from by holding down the Ctrl key and clicking each item.*

Start the Organizer

1. Start a document based on the template into which you want to copy items from another template.

2. Choose Templates And Add-Ins from the Tools menu.

3. Click Organizer.

Select and Copy Items

1. Select the template into which you'll insert the copied items.

2. Click the Close File button.

3. Click the Open File button, and open the template you want to copy from.

4. Select the items to be copied.

5. Click Copy.

6. Click a different tab, and copy any other items.

7. Click Close when you've finished.

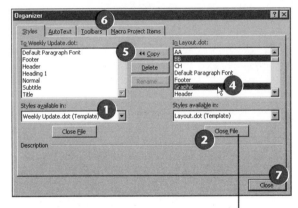

The Close File button becomes the Open File button after you close the template.

5

Creating Styles from Scratch

Whether you're creating a new template, modifying an existing one, or including a special element in a document, you can create a style and define all its elements in a few quick steps.

SEE ALSO

For more detailed information about specifying the style that follows an existing style, see "Creating a Sequence of Styles" on page 78.

For information about character styles, see "Creating an Inline Heading" on page 194.

For information about setting text effects for characters, adding animation, and changing text color, see "Making Text Stand Out" on page 236.

Create a Style

1. Choose Style from the Format menu, and click the New button in the Style dialog box.

2. Name the style and select a style type.

3. Select a style whose properties you want to start with, and then select an existing style that will automatically follow the first style.

4. Turn on the Add To Template check box.

5. Click Format, and choose Font.

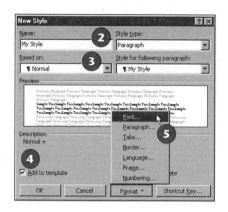

Set Up the Font

1. Select a font, style, and size.

2. If you want any underlining, select its style.

3. Select a font color.

4. Turn on the check boxes for any special effects.

5. Click OK.

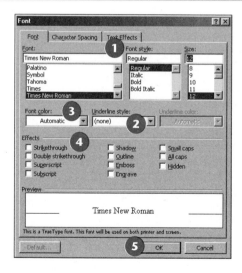

SEE ALSO

For information about controlling the way paragraph text flows across pages, see "Fine-Tuning Your Document" on page 56.

For information about transferring styles between templates and documents, see "Copying Between Templates" on page 73.

For information about modifying existing styles, see "Modifying an Existing Style" on page 76.

For information about using a style's frame settings, see "Creating Margin Notes" on page 192.

TIP

Save the style. *When you turn on the Add To Template check box, the style is saved in the template and in the document. When this check box is turned off, the style is saved in the document only.*

TIP

Print your styles. *To create a printed list of all styles and their descriptions, choose Print from the File menu, select Styles from the Print What list, and click OK.*

Set Up the Paragraph

1. Click the Format button in the New Style dialog box, and choose Paragraph.

2. Select a paragraph alignment.

3. Select an outline level.

4. Specify any indentation and a first-line paragraph indent or hanging indent.

5. Specify how much space you want before or after the paragraph.

6. Select the line spacing.

7. Click OK.

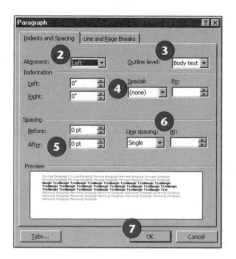

Complete the Style

1. Click the Format button, and apply any other formatting to the style.

2. Click OK to close the New Style dialog box.

3. Click the Close button to close the Style dialog box.

Set paragraph tabs.

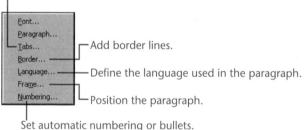

Add border lines.

Define the language used in the paragraph.

Position the paragraph.

Set automatic numbering or bullets.

Modifying an Existing Style

Sometimes, although a style might be close to what you want, it isn't exactly right. You can quickly modify the style in your document, and then save the style either as a modification of the old style or as a new style.

Modify the Style

1. To any paragraph, apply the style you want to modify.

2. Make the modifications you want to the paragraph.

3. Double-click at the left of the paragraph to select the entire paragraph.

4. Click in the Style box.

5. Press Enter to save the changes to the current style.

6. Click OK to confirm that you want to change the style.

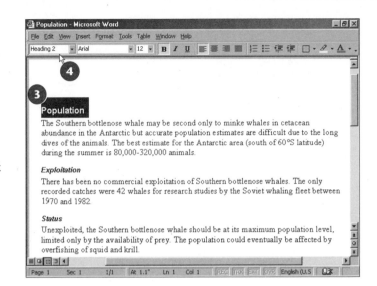

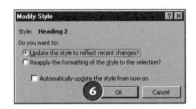

Styles, Templates, and Wizards

Styles and *templates* are useful because they're quick ways of applying formatting and layouts, and because they help you maintain consistency throughout a document and throughout all documents of the same type. *Wizards* are interactive little programs within Word that help you easily use styles and templates to create specialized documents.

Styles

Word provides two different types of styles:

◆ A *paragraph style* is the blueprint for the look of a paragraph—the font and its size, the line spacing, the borders, and even the paragraph's position on the page if you want. The formatting applied with a paragraph style applies to the entire paragraph.

◆ A *character style* defines the look of one or more characters (letters or numbers), and applies only to the characters within a paragraph to which you apply that style.

Word comes with many predefined styles. To view them, open a new blank document, hold down the Shift key, and open the Style box on the Formatting toolbar. You can use a style as is, redefine its formatting, or create your own styles.

Templates

A template is both a blueprint for your document and a container that holds the specialized tools you need to work on the document: styles, AutoText, toolbars, macros, page-layout specifications, and view settings. A template can also contain text, graphics, and any other elements that will always be included in the documents you create using that template. To view the available templates, choose Open from the File menu, and explore the tabs of the Open dialog box. Except for the ones with "Wizard" in their names, all the items are templates. Just as with styles, you can use a template as is, modify it to fit your needs, or create your own templates.

Word always uses the Normal template, which contains Word's predefined styles and default content. When you make changes to this global template, the changes are available to all your documents. You can also use a specialized template that contains information specific to a certain type of document. In this case, the contents of the Normal template *and* the contents of the specialized template are available to your document. If there is a conflict (if the two have different formatting for a Heading 1 style, for example), the contents of the specialized template take precedence over those of the Normal template. For example, when you choose New from the File menu and choose Blank Document, only the Normal template is used; when you choose a different type of document, the specialized template for that document *and* the Normal template are used.

Wizards

Wizards really live up to their name! They use the templates and styles you have, but they hide from your view the macros, fields, and whatever other tools they need, and simply step you through the creation of a document. You make choices and provide information, and Word's wizards work their magic behind the scenes, quietly taking care of all the details.

5

Creating a Sequence of Styles

A design often dictates that one style is always followed by another specific style. You can set up the first style so that after you complete the first paragraph and press Enter, the next paragraph you create uses the style specified as the *following style*. If you then specify another style to follow the second style, Word will be doing most of the work of applying styles for you. If you've specified a sequence that doesn't quite work, you can always change some of the styles yourself.

TIP

You need a new paragraph.
*Word applies the style you speci-
fy as the following-paragraph
style only when you're creating
a new paragraph. The following-
paragraph style has no effect
on an existing paragraph that
currently follows the first
paragraph.*

Select the First Style

1. Choose Style from the Format menu.

2. Select the style to be changed.

3. Click Modify.

A preview of the selected style

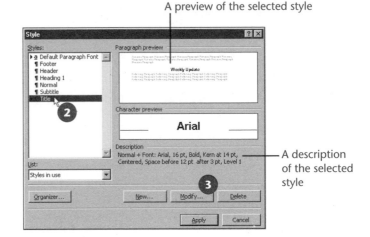

A description of the selected style

Specify a Sequence

1. Select a following-paragraph style.

2. Turn on the Add To Template check box to save the changed style in the template (rather than in the document only).

3. Click OK.

4. Click Close to close the Style dialog box.

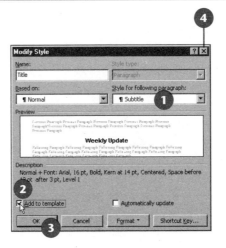

Designing for a Top Letterhead

If your letterhead is at the top of your stationery, you can modify your letter template to allow space for the letterhead on the first page. If your printer has one paper tray for letterhead stationery and another for standard paper, Word can print the first page of your letter on the letterhead stationery and subsequent pages on standard paper.

TIP

Marginal improvement.
If you're using the Letter Wizard, you can have the wizard automatically leave room for the letterhead. This, however, causes a change to the template's top margin, so all subsequent pages will have this extra space.

SEE ALSO

For information about basing a new template on an existing one, see "Customizing a Template" on page 68.

Leave Space for the Letterhead

1. Create a new template based on a letter template.

2. On a sheet of letterhead, measure the distance from the top of the page to the top of the first paragraph.

3. Subtract the height of the top margin.

4. Select the first paragraph, choose Paragraph from the Format menu, enter the resulting distance in the Space Before box, and click OK.

Specify Paper Options

1. Choose Page Setup from the File menu, and click the Paper Source tab.

2. Select the source for your letterhead paper.

3. Select the source for your standard paper.

4. Click OK.

5. Save and close the template.

Top margin + Space Before setting leaves room for the selected style

March 30, 1999¶

¶
Dear·¶
¶
Sincerely,¶

Harry·Planifrons¶
·Boss¶

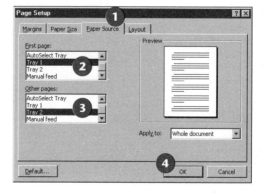

Designing for a Side Letterhead

If your letterhead is at the side of your stationery, you can modify your letter template to allow space for the letterhead on the first page but to use the full width of the page on all subsequent pages.

TIP

Design choices. *If you know that all your letters will be only one page long, or if you want to maintain the letter-head space as a design element on all the pages of longer letters, simply adjust the margins to accommodate the letterhead.*

TIP

Absolute AutoShape. *If you delete or move the first para-graph, the AutoShape might be deleted or moved. To ensure this doesn't happen, use the Advanced button on the Layout tab of the Format AutoShape dialog box to set the AutoShape to an absolute position relative to the margin.*

Leave Space for the Letterhead

1. Create a new template based on a letter template.

2. Use the Zoom box to display the whole page.

3. Click the Drawing button to display the Drawing toolbar.

4. Use the Rectangle tool to draw an AutoShape rectangle where the letterhead will appear.

5. Choose AutoShape from the Format menu, and, on the Size tab, adjust the dimensions to match those of your letterhead.

6. On the Layout tab, click the Square wrapping style, and click OK.

7. Print the template on letterhead stationery. Adjust the size of the AutoShape if necessary.

8. Choose AutoShape from the Format menu, and, on the Colors And Lines tab, set Fill Color to No Fill and Line Color to No Line. Click OK.

9. Save and close the template.

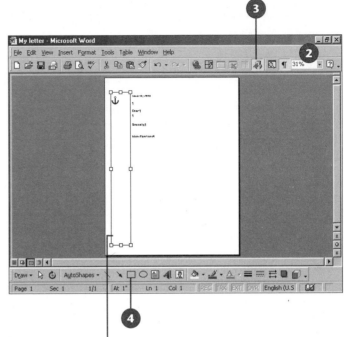

The AutoShape is a placeholder for the letterhead.

Creating Your Own Letterhead

Instead of using preprinted letterhead stationery, you can create a letterhead in your template, and the letterhead will be printed whenever you use that template. By placing the letterhead in the first-page header, you won't need to worry about margins, the position of the first paragraph, and so on.

TIP

Letterhead as footer? *To create your letterhead at the bottom of the page, place the letterhead in the footer instead of in the header. To create your letterhead at one side of the page, draw a text box to hold the letterhead, and specify a text-wrapping style around the text box.*

SEE ALSO

For information about basing a new template on an existing one, see "Customizing a Template" on page 68.

Create a First-Page Header

1. Create a new template based on a letter template.
2. Choose Page Setup from the File menu, and click the Layout tab.
3. Turn on the Different First Page check box.
4. Click OK.

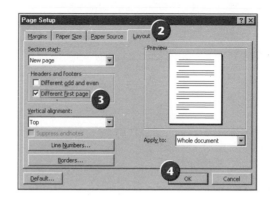

Create the Letterhead

1. Choose Header And Footer from the View menu.
2. Create your letterhead, using paragraph and font formatting.
3. Click the Close button on the Header And Footer toolbar.
4. Save and close the template.

Use a distinctive font.

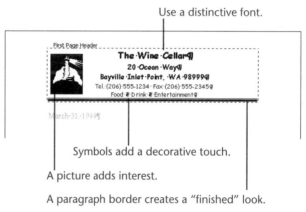

Symbols add a decorative touch.

A picture adds interest.

A paragraph border creates a "finished" look.

Addressing an Envelope

When you've taken the time and trouble to create a professional-looking letter or other document, you don't want to ruin the good impression with a hand-written envelope! Word makes it easy for you to create crisp, businesslike printed envelopes. You can easily include your return address, and, in the United States, you can even add a postal bar code.

TIP

Change of address. *If you want to change your user information, choose Options from the Tools menu, click the User Information tab, and change the information.*

Add the Address

1. Choose Envelopes And Labels from the Tools menu, and click the Envelopes tab.

2. Verify that the delivery address is correct. If it's missing, click Cancel, select the address in your document, and then reopen the Envelopes And Labels dialog box.

3. Verify that the return address is correct.

4. Do one of the following:

    ◆ Click Print to print only the envelope.

    ◆ Click Add To Document to add the envelope layout and address to your document so that you can print the letter and its envelope at the same time.

    ◆ Click Options to change the way the envelope is printed.

The delivery address from your letter

Click to use another address from your address book.

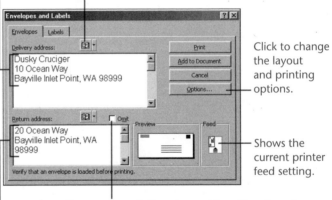

Click to change the layout and printing options.

Shows the current printer feed setting.

Turn on to omit the return address if you're using an envelope with a preprinted return address.

The return address from the user information you supplied to Word

TIP

Acronyms exposed. *The bar code is the Postal Numeric Encoding Technique (POSTNET) bar code used by the U.S. Postal Service to automate the sorting and processing of mail. The FIM-A code is the Facing Identification Mark, and is usually used in bulk mailings to identify the front of the envelope for automated sorting.*

SEE ALSO

For information about using Word's Mail Merge feature to address multiple envelopes, see "Addressing Envelopes from a Mailing List" on page 280.

Change the Setup

1. Click the Options button, and click the Envelope Options tab.

2. Change the settings as desired.

3. Click OK.

Turn on to include a bar code based on the ZIP code.

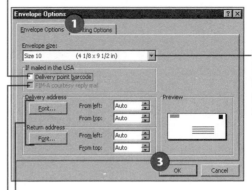

Select an envelope size, or click Custom Size to define a non-standard size.

Customize the delivery- and return-address fonts and locations.

Print a FIM-A code (available only when the Delivery Point Barcode check box is turned on).

Change the Printer Settings

1. Click the Print button in the Envelopes And Labels dialog box to test-print an envelope.

2. If the envelope doesn't print correctly, open the Envelopes And Labels dialog box again, click the Options button, click the Printing Options tab, and change the settings to correct the problem.

Click a picture to change the envelope's orientation.

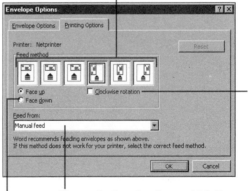

Turn on to rotate the envelopes in the three feed options on the right.

Choose the location from which the envelopes will be fed into the printer.

Click if the address was printed on the wrong side of the envelope.

6

Creating a Long Document

What's the difference between creating a long document and creating a short document? Well, a long document can give you a much bigger headache, for one thing! If your long document is simply pages and pages of text with absolutely nothing else—no headings, no graphics, no sections—the only difference between it and a short document might be that you'd add page numbers. Many long documents, however, contain elements such as tables, graphics, several levels of headings, footnotes, and so on. In addition, a long document is often made up of several smaller documents, or *subdocuments,* which might be written by several authors.

A long document involves a lot of planning, many revisions, and careful tracking of versions. Unexpected things happen: for example, the marketing department changes the name of the product you're writing about. The original name appears in about a zillion places in a report you're presenting at a big meeting in the morning. It'll take all night to make all those changes. But don't panic! You won't have to work until the wee small hours, because Microsoft Word can make those changes for you in just a few minutes.

Use Word's powerful tools to help you manage and produce a long document, and your long-document headaches will be long gone!

Organizing with Styles

Paragraph styles do more than quickly apply formatting to paragraphs; they also assign an *outline level* to each paragraph in a document. Word uses these levels to understand how you're organizing the document—which paragraphs are headings, which are subheadings, and which are text. You can use Word's defined outline hierarchy, or you can create your own structure by defining the outline levels for your styles.

SEE ALSO

For information about transferring styles between templates and documents, see "Copying Between Templates" on page 73.

For information about creating styles, see "Creating Styles from Scratch" on page 74.

For information about using Outline view to look at your heading hierarchy, see "Reorganizing a Long Document" on page 98.

Create a Heading Hierarchy

1. Switch to Normal view if you're not already in it.

2. Choose Options from the Tools menu, and click the View tab.

3. Specify a value (0.7", for example) in the Style Area Width box.

4. Turn on the Wrap To Window check box.

5. Click OK to open the style area.

6. Scroll through the document, adjusting style assignments:

   ◆ Apply appropriate heading styles to heading paragraphs.

   ◆ Apply appropriate body-text styles to body-text paragraphs.

   ◆ Apply appropriate special styles (captions, for example) to special paragraphs.

Drag left or right to resize the style area.

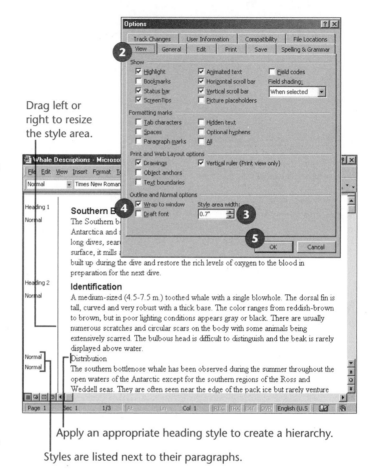

Apply an appropriate heading style to create a hierarchy.

Styles are listed next to their paragraphs.

TIP

Keep an eye on Word.
Word tries to guess which type of style you want to use. If you format and use a paragraph so that it looks like a heading, Word will probably assign it a heading style. Keeping the style area open is a good way to monitor Word's automatic style assignments.

SEE ALSO

For information about turning off the option to have Word define styles based on your formatting, see "Controlling Automatic Changes" on page 302.

TIP

A new look. *The Automatically Update The Style From Now On option causes Word to redefine a style whenever you apply any direct formatting. This can cause some startling effects because all the paragraphs in your document with that style will change to match the direct formatting. Unless you're experimenting to create a new look in a document, or unless consistency among documents isn't an issue, you'll want to keep this option turned off.*

Define a Style as a Heading

1. Select a paragraph labeled with the style name to be defined as a heading.

2. Choose Paragraph from the Format menu.

3. Select an outline level.

4. Click OK.

5. Click the style name to select it, and press Enter.

6. Click OK in the Modify Style dialog box to update the style.

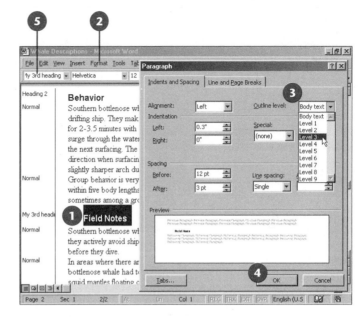

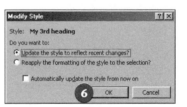

Quickly Applying Standardized Formatting

Paragraph styles are useful in any document, but they're a necessity in a long document, where each type of paragraph must be formatted consistently throughout the document. Styles are real time-savers too: just choose a style, and all the formatting is applied at once. You can save even more time and effort by assigning frequently used styles to a custom toolbar and assigning shortcut keys to less frequently used styles.

Create a Toolbar

1. Choose Customize from the Tools menu.

2. Click the Toolbars tab.

3. Click the New button.

4. Type a name for the toolbar.

5. Specify where you want to save the toolbar.

6. Click OK.

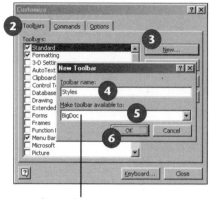

Save the toolbar in Normal.dot to make it available to all documents, in the document template (if there is one) to make it available only to documents based on that template, or in the document to make it available only in the current document.

Add a Style

1. Click the Commands tab.

2. Select Styles.

3. Click a style you want to add to the toolbar.

4. Drag the style onto the toolbar.

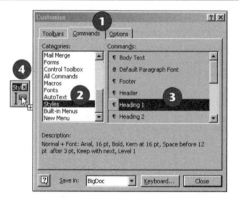

Create key combinations.

To assign a style to a shortcut key combination, click the Keyboard button, and, in the Customize Keyboard dialog box, press the key combination you want.

For information about modifying existing toolbars, see "Customizing Toolbars" on page 318.

Label the Button

1. Click the Modify Selection button.

2. Type a name for the button, and press Enter.

3. Do either of the following:

   ◆ Add another style to the toolbar, and give it a name.

   ◆ Click an existing button, and then click Modify Selection to change the button's name.

4. Click Close when you've finished.

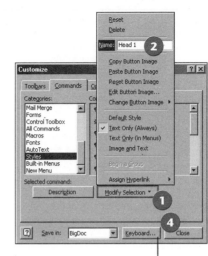

Click to assign the style to a keyboard shortcut.

Preparing for a Bound Document

Whether you put your long document in a simple ring binder or have it profession-ally bound, you'll need to allow a large enough *gutter* on the side (or at the top) of the page to accommodate the binding. Word will add this gutter for you and, if you're going to print on both sides of the paper, will automatically reverse the left and right margins and add the extra space to the appropriate side of the page.

SEE ALSO

For information about setting margins and gutters when you're printing two pages on a single sheet of paper, see "Printing Two Pages on One Sheet" on page 221.

Specify the Page Dimensions

1. Choose Page Setup from the File menu.

2. Click the Margins tab.

3. If you're going to print (or copy) the document on both sides of the paper, turn on the Mirror Margins check box. For documents that will be printed on only one side, turn off the check box.

4. Set the margin dimensions.

5. Set a gutter value equal to the room required for the binding.

6. Specify whether you want the gutter on the left side or at the top of the page.

7. Click OK.

The preview shows the size and location of the gutter.

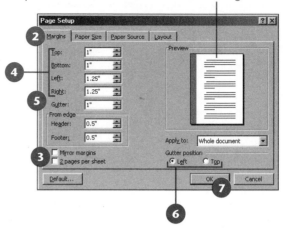

The gutter is always on the inside edge of a double-sided document.

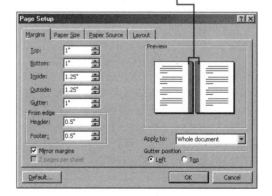

Creating a Running Head

A running head is a little message or identifier that appears at the top or bottom of a page, above or below the normal text area. All you do is create the running head once, and Word places it on the pages you designate. For the sake of consistency, we're using the term "running head" for the heading itself, and the terms "header" and "footer" to describe the running head's position on the page. Note that on the screen you can see the headers and footers on your page only in Print Layout view or in Print Preview.

TIP

Different planes of existence. *The running head exists on a different layer from that of your main document text. You can't edit your document text while you're working on the running head, and vice versa.*

Create a Header

1. Choose Header And Footer from the View menu.

2. Type the running head in the Header area. Use tabs, paragraph spacing and alignment, and font settings to customize the layout.

3. Use any of the toolbar buttons or AutoText entries to insert information.

4. If you don't want to add a footer, click Close.

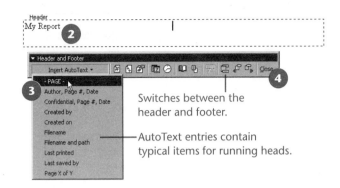

Switches between the header and footer.

AutoText entries contain typical items for running heads.

Create a Footer

1. Click the Switch Between Header And Footer button.

2. Type the running head in the Footer area.

3. Use any of the toolbar buttons or AutoText entries to insert information.

4. Click Close.

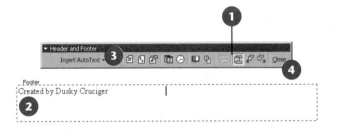

6

Creating Variable Running Heads

Look through this book and you'll see that the odd- and even-numbered pages have alternating running heads in the footer. This is a fairly standard design, especially for double-sided documents, and you can set it up quite easily in Word.

TIP

Three heads. *There must be a minimum of three pages in your document before you can insert first-page, odd-page, and even-page running heads. If your document doesn't have three pages, press Ctrl+Enter twice to create two extra pages. You can delete these manual page breaks later.*

Specify Different Headers and Footers

1. Choose Page Setup from the File menu.

2. Click the Layout tab.

3. Turn on the check box for different odd and even running heads.

4. Turn on the check box for a different or blank first-page running head.

5. Click OK.

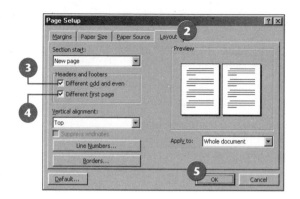

Create a First-Page Running Head

1. Press Ctrl+Home to move to the beginning of the document.

2. Choose Header And Footer from the View menu.

3. Enter the header information.

4. Click the Switch Between Header And Footer button.

5. Enter the footer information.

The label tells you which header you're working on.

Use any formatting and alignment you want.

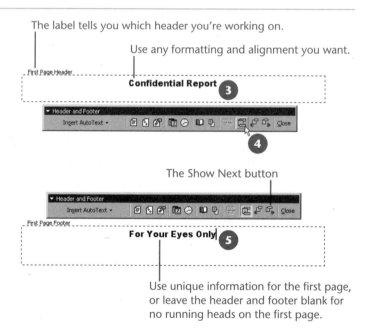

First Page Header

Confidential Report

The Show Next button

First Page Footer

For Your Eyes Only

Use unique information for the first page, or leave the header and footer blank for no running heads on the first page.

Create an Even-Page Running Head

1. Click the Show Next button.

2. Enter the footer information.

3. Click the Switch Between Header And Footer button.

4. Enter the header information.

Create an Odd-Page Running Head

1. Click the Show Next button.

2. Enter the header information.

3. Click the Switch Between Header And Footer button.

4. Enter the footer information.

5. Click the Close button on the Header And Footer toolbar.

Place the text on the left side of the header for a running head on the outside edge of the even-numbered page.

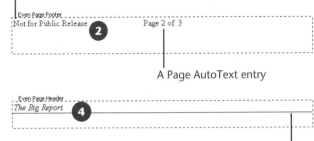

A Page AutoText entry

A paragraph bottom border adds a nice effect.

Place the text on the right side of the header for a running head on the outside edge of the odd-numbered page.

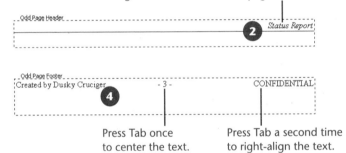

Press Tab once to center the text.

Press Tab a second time to right-align the text.

6

Inserting a Word Document

Sometimes parts of a large document are created as separate documents: chapters of a book, for example, or sections of a report. You can insert the contents of a separate document into the main document. When you do, the styles in the inserted document are copied into your main document, but the formatting and the running heads are set by the main document. You can also link the inserted content to the source document so that any changes made to it will appear in the main document.

TIP

Dual existence. *A document you insert continues to exist as a separate document. Only when you link to it are any changes you make to the source document reflected in the main document.*

Insert a Word Document

1. Click in the document where you want the inserted document to appear.

2. Choose File from the Insert menu.

3. In the Insert File dialog box, select the type of document, if necessary.

4. Locate and select the document to be inserted.

5. Do either of the following:
   - ◆ Click the Insert button to insert the content.
   - ◆ Click the down arrow next to the Insert button, and click Insert As Link to insert the content and keep the main document linked to the inserted (source) document.

6. Click OK.

7. Verify that the contents of the inserted file are correct.

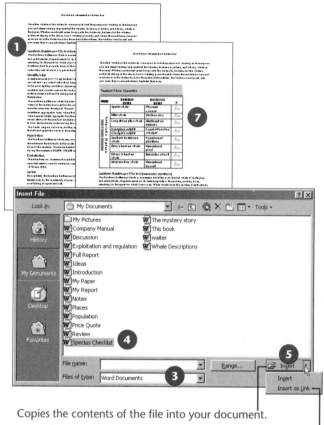

Copies the contents of the file into your document.

Copies the contents and creates a connection to the source file.

Inserting Part of a Word Document

You can insert part of another document into your main document, and, if the inserted content changes in the original document, the changes will be updated in your main document. Updates usually occur as soon as you open the main document, or when you're working in the main document and the linked information changes in the source document.

TRY THIS

Test the link. *After you've linked part of the source document to the main document, switch back to the source document and make some changes to the part you linked. You'll see the changes when you switch back to your main document.*

Insert Part of a Document

1. Open the document containing the content to be included.

2. Select and copy the content.

3. Switch to your main document, and click where you want the content to appear.

4. Choose Paste Special from the Edit menu.

5. Click the Paste Link option.

6. Select a format:
   - Use Formatted Text (RTF) if you're using Word documents (.doc) as your standard.
   - Use HTML Format if you're using HTML (Web pages) as your standard.

7. Click OK.

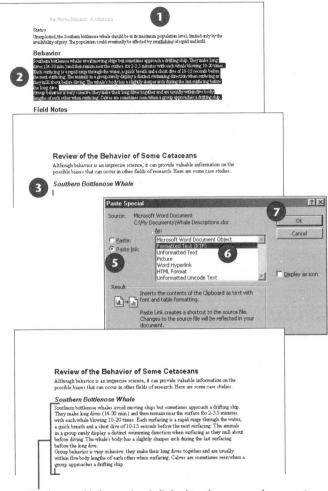

The inserted information is linked to the source document.

Finding Items in a Document

When you're editing or proofreading a document, you often do so in stages: you might check the tables, for example, and then the graphics, and so on. You can browse through your document, jumping to the next occurrence of a specific element, with the help of a tiny button that does a big job. Use the table at the right to achieve the results you want.

SEE ALSO

For information about using the Document Map to find topics in a long document, see "Finding Topics in a Document" on the facing page.

Browse by Element

1. Click the Select Browse Object button.

2. Click the type of element you're looking for.

3. Click the appropriate button to go to the next or previous occurrence of the element.

4. Continue clicking the buttons to move through the document, locating each instance of the element you want to review.

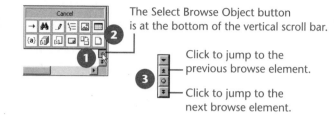

The Select Browse Object button is at the bottom of the vertical scroll bar.

Click to jump to the previous browse element.

Click to jump to the next browse element.

THE SELECT BROWSE OBJECT BUTTON	
Use this button	**To do this**
→	Display the Go To tab of the Find And Replace dialog box.
🔍	Display the Find tab of the Find And Replace dialog box.
✎	Go to the next or previous edit.
☰	Go to the next or previous heading.
▨	Go to the next or previous graphic.
▦	Go to the next or previous table.
{a}	Go to the next or previous field.
⬛	Go to the next or previous endnote.
⬛	Go to the next or previous footnote.
⬛	Go to the next or previous comment.
⬛	Go to the next or previous section.
⬛	Go to the next or previous page.

Finding Topics in a Document

The longer a document gets, the more difficult it can be to find a specific topic within it. This is when you'll really appreciate Word's Document Map. When you display the Document Map, you can see an outline view of your document, and, with a click or two, you can jump to the appropriate topic. The outline structure is based on the heading levels assigned to the styles you used.

SEE ALSO

For information about structuring your document, see "Organizing with Styles" on page 86.

TIP

Map border. *Drag the border between the Document Map and the text area to see more or less of the Document Map.*

Navigate with the Document Map

1. Switch to the view you want to use:
   - Web Layout view to easily view all the content of the document
   - Print Layout view to see the formatting and line breaks that will be used in a printed document

2. Click the Document Map button.

3. Point to a topic to see its full text if the heading is too long to be displayed completely in the Document Map area.

4. Click the topic.

5. When you've finished locating and reviewing topics, click the Document Map button to hide the Document Map.

Click a minus sign to collapse the headings directly below it.

...to jump to it in the document.

Click a topic...

Click a plus sign to expand the headings directly below it.

Reorganizing a Long Document

Outline view provides a powerful way for you to view the structure of your document and to rearrange the order of presentation of topics in the document. The outline structure assumes that you've used specific styles to organize your document into a hierarchy of topics and subtopics.

Change the level. *To quickly change a topic's outline level, drag its plus or minus sign to the left to promote the level, to the right to demote it, or to the far right to turn it into body text.*

View a Document's Outline

1 Switch to Outline view.

2 Click in a heading, and use the tools on the Outlining toolbar to expand or collapse the outline or to promote or demote heading levels.

Move a Topic

1 Place the mouse pointer over a plus or minus sign. The pointer becomes a four-headed arrow.

2 Drag the topic up or down and into a new location. (The pointer becomes a two-headed arrow, pointing up and down.)

Promotes or demotes the heading level.

Expands or collapses the topic.

Specifies the lowest heading level displayed.

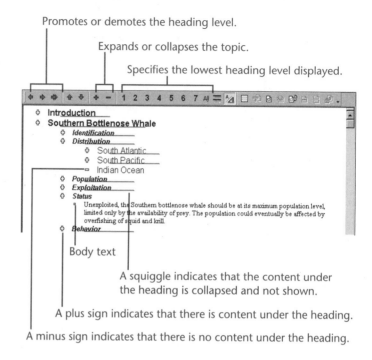

Body text

A squiggle indicates that the content under the heading is collapsed and not shown.

A plus sign indicates that there is content under the heading.

A minus sign indicates that there is no content under the heading.

Shows where the topic will be moved to.

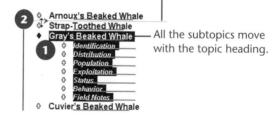

All the subtopics move with the topic heading.

Adding Page Numbers

If you've ever dropped a stack of unnumbered pages, you'll vow to add page numbers to any document that's more than a couple of pages long! Page numbers are essential, too, in a book such as this one, where there's a great deal of cross-referencing. Word will automatically number the pages for you.

TIP

I'll have a double. *If you're creating a double-sided document, choose Inside or Outside for the alignment of page numbers.*

SEE ALSO

For information about adding page numbers to a custom header or footer, see "Creating a Running Head" on page 91.

Place the Page Number

1. Choose Page Numbers from the Insert menu.

2. Specify a position for the page numbers.

3. Select an alignment.

4. Click Format.

5. Do any of the following to customize the page numbers:

   ◆ Specify a different numbering format.

   ◆ Turn on the Include Chapter Number check box, and specify a unique style to identify the first page of each chapter.

   ◆ Specify whether pages will be numbered consecutively throughout the document or will start with a specific page number.

6. Click OK.

7. Click OK.

The preview shows the placement of the number.

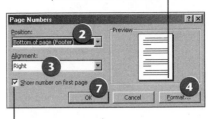

Turn off if you don't want a number on the first page.

Turn on to automatically include chapter numbers.

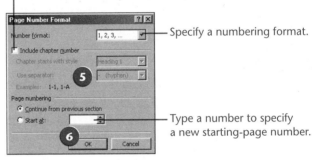

Specify a numbering format.

Type a number to specify a new starting-page number.

Finding Text

If you're not sure where to find some text in your document, Word can locate it for you. You can broaden the search so that Word finds similar words, or you can narrow the search to a designated part of the document or to text that uses specific formatting.

TIP

Wild! *"Wildcard" characters are used to represent other characters. The most commonly used wildcards are ? and *. The ? wildcard specifies any single character, and the * wildcard specifies any number of characters. For a complete list of wildcards, turn on the Use Wildcards check box and click the Special button.*

SEE ALSO

For information about quickly locating different types of elements in a document, see "Finding Items in a Document" on page 96.

Search for Text

1 Specify what part of the document is to be searched:

◆ Select some text to limit the search to the selection.

◆ If you want to search the entire document, click in the document so that nothing is selected.

2 Choose Find from the Edit menu.

3 Type the text you want to find.

4 Click Find Next.

Broaden the Search

1 Click the More button (if it's displayed).

2 Select the appropriate option to achieve the result shown in the table at the right.

3 Click Find Next.

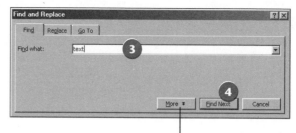

Click to see more search options.

OPTIONS TO BROADEN A SEARCH	
Option	**Result**
Use Wildcards check box	Uses certain characters as wildcard characters.
Sounds Like check box	Finds words that sound the same but are spelled differently (*their* and *there,* for example).
Find All Word Forms check box	Finds all words that are forms of the word (its plural or past tense, for example) in the Find What box.
All (from the Search list)	Searches the entire document.

Play your cards. *In your document, type the text "To be or not to be" is asked too often. In the Find What box, type o?t and turn on the Use Wildcards check box. Click Find Next until the entire selection has been searched. Then change the Find What text to o*t and repeat the search. Then use to as the search text, turn on the Sounds Like option, and search the document. Finally, use is as the search text, turn on the Find All Word Forms option, and search the document. Note the different results.*

Find it again. *When you use the Find Next command, the Select Browse Object button at the bottom of the vertical scroll bar automatically uses the information you entered in the Find And Replace dialog box. To find text again after you've closed the dialog box, click the Next Find/GoTo button below the Select Browse Object button.*

Narrow the Search

1 Use any combination of the following:

◆ Select text to limit the search to the selection.

◆ Be as specific as possible in the text you type in the Find What box.

◆ Choose the appropriate option to achieve the result shown in the table at the right.

◆ Click Format and specify the format of the text.

◆ Click Special and select any special formatting element that is associated with the text.

2 Click Find Next. Repeat the search if necessary.

3 Click Close.

OPTIONS TO NARROW A SEARCH	
Option	Result
Match Case check box	Finds only text that exactly matches the capitalization of the text in the Find What box.
Find Whole Words Only	Finds text only if the matching text consists of whole words, not parts of words.
Down (from the Search list)	Searches only from the location of the insertion point to the end of the document.
Up (from the Search list)	Searches only from the location of the insertion point to the beginning of the document.

6

Replacing Text

When you need to replace a word or phrase with a different word or phrase in several places in your document, let Word do it for you. It's a great way to use Word's speed and power to make quick work of those tedious document-wide changes.

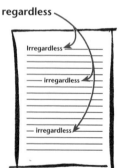

SEE ALSO

For information about broadening or narrowing a search, see "Finding Text" on pages 100–101.

Replace Text

1. Specify what part of the document is to be searched:

   ◆ Select text to limit the search to the selection.

   ◆ If you want to search the entire document, click in the document so that nothing is selected.

2. Choose Replace from the Edit menu.

3. On the Replace tab, click in the Find What text box, and type the text to be found.

4. Press the Tab key to move to the Replace With text box, and type the replacement text.

5. Click the Replace, Replace All, or Find Next button.

6. Click the Cancel or Close button when you've finished.

7. Review the document. If you used the Replace All button and the results are not what you expected, click the Undo button on the Standard toolbar. Then repeat the Find and Replace sequence using narrower search parameters.

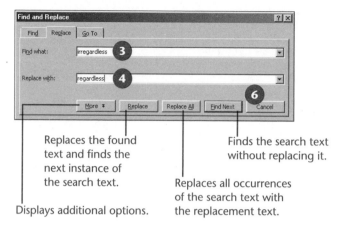

Replaces the found text and finds the next instance of the search text.

Displays additional options.

Replaces all occurrences of the search text with the replacement text.

Finds the search text without replacing it.

Replacing Text and Formatting

Let's say that the word *computer* is lowercased in all your headings and you realize that it should have an initial capital letter. You don't want to replace every instance of the word throughout the entire document, because it's perfectly correct as is in the body text. When you need to replace a frequently used word, but only in instances where it has a specific style or format, you can use Word's Replace command. Simply specify the search text and its formatting and the replacement text, and Word will produce precise and powerful modifications.

TIP

Quick change. *To quickly replace one style with another, specify the style as the format in the Find What and Replace With boxes, but don't type any text.*

Replace Text and Formatting

1 Specify what part of the document is to be searched:

 ◆ Select text to limit the search to the selection.

 ◆ If you want to search the entire document, click in the document so that nothing is selected.

2 Choose Replace from the Edit menu.

3 In the Find What text box, type the search text, or leave the box blank to search for formatting only.

4 Click the More button, and specify any search options.

5 Click the Format button, and specify the formatting to be searched for.

6 Type the replacement text.

7 Click the Replace or Replace All button.

8 Click the Close or Cancel button when you've finished.

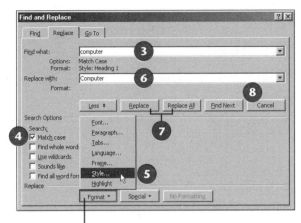

Displays the selected format to be searched for.

6

Using Different Layouts in One Document

In a long document, different parts of the document sometimes require different layouts. By dividing the document into sections, you can set up each section in its own way.

SEE ALSO

For information about using a multiple-column layout, see "Flowing Text into Columns" on page 188.

TIP

Selection section. *When you change the orientation of selected text, you're actually creating two new sections: one section for the selected text and another one for the text that follows the selection.*

Change the Page Orientation

1. Select the part of the document whose page orientation you want to change.

2. Choose Page Setup from the File menu.

3. Click the Paper Size tab.

4. Select the orientation you want.

5. Select Selected Text.

6. Click OK.

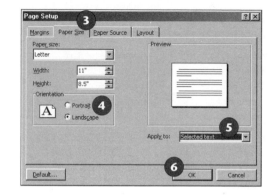

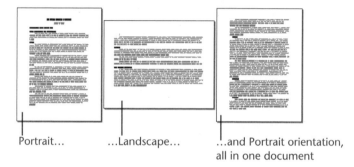

Portrait...   ...Landscape...   ...and Portrait orientation, all in one document

Change the Margins

1. Select the part of the document whose margins you want to change.

2. Choose Page Setup from the File menu.

3. Click the Margins tab.

4. Set the new margins.

5. Select Selected Text.

6. Click the Layout tab.

7. Select the point where the changed section will start.

8. Click OK.

9. Click in the following section, choose Page Setup again, and, on the Layout tab, select where you want this section to start. Click OK when you've finished.

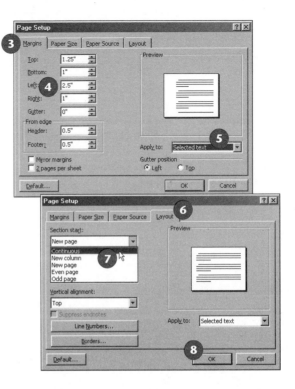

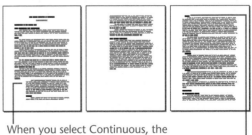

When you select Continuous, the new format starts on the same page.

By default, the following section starts on the next page.

6

Creating Chapters

A long document is usually divided into chapters or sections, each of which should begin on an odd-numbered (right-hand) page. Word will start your chapters or sections on odd-numbered pages, and will create running heads to your specifications.

TIP

Change heads. *If the document is set for a different running head on the first page, or for different running heads on odd and even pages, make any changes to running heads after turning off the Same As Previous button.*

SEE ALSO

For information about running heads, see "Creating a Running Head" on page 91 and "Creating Variable Running Heads" on page 92.

For information about including the chapter number with the page number, see "Adding Page Numbers" on page 99.

Start a New Chapter

1. Place the insertion point at the beginning of a new chapter or section.

2. Choose Break from the Insert menu.

3. Select the Odd Page option under Section Break Types.

4. Click OK.

Change the Running Heads

1. Choose Header And Footer from the View menu.

2. Click the Same As Previous button to turn it off.

3. Make changes to the running head.

4. Switch to the footer and repeat steps 2 and 3 for the footer.

5. Click Close.

The section break is inserted in front of the insertion point. (Turn on the Show/Hide ¶ button on the Standard toolbar if the section break isn't visible.)

The text comes from the previous header.

The label tells you that this header is the same as the previous header.

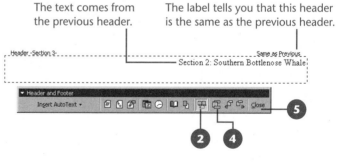

When the Same As Previous button is turned off, you can create unique headers and footers for each chapter.

Creating a Summary

Hard to believe, but some people might not take the time to savor every word of your document! To make sure they don't miss the important parts, you can create a summary of the completed document that contains all the pertinent information. You can use the AutoSummary as a starting point, but you'll need to review the summary and tailor it as desired.

TIP

To summarize... *When you're reviewing a highlighted summary on line, you can use the AutoSummarize toolbar to show or hide the text that isn't highlighted and to change the percentage of the original text that's included in the summary. The AutoSummarize toolbar is not available for an executive summary or for a summary created in a new document.*

Create a Summary

1 Choose AutoSummarize from the Tools menu. Depending on the length of the document, Word might take a little while to review it.

2 Specify the type of summary you want.

3 Specify the length of the summary.

4 Click OK.

5 Point to the split box at the top of the vertical scroll bar. When you see the split bar, drag it halfway down the window to split the window in two horizontally.

6 Review the summary, and compare it carefully with the contents of the original document. Delete any unnecessary information from the summary; copy any missing information from the main text into the summary.

Select for an online document or to print a summary showing highlighted text.

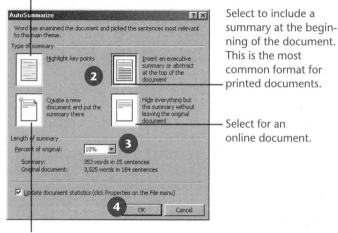

Select to include a summary at the beginning of the document. This is the most common format for printed documents.

Select for an online document.

Select to circulate the summary separately from the document.

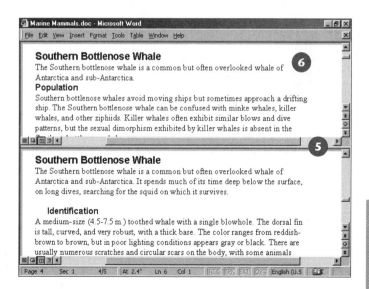

6

Creating a Table of Contents

Provided your document is organized by styles, it's a snap to have Word create a well-organized table of contents for you. You design your table of contents by selecting a format and designating which levels are assigned to the headings. Word adjusts the appearance of the table of contents depending on how you're viewing it. In Web Layout view, for example, the table consists of links, but in Print Layout view it looks like a table of contents you'd see in a book. Either way, when your document is viewed on line, the table of contents is active, with jumps to the headings listed in your table.

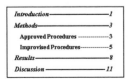

Choose a Layout

1. Click in the document where you want the table of contents to appear.

2. Choose Index And Tables from the Insert menu.

3. Click the Table Of Contents tab.

4. Select a format.

5. Choose the options to be included.

Displays samples of tables of contents based on the outline levels assigned to document styles, and on the format and options selected.

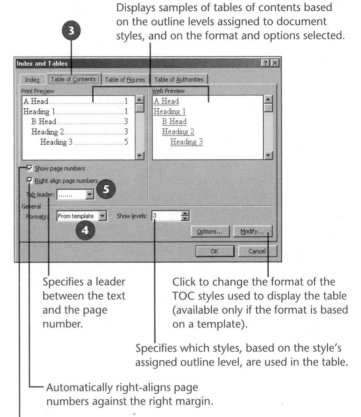

Specifies a leader between the text and the page number.

Click to change the format of the TOC styles used to display the table (available only if the format is based on a template).

Specifies which styles, based on the style's assigned outline level, are used in the table.

Automatically right-aligns page numbers against the right margin.

Includes the current page number for each entry.

TOC levels. *You can assign the same table-of-contents (TOC) level to different styles.*

Excluded content. *Keep in mind that Word doesn't search text boxes, so any text you've placed in a text box won't appear in the table of contents. You can decide not to put items into text boxes if you want them to appear in your table of contents, or, for a printed document, you can add text-box entries manually after you've compiled the final table of contents.*

Active table. *Create your table of contents. Switch to Online Layout view, and click a link in the table to jump to a topic. Switch to Print Layout view, return to the table of contents, and click another entry to jump to that topic.*

For information about assigning outline levels to styles, see "Define a Style as a Heading" on page 87.

For information about editing a table of contents, see "Updating a Table of Contents" on page 110.

Specify Styles

1. Click the Options button.

2. Enter the level number for each style you want to use.

3. Change the level number for a style you want to use at a different level.

4. Delete the numbers from styles you don't want to use.

5. Click OK.

6. Look at the preview again, and adjust the settings if necessary.

7. Click OK.

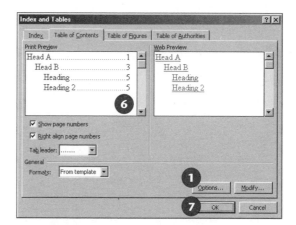

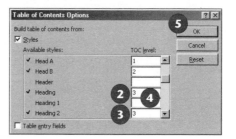

Updating a Table of Contents

Once you've set up a table of contents, Word can update it to reflect changed page numbers, or can rebuild the entire table if you've added, deleted, or moved headings. You can also freeze the table of contents so that you can edit it before you print it.

TIP

Roman or Arabic? *If the page numbers in your table of contents are Roman numerals but you want the main part of your document to start on page 1, insert a section break after the table of contents, and reset the page numbering.*

SEE ALSO

For information about changing the page-numbering format see "Adding Page Numbers" on page 99.

For information about section breaks, see "Creating Chapters" on page 106.

Update the Contents

1 In a document that already has a table of contents, edit the document and save the changes.

2 Move the mouse pointer to the left of the first line of the table of contents until the pointer becomes the standard Text Selection pointer, and click to select the table.

3 Right-click anywhere in the table of contents, and choose Update Field from the shortcut menu.

4 Specify how you want to update the table of contents:

◆ Update the page numbers for the existing entries.

◆ Re-create the table of contents to update both the changed entries and their page numbers.

5 Click OK.

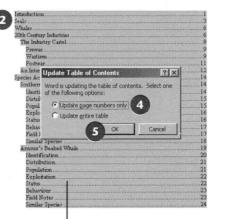

The entire field is shaded when selected.

TIP

Field your questions. *The table of contents is generated by the TOC field. A field is a tool Word uses to automate a process. Word uses fields for other common processes—inserting page numbers in a document, for example, or inserting a date that updates itself automatically.*

TRY THIS

Question your fields. *Select the table-of-contents field, and press Shift+F9 to see the field code. Now choose Field from the Insert menu, and click TOC in the Field Names list. Click the Options button, click some of the switches to see what they do, and compare them with the switches in your TOC field. When you've satisfied your curiosity, click Cancel in both dialog boxes, select the entire TOC field, and press Shift+F9 to redisplay the table of contents.*

SEE ALSO

For more information about fields, see "Wandering and Wondering Through Word's Fields" on page 293 and "Inserting Changing Information" on page 296.

Freeze and Edit the Table

1 Make sure that your long document is complete, that the page breaks are all in the correct places, and that you don't want to use the table-of-contents links in an online document.

2 Click at the left of the first line of the table of contents to select the table.

3 Press Ctrl+Shift+F9 to unlink the field so that the information won't be updated.

4 With the text still selected, press Ctrl+Spacebar to remove any direct text formatting.

5 Edit the table as you would edit any text.

With the table of contents no longer a field, you can change its content and formatting.

6

Tracking Versions

During the creation of a long document, you might change the text a dozen times. Each time you save the document, your changes are saved in the current version, and the original text is lost. If you want to refer to the original text, you can save each changed version of the document. When you print the document, you can include information that clarifies which version you're printing.

TIP

Saving the version. *A new version is created only when you click the Save Now button in the Versions dialog box or, if the Automatically Save A Version check box is turned on, when you close the document.*

TIP

Quick version. *To quickly open the Versions dialog box after you've saved the first version, double-click the Versions icon on the status bar.*

Save a Version

1. Choose Versions from the File menu.

2. Turn on the check box to save a version whenever the document is closed.

3. Click Save Now.

4. Enter any comments.

5. Click OK.

6. If the Save As dialog box appears, type a name for the file, and click Save.

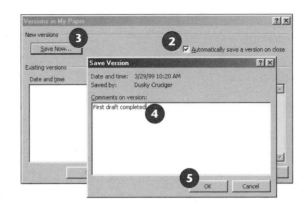

Review a Previous Version

1. Choose Versions from the File menu.

2. Double-click the version you want to review.

3. Close the document when you've finished your review.

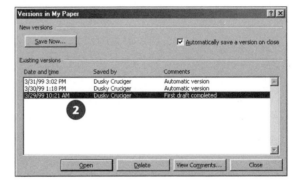

TIP

View the fields. *Most of the AutoText information is inserted as fields. Word has several additional fields, which provide information about your document that you can insert directly.*

TIP

Fields in templates. *If you want the same information in every document, you can place the entries in your template. Because the information is completed by fields, the information will be included in each document created from the template.*

SEE ALSO

For information about adding content to a template, see "Customizing a Template" on page 68.

For information about recording and inserting information about your document, see "Inserting Document Information" on page 299 and "Keeping Track of Document Information" on page 300.

Print Version Information

1. Choose Page Setup from the File menu, and, on the Layout tab, turn on the Different First Page check box. Click OK.

2. Press Ctrl+Home to move to the beginning of your document.

3. Choose Header And Footer from the View menu.

4. Switch to the footer.

5. Click the Insert AutoText button.

6. Click the items you want to be printed in the document.

7. Format the paragraph in a different or smaller font, if necessary.

8. Click Close.

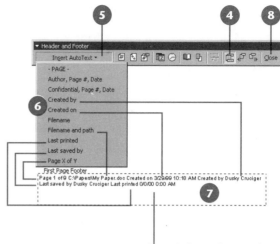

Some information won't appear until you save and print the document.

Organizing a Multiple-Authors Document

A single long document often comprises several smaller documents: each section of a report, for example, might be created by a different person. In this situation, there's a strong possibility of inconsistency in writing or formatting and of repetition of content. To organize the individual sections and to ensure that they cover the required material without being redundant, you can create an outline, divide the parts of the document into separate but connected *subdocuments,* and review the completed documents as one. The main document in which the subdocuments are contained is called the *master document.*

Create an Outline

1. Start a new document, using the appropriate template, and switch to Outline view.

2. Create an outline, using the appropriate heading styles. Use a top-level heading to start each new section.

3. Save the outline in the folder where you want all the related documents to be saved.

Divide a Document into Subdocuments

1. Click the Master Document View button.

2. Select the part of the outline that's to be written by one author.

3. Click the Create Subdocument button.

4. Repeat steps 2 and 3 until all the parts of the outline have been made into subdocuments.

5. Save and close the document.

Turn on the Show/Hide ¶ button to see (and to avoid deleting) all the hidden formatting marks.

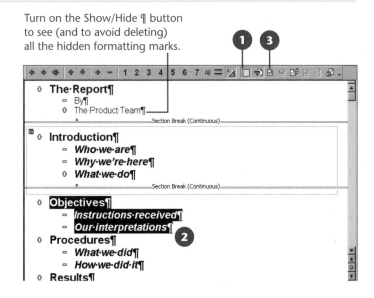

Distribute the Subdocuments

1. Open the folder that contains the master document.

2. Distribute the subdocuments to the appropriate authors.

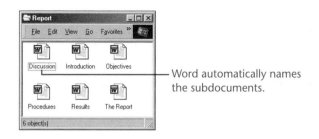

Word automatically names the subdocuments.

Compile the Completed Document

1. Make sure the most recent version of each subdocument is in the original folder, using its original subdocument name.

2. Open the master document.

3. Review the document:
   - Click a hyperlink to open an individual subdocument.
   - Click the Expand Subdocuments button to review the content of each subdocument.

A hyperlink to a subdocument

Click to show the content of all the subdocuments.

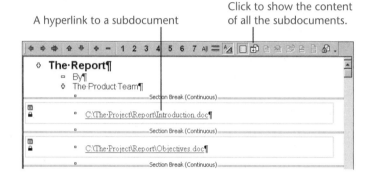

Click to show hyperlinks to the subdocuments.

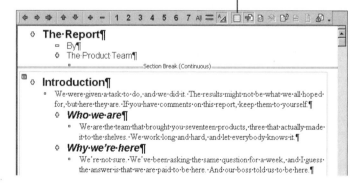

Using Multiple Documents as a Single Document

When several documents are part of the same project, you can combine them by making them into *subdocuments* of a *master document*. You can then work on the entire project as if it were a single document: create a table of contents, use the same template and styles, and copy information from one subdocument into another. But several authors can still work on the subdocuments individually. All changes are coordinated, so whether you edit documents separately or as part of the master document, all the changes are saved. You can assemble the master document periodically, check the page count, and so on, and then return to working on the individual documents.

Create a Master Document

1. Start a new document, using the template that will be used for the entire document.

2. Switch to Outline view to display the Outlining toolbar.

3. Add text and any other items to the master document, and then save the document.

The Outlining toolbar contains all the master-document tools.

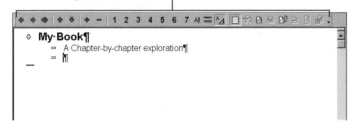

Add Subdocuments

1. Click the Insert Sub-document button, and open the subdocument.

2. Click OK if Word informs you that the subdocument has a different template.

3. Move to the paragraph following the inserted subdocument if the insertion point isn't already there, and repeat steps 1 and 2 until all the subdocuments have been added.

A subdocument in the master document

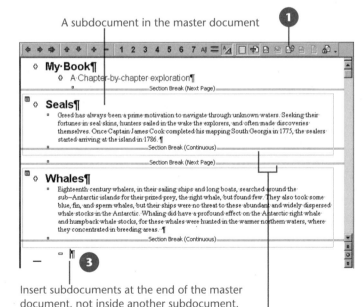

Insert subdocuments at the end of the master document, not inside another subdocument.

Section breaks between separate subdocuments

Don't try this! *Never, never, never delete a section mark when you're working in the master document! You might combine different documents and create some very strange repercussions. If a subdocument contains sections that you want to combine, open the subdocument and delete the appropriate section marks, but do not delete the one at the end of the document.*

Locked out. *If you can't edit a subdocument, or if it opens as a Read-Only document, it might be locked. Turn off the Lock Document button on the Outlining toolbar to unlock the subdocument.*

See more. *If you see any hyperlinks to the subdocuments, click the Expand Subdocuments button.*

For information about creating a master document from an outline, see "Organizing a Multiple-Authors Document" on page 114.

Edit the Document

1 Use the tools on the Outlining toolbar to hide or display material.

2 Use standard editing techniques to change the content of the subdocuments.

3 Save the master document. Any changes to the subdocuments will be saved in the original subdocument files.

Insert document-wide information, such as a table of contents or an index, outside all the subdocuments.

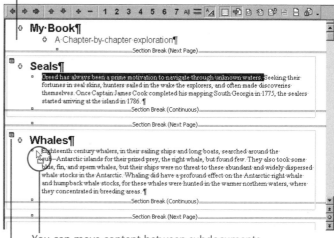

You can move content between subdocuments.

Click to select an entire subdocument, and drag it to change its location in the master document.

6

Creating Cross-References

Cross-references are valuable tools in a long and informative document, but you have to be *extremely* well organized if you're planning to insert them manually, especially if you do a lot of editing and rewriting. It's much easier to let Word do the work for you. Word will keep track of all your cross-references and will keep all the information current. Word can even insert your cross-references as hyperlinks in an online document.

TRY THIS

Easy x-ref. *Create a cross-reference to a heading. Type* For more information, see *, open the Cross-Reference dialog box, and insert the heading text. Click in the document, add a space, type* on page *, and use the Cross-Reference dialog box to insert the page number for the heading.*

Create a Cross-Reference

1. Type the beginning text of your cross-reference.

2. Choose Cross-Reference from the Insert menu.

3. Select the type of item to be cross-referenced.

4. Select the type of cross-reference to be inserted.

5. Select the cross-reference.

6. Click Insert.

7. Continue using the Cross-Reference dialog box to insert cross-references.

8. Click Close.

A reference can be a numbered item, a heading, a bookmark, a footnote, an endnote, an equation, a table, or any caption label you create.

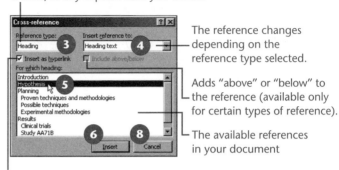

The reference changes depending on the reference type selected.

Adds "above" or "below" to the reference (available only for certain types of reference).

The available references in your document

Turn on if the document is to be read on line. Clicking the cross-reference takes the reader directly to the referenced item.

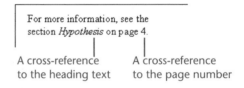

For more information, see the section *Hypothesis* on page 4.

A cross-reference to the heading text

A cross-reference to the page number

7

Creating a Technical Document

Elsewhere in this book we've discussed frequently used documents, long documents, and working with elements other than text. A technical document can integrate some or all of these elements, while still having its own set of requirements. Conversely, elements of a technical document might often be incorporated into a nontechnical document. In reality, there are few elements that are unique to any one type of document, and you can use the techniques we describe to achieve the results you want regardless of the headings under which you find them.

So what *is* a technical document? It could be a doctoral dissertation, a high-school paper, a scientific report, your company's quarterly financial statement, or an annual report to stockholders. It could be an ongoing analysis of a medical experiment, the written specifications for an architectural design, a grade-school teacher's compilation of test scores, or a comparison of various sets of data. What all these examples have in common is that they must present a lot of sometimes complicated information in a format that is inviting rather than daunting, that is organized for ease of reference rather than confusion, and that conveys the information with simplicity and clarity so that it can be understood by a receptive and interested audience.

Inserting Special Characters

With at least 101 keyboard keys at your fingertips, you'd think that every character you could possibly need would be available. But what about the accented characters in other languages? Different currency symbols? Trademark and copyright symbols? You'd need a keyboard with thousands of keys! As you can see in the illustrations at the right, Microsoft Word gives you a huge assortment of symbols and special characters, and several ways to insert them into your documents.

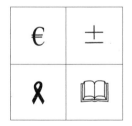

Insert a Text Character

1. Click in your document where you want to place the character.

2. Choose Symbol from the Insert menu, and click the Symbols tab.

3. Select Normal Text from the Font list.

4. Select the character's category.

5. Click the character you want to use.

6. Click Insert.

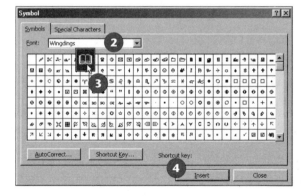

Click the character to see its enlarged view.

Keyboard shortcut for inserting the character

Insert a Symbol Character

1. Move the Symbol dialog box out of the way. Click in your document to activate it, and then click where you want to place the symbol.

2. Select a symbol font.

3. Click the symbol you want to use.

4. Click Insert.

For information about the symbols Word can insert automatically, see "Inserting Special Characters Automatically" on page 122.

For information about assigning and using keyboard shortcuts to insert special characters and symbols, see "Inserting Special Characters with Keys" on page 123.

More characters. *More text fonts with their own character sets are available in addition to the fonts included under Normal Text. Open the Font drop-down list to see what's available.*

Elusive characters. *Some of the characters in the Symbol dialog box might not be supported by all fonts and printers. If you see an empty box instead of a symbol in your document, try using a different font. If you see the symbol on screen but it doesn't print, try using only the TrueType fonts that came with Word. Also, make sure that Windows is set to download TrueType fonts to the printer.*

Insert a Typographic Character

1. Click in your document to activate it, and then click where you want to place the special character.

2. Click the Special Characters tab.

3. Double-click the character you want to insert.

4. Click Close after you've inserted all the special characters and symbols.

5. If you want to change the size of a special text, symbol, or typographic character, select the character in your document, and specify a different size in the Font Size drop-down list on the Formatting toolbar.

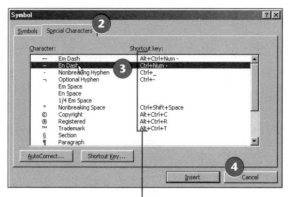

Keyboard shortcuts for inserting characters

Inserting Special Characters Automatically

Word has a list of characters that it inserts automatically when you type the text that represents the character. If a special character you want to use isn't in the list, you can add it and assign normal characters to represent it.

Insert a Listed Character

1. Choose AutoCorrect from the Tools menu.

2. Examine the list of special characters.

3. Verify that the Replace Text As You Type check box is turned on.

4. Click OK.

5. Type the text for the special character.

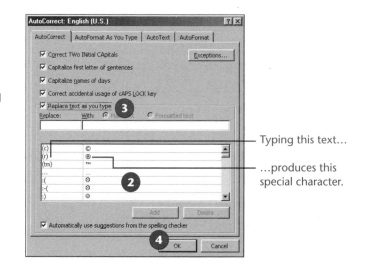

Typing this text...

...produces this special character.

Add a Character to the List

1. Choose Symbol from the Insert menu, and click the Symbols tab.

2. Select the font and the character you want.

3. Click AutoCorrect.

4. Type the characters you want the special character to replace.

5. Click Add.

6. Click OK, and then close the Symbol dialog box.

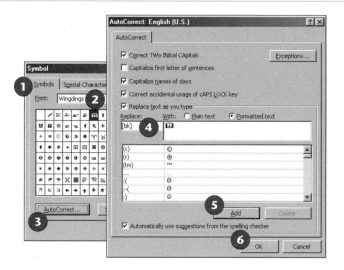

Inserting Special Characters with Keys

If you use a special character frequently, you can insert it quickly with a key combination. If a special character doesn't have a key combination already assigned to it, or if you prefer a different or more convenient key combination, you can assign one of your own.

Assign the Keys

1. Choose Symbol from the Insert menu, select the special character you want, and click the Shortcut Key button.

2. In the Press New Shortcut Key box, press the key combination you've chosen.

3. Click Assign.

4. Click Close, and then close the Symbol dialog box.

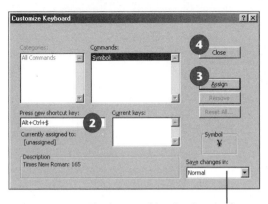

The key combination is stored in the Normal template unless you specify a different location.

Insert the Character

1. Click where you want to place the symbol.

2. Press keys as follows:

   ◆ Hold down the Alt key and use the numeric keypad when keys are in the form Alt+0xxx, where x is a number.

   ◆ Press keys simultaneously when they're separated by a plus sign (+).

   ◆ Press keys sequentially when they're separated by a comma (,).

Using a key combination quickly places the special character where you want it.

Enclosed is a money order for the amount of ¥25000 to guarantee our room reservation. We will arrive on

Creating Superscript and Subscript Characters

If you need superscript or subscript characters for annotations or to create equations without using Word's footnote-, endnote-, or equation-editing tools, you can manually insert any number, character, or symbol, and format it as a superscript or subscript character. Here's how.

SEE ALSO

For information about foot-notes and endnotes, see "Creating Footnotes" on the facing page and "Creating Endnotes" on page 128.

For information about format-ting equations, see "Creating an Equation" on page 134.

Format the Text

1 Type the text you want to format as a superscript or subscript character, and then select it.

2 Do either of the following:

- Press Ctrl+Shift+equal sign (=) to create a superscript.
- Press Ctrl+equal sign (=) to create a subscript.

3 Press the Right arrow key to deselect the text.

4 Select the superscript or subscript text, and do any of the following if you want to modify it:

- Specify a different font or font size.
- Choose Font from the Format menu, and, on the Character Spacing tab, choose Raised (for a superscript) or Lowered (for a sub-script) from the Position list, specify a different distance, and click OK.
- Press Ctrl+Spacebar if you want to change the superscript or subscript characters back into normal text.

Use superscripts to refer to nonsequential endnotes or literary annotations.

Subscripts are common in formulas and equations.

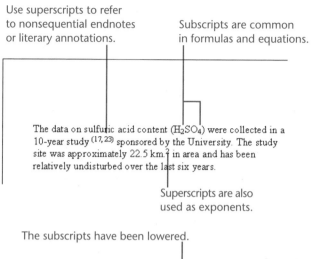

The data on sulfuric acid content (H_2SO_4) were collected in a 10-year study [17, 23] sponsored by the University. The study site was approximately 22.5 km.[?] in area and has been relatively undisturbed over the last six years.

Superscripts are also used as exponents.

The subscripts have been lowered.

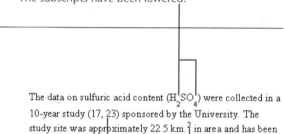

The data on sulfuric acid content (H_2SO_4) were collected in a 10-year study (17, 23) sponsored by the University. The study site was approximately 22.5 km.[?] in area and has been relatively undisturbed over the last six years.

The superscripts have been returned to normal text.

The superscript font and font size have been changed.

Creating Footnotes

Word makes it so easy to add footnotes to a document! Word can mark the footnoted material for you with an automatic series of numbers or symbols, or you can insert your own choice of symbols. When you leave it to Word to insert the footnote number, it updates the number whenever you add or delete a footnote. Word also figures out how much space is required at the bottom of the page for the footnote, and when a footnote is too long for the page, Word automatically continues it on the next page. How clever!

Insert a Footnote

1. Click in your document where you want to place the footnote mark.

2. Choose Footnote from the Insert menu.

3. Select Footnote.

4. Select AutoNumber, or choose a symbol.

5. Click OK.

6. Type the footnote text.

7. Double-click the footnote number to return to the place in your document where you inserted the footnote.

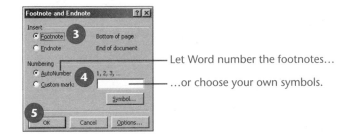

Let Word number the footnotes...

...or choose your own symbols.

The footnote number or mark is added to the text.

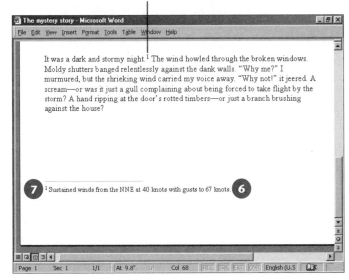

Changing the Look of Footnotes

Word inserts your footnotes using the most commonly accepted conventions: consecutive numbering throughout the document; footnotes at the bottom of each page; a short line, or rule, to separate footnotes from text; and a long line to separate from the text a footnote that was continued from the previous page. If you want, you can change these default settings to create your own look.

TIP

Reset the separator. *If you want to use the default separator after you've deleted it, click the Reset button.*

TIP

Zoom in. *Increase the Zoom control to 200% if you need to see the footnote marks more clearly.*

Change the Look

1. Choose Footnote from the Insert menu.

2. Click the Options button.

3. Select the options.

4. Click OK.

5. Click Close to close the Footnote And Endnote dialog box.

6. Change the Footnote Reference text style to change the footnote mark. Change the Footnote Text paragraph style to change the text of the footnote.

Change the Separator

1. In Normal view, choose Footnotes from the View menu.

2. Select the item you want to change.

3. Select and delete the current separator.

4. Create a new separator.

5. Click Close.

The footnote text can appear at the bottom of a page or directly below the text it refers to, provided the text doesn't completely fill the page.

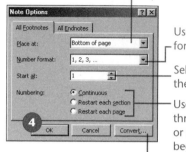

Use a number, letter, or symbol scheme for AutoNumbered footnote marks.

Select a number, letter, or symbol for the first AutoNumbered footnote mark.

Use continuous numbering throughout the document, or restart numbering at the beginning of each section or page.

Converts all footnotes into endnotes.

Select to change the separator between the text and the footnotes, the separator between the text and a footnote continued from the previous page, or the notice that the footnote is continued on the next page.

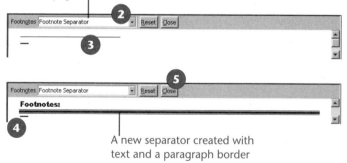

A new separator created with text and a paragraph border

Editing Footnotes

Footnotes, like most text, usually need some review and editing. When you're reviewing a document, you'll really like the way the footnote pops up in your text so that you can read it in context.

Review a Footnote

1. Click the Select Browse Object button at the bottom of the vertical scroll bar, and click Browse By Footnote.

2. Use the Previous Footnote or Next Footnote arrow to locate the footnote mark.

3. Point to the footnote mark, and read the footnote.

Edit a Footnote

1. Double-click the footnote mark.

2. Edit the footnote text.

3. Double-click the footnote number to return to the main text.

Move a Footnote

1. Select the footnote mark.

2. Drag it to a new location.

It was a dark and stormy night.[1] The wind howled through the broken windows. Moldy shutters banged relentlessly against the dank walls. "Why me?" I murmured, but the shrieking wind [Probably Larus delawarensis] carried my voice away. "Why not!" it jeered. A scream—or was it just a gull[2] complaining about being forced to take flight by the storm? A hand ripping at the door's rotted timbers—or just a branch[3] brushing against the house?

Placing the mouse pointer near the footnote mark...

...displays the footnote text.

Double-click here...

It was a dark and stormy night.[1] The wind howled through the broken windows. Moldy shutters banged relentlessly against the dank walls. "Why me?" I murmured, but the shrieking wind carried my voice away. "Why not!" it jeered. A scream—or was it just a gull[2] complaining about being forced to take flight by the storm? A hand ripping at the door's rotted timbers—or just a branch[3] brushing against the house?

[1] Sustained winds from the NNE at 40 knots with gusts to 67 knots.
[2] Probably *Larus delawarensis*
[3] *Cerocarpus ledifolius*

...to move to here.

It was a dark and stormy night. The wind howled

Creating Endnotes

An endnote is just like a footnote, except that all the endnotes are listed together at the end of the document instead of being listed at the foot of each page. If the document has more than one section, you can also group your endnotes at the end of each section.

TIP

They're the same... *End-notes and footnotes are similar in purpose and content. They differ only in their location in a document. You use the same techniques to create, modify, and edit endnotes as you do for footnotes.*

TIP

...but different. *By default, Word uses different numbering schemes for footnotes and for endnotes so that if both exist in the same document, it's easy to tell them apart.*

Insert an Endnote

1. In Normal view, click in your document where you want to place the endnote mark.

2. Choose Footnote from the Insert menu.

3. Select Endnote.

4. Select AutoNumber, or choose a symbol.

5. Click OK.

6. Type the endnote text.

7. Click Close.

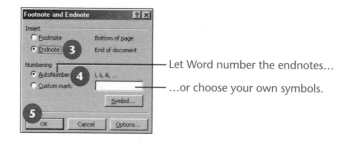

Let Word number the endnotes...

...or choose your own symbols.

Control Where Endnotes Appear

1. Choose Footnote from the Insert menu.

2. Click the Options button.

3. On the All Endnotes tab, select a location for the endnote.

4. Click OK.

5. Click Close in the Footnote And Endnote dialog box.

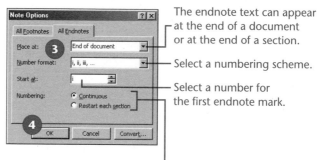

The endnote text can appear at the end of a document or at the end of a section.

Select a numbering scheme.

Select a number for the first endnote mark.

Use continuous numbering throughout the document, or restart numbering at the beginning of each section.

Creating Captions

Figures, tables, equations, and other similar elements in a technical document often need captions that number them consecutively and provide identifying, qualifying, and explanatory text. Word can label and number these items and can keep track of the numbering so that if you add or delete an item in the sequence, Word will automatically renumber the entire sequence.

SEE ALSO

For information about creating a listing of the figures in your document, see "Creating a Table of Figures" on page 154.

For information about working with a caption for an item that's set for text wrapping, see "Creating Floating Captions" on page 198.

For information about adding captions automatically, see "Adding Captions Automatically" on page 304.

Create a Caption

1. Select the item to be captioned.

2. Choose Caption from the Insert menu.

3. Select a caption label for the caption. If there isn't an appropriate label in the list, click New Label, type the label name you want, and click OK.

4. Select a location for the caption.

5. Type the caption text. Don't change the caption label or number.

6. Click OK.

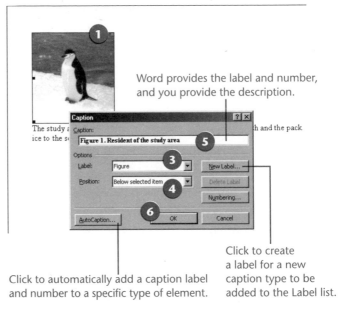

Word provides the label and number, and you provide the description.

Click to automatically add a caption label and number to a specific type of element.

Click to create a label for a new caption type to be added to the Label list.

Figure 1. Resident of the study area
The study area is bounded by the Antarctic Convergence to the north and the pack ice to the south.

Numbering Headings

It's a commonly accepted practice to number each heading level in a long technical document so that when the document is being technically reviewed or is under discussion at a meeting, it's easy to refer to the relevant sections. Word uses the outline-level setting for each style as the basis for the numbering hierarchy.

SEE ALSO

For information about setting outline levels, see "Organizing with Styles" on page 86.

For information about creating and printing a numbered outline, see "Creating a Numbered Outline" on the facing page.

For information about numbering the lines in a technical document, see "Numbering Lines" on page 132.

TIP

Quick selection. *To quickly select all the text, press Ctrl+A.*

Number the Headings

1. Verify that all headings have the correct heading styles applied.

2. Choose Select All from the Edit menu.

3. Choose Bullets And Numbering from the Format menu.

4. Click the Outline Numbered tab.

5. Select one of the numbering schemes shown in the bottom row.

6. Click OK.

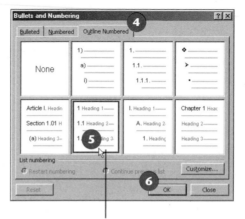

Selecting a numbering scheme here...

...numbers the headings in your document.

Creating a Numbered Outline

Word's Outline view is an excellent tool for organizing a document, but let's say you want to create a printed outline from an existing document—to use as an agenda at a meeting, perhaps. Here's a great way to do it. You create a specialized table of contents, designate which headings are to be shown, and then format the table with the look you want.

SEE ALSO

For information about working with a table of contents, see "Creating a Table of Contents" on page 108 and "Updating a Table of Contents" on page 110.

For information about numbering headings, see "Numbering Headings" on the facing page.

For information about fields, see "Wandering and Wondering Through Word's Fields" on page 293.

Create an Outline

1. Number the headings, using one of the outline-numbering schemes, and then move the insertion point to the end of your document.

2. Choose Index And Tables from the Insert menu, and click the Table Of Contents tab.

3. Select the heading levels you want to include.

4. Turn off the Show Page Numbers check box.

5. Click OK.

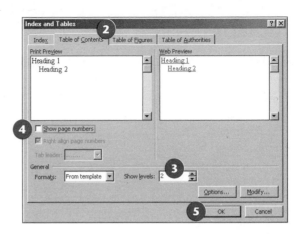

Save the Outline as a New Document

1. Select the entire table of contents, and press Ctrl+Shift+F9 to make the text normal text instead of a field.

2. Click the Cut button, and then paste the copied text into a new document.

3. Modify the styles or assign new styles to format the document.

4. Save the document.

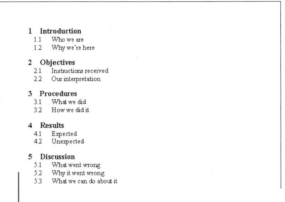

Modifying the styles emphasizes the outline structure.

Numbering Lines

It's a nice convenience to be able to number the lines in a technical document for easy reference when the document is being reviewed or discussed. Word will number the lines for you in whatever increments you want, and will skip any paragraphs in which you *don't* want the line numbering to appear.

TIP

No numbers. *You can set a style's paragraph formatting to suppress line numbers if paragraphs of that style are never to be numbered.*

TIP

Changed numbers. *To change the appearance of the line numbers, modify the Line Number character style.*

Number a Document

1. In Print Layout view, choose Page Setup from the File menu.

2. Click the Layout tab.

3. Select Whole Document in the Apply To list.

4. Click the Line Numbers button.

5. In the Line Numbers dialog box, turn on the Add Line Numbering check box.

6. Specify the options you want.

7. Click OK.

8. Click OK in the Page Setup dialog box.

Set the distance between the number and the text.

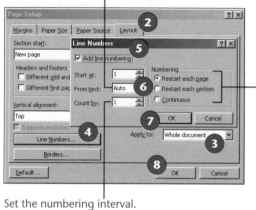

Set the numbering interval.

Use continuous numbering throughout the document, or restart numbering at the beginning of each page or section.

Read by the numbers. *In a long document, number the headings, using the Bullets And Numbering command on the Format menu. Set up all the heading styles you use to suppress line numbers. Turn on the line numbering and set it to restart at each new section. Insert a Continuous section break before each Level 1 heading. Note that when the document is printed, you'll be able to refer to a specific line number under a specific topic number.*

Lines in columns. *When you have multiple columns of text, each line in each column is numbered. Line numbers are always at the left of the text, regardless of the number of columns on a page or whether you're using mirror margins.*

For information about adding numbers to headings only, see "Numbering Headings" on page 130.

Exclude Paragraphs from Numbering

1. Select the paragraphs whose lines are not to be numbered.

2. Choose Paragraph from the Format menu.

3. Click the Line And Page Breaks tab.

4. Turn on the Suppress Line Numbers check box.

5. Click OK.

6. Click the Print Preview button on the Standard toolbar, and verify that the line numbering is correct.

Running heads are not numbered…

…but headings and titles are numbered.

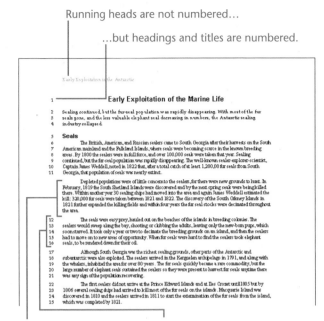

When a paragraph is formatted to suppress line numbers…

…the line numbering resumes in the next paragraph that isn't formatted to suppress line numbers.

Creating an Equation

Mathematical equations can be difficult to construct on a computer. For simple equations, you can generally use standard characters and formatting, but for more complex equations, you'll want to use Microsoft Equation Editor 3.0. Be aware, though, that you are simply *constructing* the equation. Word doesn't do any calculations based on the equation.

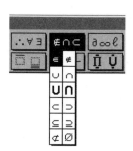

SEE ALSO

For information about installing Equation Editor if it doesn't appear in the Object Type list, see "Adding or Removing Components" on page 306.

Create an Equation

1 Choose Object from the Insert menu.

2 Click the Create New tab, select Microsoft Equation 3.0 from the list, and click OK.

3 Use the template menus to insert the symbols with the correct configuration, and use the keyboard to enter characters, keeping these points in mind:

- Work from left to right—that is, from the outside of the equation to the inside.

- Use the Tab and Shift+Tab keys to move to different elements and levels.

4 Click outside the equation area when you've finished.

$$s =$$

$$s = \sqrt{\Box}$$

$$s = \sqrt{\frac{\Box}{\Box}}$$

$$s = \sqrt{\frac{\sum \Box}{\Box}}$$

$$s = \sqrt{\frac{\sum(\Box)}{\Box}}$$

$$s = \sqrt{\frac{\sum(X_i)}{\Box}}$$

$$s = \sqrt{\frac{\sum(X_i - X)}{\Box}}$$

$$s = \sqrt{\frac{\sum(X_i - \bar{X})}{\Box}}$$

$$s = \sqrt{\frac{\sum(X_i - \bar{X})^{\Box}}{\Box}}$$

$$s = \sqrt{\frac{\sum(X_i - \bar{X})^2}{\Box}}$$

$$s = \sqrt{\frac{\sum_{i=1}^{N}(X_i - \bar{X})^2}{\Box}}$$

$$s = \sqrt{\frac{\sum_{i=1}^{N}(X_i - \bar{X})^2}{N-1}}$$

Creating a Chart

A chart can make the results of your data more instantly understandable than can a spreadsheet of figures that presents the same information. And, while a spreadsheet tends to put your readers to sleep, a chart makes them sit up and take notice. You can use Microsoft Graph, an accessory program that comes with Word, to produce a variety of different charts based on your data.

SEE ALSO

For information about using a chart created in Microsoft Excel, see "Adding an Excel Chart" on page 146 and "Connecting to an Excel Chart" on page 148.

Create a Chart

1. Point to Picture on the Insert menu, and choose Chart from the submenu.

2. Replace the sample data in the worksheet with your own data.

3. Click to select individual components of the chart, and use the toolbars and menus to format the chart.

4. Click outside the chart area when you've finished.

Edit the Chart

1. Double-click the chart to activate it.

2. Edit the data and the chart.

3. Click outside the chart area when you've finished.

Toolbars and menus change to include tools for editing the chart.

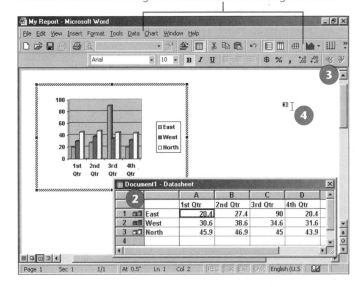

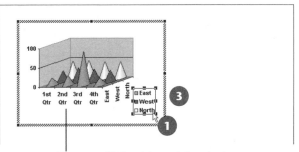

You can edit the data and the chart formatting when you activate the chart.

Summing Table Rows and Columns

Word, as its name suggests, is much more literary than it is mathematical—but it can do some simple table summarizing for you. For more complex calculations, you'll want to insert a Microsoft Excel worksheet.

TIP

Cell conditions. *If you're going to do some math in a table, don't split or merge any cells that contain data, or any cells in which there is more than one entry—you might get some surprising results!*

TIP

Best guess. *The AutoSum button tries to guess what you want to calculate, but it usually decides to sum the column. When it does, it inserts the formula =SUM(ABOVE). If its guess is incorrect, you can edit the formula in the Formula dialog box.*

Sum Columns

1. Display the Tables And Borders toolbar.

2. Create a table containing your data, with a blank row at the bottom and a blank column at the right.

3. Click in the first cell to be summed in the blank bottom row.

4. Click the AutoSum button.

5. Move to the blank cell at the bottom of the next column, and click the AutoSum button.

6. Repeat step 5 until you've summed all but the last column.

Item	Cost	Handling	Total
A1223	$23.95	$18.00	
B3312	$6.95	0	
XY9989	$234.50	$25.00	
Total	$265.40		

Use zeros for blank entries.

Put only one entry in a cell.

SEE ALSO

For information about displaying toolbars, see "Using Toolbars" on page 16.

For information about calculating results from individual cells, see "Calculating Table Values Outside a Table" on page 139.

TIP

Sum location. *With the =SUM( ) formula, you can also use the word BELOW to place the sum of a column in the top row, and the word RIGHT to place the sum of a row in the left column.*

TIP

Decimal values. *To align decimal values, select the column, and then insert a decimal tab. The numbers will automatically align to the tab.*

TIP

Use F9. *Pressing the F9 key updates the fields used to calculate the values. Press Shift+F9 to switch between the field code and the result, Ctrl+F9 to insert an empty field, and Ctrl+Shift+F9 to unlink a field.*

Sum Rows

1. Click in a blank cell whose row is to be summed.

2. Choose Formula from the Table menu.

3. Set the formula to sum the cells to the left.

4. Choose or type a number format for the result if you don't want to use the default format.

5. Click OK.

6. Move through the remaining blank cells, repeating steps 3 and 4.

Item	Cost	Handling	Total
A1223	$23.95	$18.00	$41.95
B3312	$6.95	0	
XY9989	$234.50	$25.00	
Total	$265.40	$43.00	

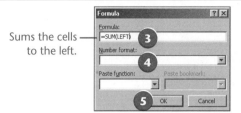

Sums the cells to the left.

Edit the Table

1. Change any values in the table.

2. To change a formula, select the field and choose Formula from the Table menu. In the Formula dialog box, make your changes, and then click OK.

3. Select the entire table.

4. Press the F9 key to update the calculations.

Selecting the entire table...

Item	Cost	Handling	Total
A1223	$23.95	$18.00	$41.95
B3312	$6.95	$3.95	$10.90
XY9989	$234.50	$30.00	$264.50
Total	$265.40	$51.95	$317.35

...lets you update all the calculations at one time.

Calculating a Value

When you need to make a calculation, Word can do the math for you. Your calculation can be as simple as adding two numbers or as complex as using mathematical functions. You can place the results anywhere in your document, but they usually fit best in a table.

TIP

More functions. *Additional functions are available, some of which can produce fairly complex calculations. See Word's Help for details.*

SEE ALSO

For information about inserting the results of calculations into your text, see "Calculating Table Values Outside a Table" on the facing page.

Do the Arithmetic

1. Click in your document where you want to place the result of your calculation.

2. Choose Formula from the Table menu.

3. Enter your calculation.

4. Choose or type a number format.

5. Click OK.

Use + for addition, - for subtraction, * for multiplication, / for division, and ( ) to group operations.

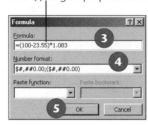

You wanted a quick estimate, so here it is: $ 82.80

The calculated result is inserted into your document.

Use Functions

1. Click in your document where you want to show the result.

2. Choose Formula from the Table menu.

3. Choose a function from the Paste Function list.

4. Insert the values inside the parentheses.

5. Select a number format.

6. Click OK.

COMMONLY USED FUNCTIONS FOR CALCULATIONS	
Example	**Result**
AVERAGE(10,20,33)	The average value of the numbers
INT(123/7)	The integer value of the result
MOD(17,3)	The remainder after the first number is divided by the second number (modular arithmetic)
PRODUCT(10,20,30)	The value after multiplying the numbers together
ROUND(22/7,4)	The result of the division rounded to the nearest four decimal places
SUM(1,2,3,4,5,6)	The value after adding all the numbers together

Calculating Table Values Outside a Table

If you want to calculate values in a table and then place the results in your regular text, you name the table and then refer to individual cells or a range of cells within the table.

> **TIP**
>
> **A single cell.** *To refer to a single cell, use the SUM function, and reference the table name and the one cell you want.*

> **TIP**
>
> **Separators.** *Use a colon (:) to separate a range of cells, and a comma (,) to separate individual cell references.*

Name the Table

1. Select the entire table.
2. Choose Bookmark from the Insert menu.
3. Type a name for the table.
4. Click Add.

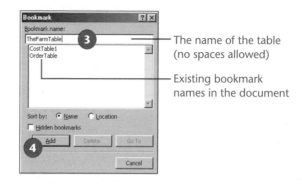

The name of the table (no spaces allowed)

Existing bookmark names in the document

Calculate the Value

1. Click in your text where you want to show the value of the cell.
2. Choose Formula from the Table menu.
3. Use the Paste Function list to insert any functions you want to use.
4. Use the Paste Bookmark list to insert the name of the table into the formula.
5. Type the reference to the cell or cells, enclosed in square brackets.
6. Click OK.

Cell A1 Cell B2 Cell C2

Cell A2 Cell B3 Cell C6

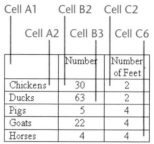

	Number	Number of Feet
Chickens	30	2
Ducks	63	2
Pigs	5	4
Goats	22	4
Horses	4	4

As you can see, the number of two-legged animals we have is 93

Function   Bookmark

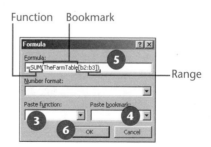

Range

Crunching Data

Word is great for presenting information and doing simple calculations, but if you want to do some more advanced number crunching, add a Microsoft Excel worksheet to your document. You'll be using the power of Excel for the number crunching and the finesse of Word for the presentation.

SEE ALSO

For information about working with objects such as Excel worksheets, see "Alien Objects" on pages 142–143.

For information about copying data from an existing Excel worksheet into a Word document, see "Copying Data from Excel" on page 144.

Add a Worksheet

1. Click in your document where you want to place the worksheet.

2. Click the Insert Microsoft Excel Worksheet button.

3. Drag the mouse to select the number of rows and columns to be included.

4. Complete the worksheet as you would any Excel worksheet.

5. Click outside the worksheet area.

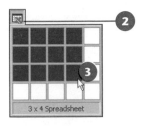

3 x 4 Spreadsheet

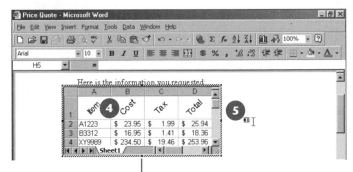

Drag a sizing square to change the number of cells displayed.

Edit a Worksheet

1. Double-click the worksheet.

2. Change any values or calculations.

3. Format the cells in any way you want: add borders and shading, for example, or rotate the text in the column headings.

4. Click outside the worksheet area.

Here is the information you requested:

Item	Cost	Tax	Total
A1223	$ 23.95	$ 1.99	$ 25.94
B3312	$ 16.95	$ 1.41	$ 18.36
XY9989	$ 234.50	$ 19.46	$ 253.96

Copying Information from Multiple Sources

When you assemble a document, you often need to include information from different sources. The *Windows* Clipboard allows you to store only one item at a time, but the *Office* Clipboard lets you gather as many as 12 different items from any Microsoft Office programs. The Office Clipboard toolbar pops up automatically after you copy a second item, or you can open it yourself using the Toolbars command on the View menu.

Copy and Paste the Material

1 Copy the material you want to use from one of your Office programs.

2 Switch to other Office documents or other Office programs, and copy material from up to 11 other sources.

3 Switch to your Word document, and click where you want to insert one or more of the copied items.

4 Do either of the following:

◆ Click the item you want to insert. If the Clipboard toolbar is docked, click the Items button to see the list of copied items.

◆ Click Paste All to insert all the items from the Clipboard.

5 Click in your Word document or in another Office program where you want to insert another copied item, and click the item.

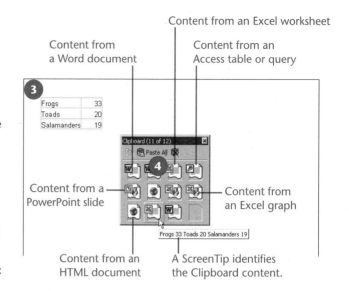

Content from an Excel worksheet

Content from a Word document

Content from an Access table or query

Content from a PowerPoint slide

Content from an Excel graph

Content from an HTML document

A ScreenTip identifies the Clipboard content.

Alien Objects

Several accessory programs come with Word, and others are already installed on your computer, thanks to Windows. These accessory programs are designed specifically to create and insert special content—graphs and mathematical equations, for example. Because such content is *alien* to Word—that is, Word doesn't have the ability to work directly with graphs, complex equations, and whatever else these programs insert—it resides as a separate *object* that is contained (or embedded) in Word. By categorizing this type of content as an object, Word avoids the need to know much about it: Word simply reserves the space for the object and lets the accessory program take care of creating and editing it.

However, Word isn't limited to objects from these accessory programs. Word can contain objects from other major programs such as Microsoft Excel and PowerPoint, and it can even contain objects from Word. And not only can you create an object by using any of these programs in Word, you can also add an object that was previously created—that is, you can use a document file as the source of an object.

This might sound scary, but it's not. Word has made it easy to work with any of these programs and their objects. You can run many of the programs with a click of a toolbar button or from a simple menu command. When one of these programs is running, you're still working in Word, but the accessory program's tools have been added to Word. You'll see changes to the menus, and maybe an extra toolbar or two. When you've finished with the accessory program, Word comes back as its old self, and you have some new content in your document.

If you've ever added a piece of clip art to a document, you've already created an object from a file—it's just that Word did most of the work for you. So if Word does so much of the work for you, why do you need to know about objects? For one thing, Word often refers to them—you "insert objects," "format objects," "edit objects." And, despite the benefits of using objects—and there are many—you can also run into some problems. If your document is used on another computer, for example, an inserted object can be displayed but can't be edited unless that computer has the same program as (or a program similar to) the one that created the object. That means, for instance, that you can read the data in an Excel worksheet object, but if you want to edit the data, Excel must be installed on that computer.

So work with objects with a little care and the knowledge that they're from other programs, and you'll find the added power to achieve exactly the results you want. We'll be working with objects throughout this book, because it's often the best, fastest, and easiest way to get things done.

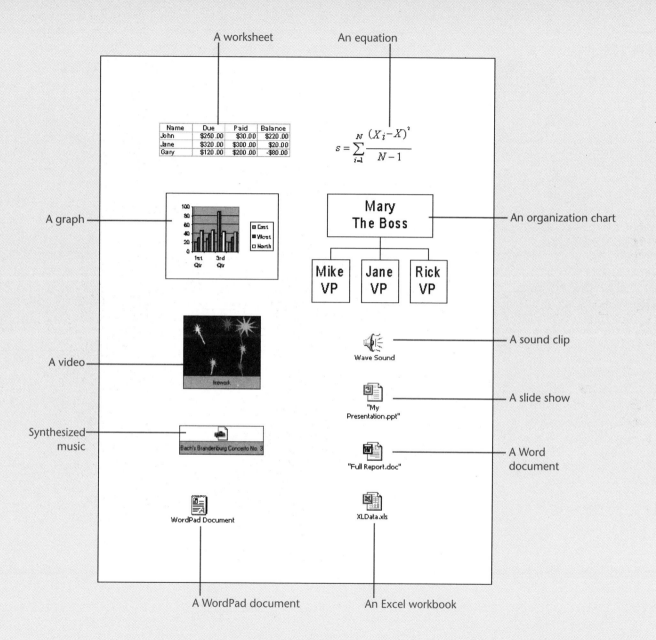

A worksheet

An equation

Name	Due	Paid	Balance
John	$250.00	$30.00	$220.00
Jane	$320.00	$300.00	$20.00
Gary	$120.00	$200.00	-$80.00

$$s = \sum_{i=1}^{N} \frac{(X_i - X)^2}{N-1}$$

A graph

An organization chart

Mary
The Boss

Mike
VP

Jane
VP

Rick
VP

A video

A sound clip

Wave Sound

A slide show

"My Presentation.ppt"

Synthesized music

Bach's Brandenburg Concerto No. 3

A Word document

"Full Report.doc"

WordPad Document

XLData.xls

A WordPad document

An Excel workbook

Copying Data from Excel

If you want to include information that's stored in a Microsoft Excel worksheet, you can copy the data and then insert it into Word in the form of a standard table rather than as a worksheet.

Get the Data

1. Open the Excel worksheet.

2. Select the cells you want to copy.

3. Choose Copy from the Edit menu.

4. Switch to Word.

Only the selected cells are copied.

	A	B	C	D	E	F	G	H	I
1	Subject	Test 1	Test 2	Test 3	Average	Std. Dev.			
2	1	55	77	61	64.3	11.37			
3	2	66	55	64	61.7	5.86			
4	3	44	56	61	53.7	8.74			
5	4	54	62	65	60.3	5.69			
6	5	64	44	60	56.0	10.58			
7	6	99	98	100	99.0	1.00			
8	7	100	99	100	99.7	0.58			
9	8	55	61	46	54.0	7.55			
10	9	60	82	48	63.3	17.24			
11	10	59	66	50	58.3	8.02			
12									

Insert the Data

1. Click in your document where you want to place the data.

2. Click the Paste button on the Standard toolbar.

3. Use the Tables And Borders toolbar to format the table.

Here are the test results:

Average	Std. Dev.
64.3	11.37
61.7	5.86
53.7	8.74
60.3	5.69
56.0	10.58
99.0	1.00
99.7	0.58
54.0	7.55
63.3	17.24
58.3	8.02

Format the table as you would any other Word table.

Connecting to Excel Data

If you want to include data from a Microsoft Excel worksheet in your document, and that data is likely to change periodically, you can *link* to the Excel worksheet. Then, whenever the data changes in the worksheet, the information in your document will be updated automatically.

TIP

Missing link. *Save the Excel workbook before linking to Word so that the link will use the correct filename and location, and don't move the workbook from its folder after you've created the link. If you do move the workbook, you can change the link to the new location by choosing Links from the Edit menu.*

Link to the Data

1. Open the Excel worksheet.

2. Select the cells you want to copy.

3. Choose Copy from the Edit menu.

4. Switch to Word.

5. Click in your document where you want to place the data.

6. Choose Paste Special from the Edit menu.

7. Select the Paste Link option.

8. Click OK.

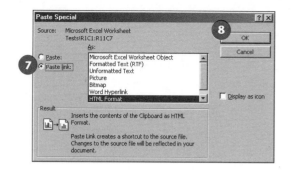

Here are the results of the testing that have been completed:

Subject	Test 1	Test 2	Test 3	Test 4	Average	Std. Dev.
1	55	77	61		64.3	11.37
2	66	55	64		61.7	5.86
3	44	56	61		53.7	8.74
4	54	62	65		60.3	5.69
5	64	44	60		56.0	10.58
6	99	98	100		99.0	1.00
7	100	99	100		99.7	0.58
8	55	61	46		54.0	7.55
9	60	82	48		63.3	17.24
10	59	66	50		58.3	8.02

Although the data is contained in a Word table, it will change if the data in the Excel worksheet changes.

Adding an Excel Chart

If you have the final results of your data in a Microsoft Excel worksheet but you want to display the data as a chart, you can copy it into your Word document. Once you've done so, the chart resides in Word, so you can edit it as necessary, and you no longer need the original Excel document.

TIP

Install Excel. *Microsoft Excel must be available to your computer for you to be able to edit the chart.*

Get the Chart

1. In Excel, use the Chart Wizard to create the chart as a chart object. Format the chart as you want it to appear in Word.

2. Save the workbook.

3. Select and copy the chart object.

4. Switch to Word.

Copy the chart object.

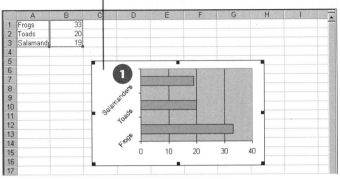

Insert the Chart

1. Click in your document where you want to place the data.

2. Click the Paste button on the Standard toolbar.

The chart object in Word

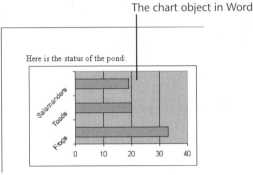

SEE ALSO

For information about inserting a chart using Microsoft Graph, see "Creating a Chart" on page 135.

For information about linking to an Excel chart, see "Connecting to an Excel Chart" on page 148.

TIP

Modify the chart. *To insert an Excel chart without first creating it in an Excel workbook, choose Object from the Insert menu, and, on the Create New tab, select Microsoft Excel Chart, and click OK. You can then edit the sample data on the Sheet1 tab and modify the chart on the Chart1 tab. Microsoft Excel must be installed on your computer for a chart object to be listed in the Object dialog box.*

TIP

Display the chart. *If you don't click the Chart tab after you've edited the data, the data will be displayed instead of the chart.*

Edit the Chart

1. Double-click the chart.

2. Right-click a chart element, and choose an appropriate command from the shortcut menu. You can also modify the chart by using the menu commands or toolbars that Excel has added to the Word window.

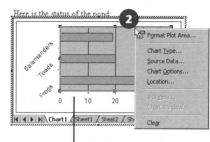

The chart is active for editing.

Edit the Data

1. Click the worksheet that contains the data.

2. Make your changes.

3. Click the Chart tab.

4. Click outside the chart area to deactivate the chart object and return Word to its standard form.

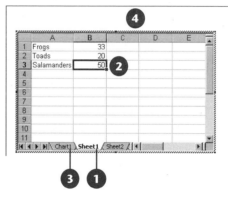

Connecting to an Excel Chart

When you insert a chart from Microsoft Excel, and the data the chart is based on changes, the chart will be updated automatically in your document. If you ever want to update the chart manually, however, the original Excel worksheet must be available to you.

Insert the Chart

1. In Excel, use the Chart Wizard to create the chart as a chart object. Format the chart as you want it to appear in Word.

2. Save the workbook.

3. Select and copy the chart object.

4. Switch to Word.

5. Click in your document where you want to place the data.

6. Choose Paste Special from the Edit menu.

7. Select the Paste Link option.

8. Click OK.

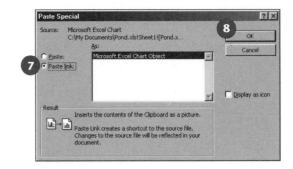

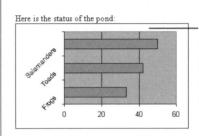

Here is the status of the pond:

The chart will be updated automatically to show changes in the Excel worksheet. Double-click to edit the chart or the data in Excel.

Creating an Organization Chart

An organization chart is a graphical representation of your group's structure. In very little time, you can create an impressive chart that illustrates the chain of command—and you can change it even faster than people can move up or down the corporate ladder.

TIP

People mover. *To select a box or a line in order to move or format it, click the Select button on the Organization Chart toolbar.*

SEE ALSO

For information about installing MS Organization Chart, see "Adding or Removing Components" on page 306.

Create the Chart

1. Choose Object from the Insert menu.

2. Click the Create New tab, select MS Organization Chart 2.0 from the list, and click OK. (If MS Organization Chart isn't listed, you'll need to install it.)

3. Complete the chart:

   ◆ Replace the placeholder text by clicking the selected box and typing. Use the Tab key to move between text fields.

   ◆ Add a new element by selecting an element and clicking the box it's attached to.

   ◆ Format a connecting line by selecting it and using the Lines menu.

   ◆ Format a box by selecting it and using the Boxes menu.

4. Choose Update Document from the File menu.

5. Choose Exit And Return To Document from the File menu.

Use the buttons to add components.

Format the boxes to add emphasis.

Replace the placeholder text.

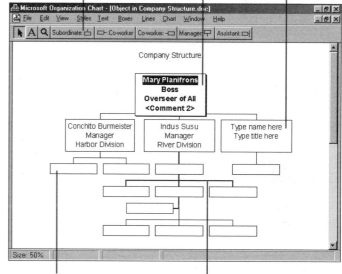

Drag a box to change its position.

Format the lines to designate paths.

Creating an Index

If you're not blessed with the expertise of a professional indexer, Word is the next best thing. It simplifies and automates the arduous mechanics of indexing. Word places a hidden-text tag next to each indexed item, so no matter how the page numbers change, the index is kept current. Your index can include multiple levels, cross-references, and even a range of pages when an indexed item extends beyond a single page.

Tag the Entries

1. Choose Index And Tables from the Insert menu, and click the Mark Entry button on the Index tab.

2. Turn on the Show/Hide ¶ button on the Standard toolbar if it's not already turned on.

3. In your document, select the text you want to index.

4. Modify the wording or capitalization of the main entry, if necessary.

5. Type any subentries. To specify more than one level of subentry, separate subentry levels with colons.

6. Select options as follows:

   ◆ Click Cross-Reference, and type the topic to be cross-referenced.

   ◆ Click Current Page to list the page number next to the entry.

7. Click in the document, find your next index entry, and repeat steps 3 through 6.

This index tag contains the cross-reference information.

All index tags are in hidden text.

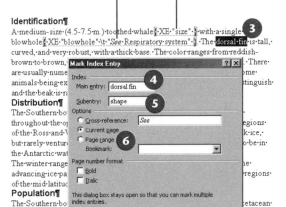

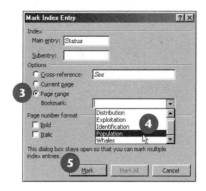

TIP

Automated first step.
The Mark All button in the Mark Index Entry dialog box finds every instance in your document of the text you've selected and marks each one with the tag information you entered in the dialog box. The AutoMark button in the Index And Tables dialog box lets you specify a document that contains a list of items you want Word to mark automatically for your index. If you use either of these automated techniques, you'll need to go through your document and carefully verify these index entries.

TIP

Index insights. *Always compile the index just before you print your document, because the page numbers might have changed. When you compile the index, it's important that you use the same printer setup that you'll use when you print the document—last-minute changes can affect the page breaks. Last, make sure your computer isn't set to print hidden text (check the Print tab of the Options dialog box on the Tools menu).*

Tag a Page Range

1. Select the *entire* text of the item to be indexed.

2. Choose Bookmark from the Insert menu, type a unique name (without spaces) to describe the topic, and click Add.

3. In the Mark Index Entry dialog box, type your main entry and any subentries, and select Page Range.

4. Select the corresponding bookmark name.

5. Click Mark.

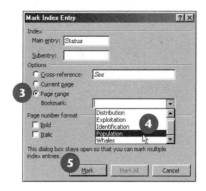

Compile the Index

1. Close the Mark Index Entry dialog box, and save the document.

2. Press Ctrl+End to move to the end of the document, and choose Index And Tables from the Insert menu.

3. On the Index tab, select an index type and style, and click OK.

Preview your index.　　Specify an index type.

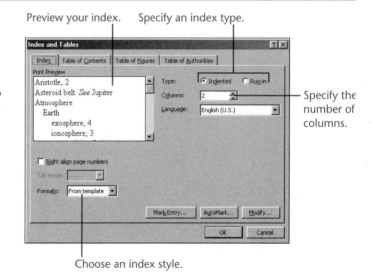

Specify the number of columns.

Choose an index style.

Creating a Multilevel Bulleted List

How you present your information can determine whether or not your readers clearly understand what you're trying to convey. A great way to display information and clarify the relationship between items is with a multilevel bulleted list. Here's how to do it.

SEE ALSO

For information about creating a bulleted list, see "Creating a Bulleted List" on page 38.

For information about using different bullet styles, see "Creating a Custom Bulleted List" on page 39.

Create a List

1. In an empty paragraph, click the Bullets button on the Standard toolbar.

2. Type the text for a first-level entry, and press Enter.

3. Press the Tab key, type the text for a second-level entry, and press Enter.

4. Do any of the following:

   ◆ Enter additional second-level text.

   ◆ Press Tab to move to the next level, and enter the text.

   ◆ Press Shift+Tab to move back one level, and enter the text.

5. When you've completed all the entries, press Enter twice to end the bulleted list.

- Baleen whales
  - Balaenidae
    - Bowhead whale
    - Northern right whale
    - Pygmy right whale
    - Southern right whale
  - Balaenopteridae —————— Press Tab to move to the next level.
    - Blue whale
    - Bryde's whale
    - Fin whale
    - Humpback whale
    - Minke whale
      - Northern
      - Southern
      - Pygmy
    - Sei whale —————— Press Shift+Tab to move back a level.
  - Eschrichtiidae
    - Gray whale
- Odontocete whales
  - Physeteridae
    - Dwarf sperm whale
    - Pygmy sperm whale

Change the Bullets

1. Click in a paragraph whose bullets you want to change.

2. Choose Bullets And Numbering from the Format menu.

3. On the Bulleted tab, click the bullet you want.

4. Click OK.

5. Repeat steps 1 through 4 to change any other bullets. Note, though, that Word doesn't automatically change the bullet for first-level headings.

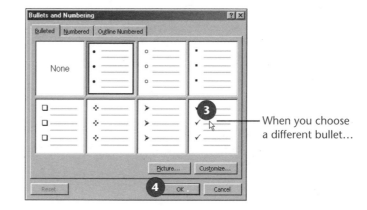

When you choose a different bullet...

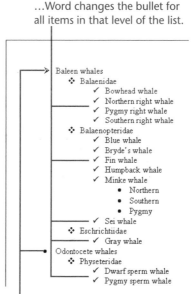

...Word changes the bullet for all items in that level of the list.

You can manually change the bullet for first-level headings.

Creating a Table of Figures

A technical document often contains a table that lists all the figures or illustrations that appear in the document. Word can generate a table of figures for you. You can also use the method described here to generate a table of equations, a table of captions, or a table of tables.

TIP

Floating away. *Word doesn't search for floating captions, so any figures with floating captions will be missed.*

SEE ALSO

For information about adding captions to your figures, see "Creating Captions" on page 129 and "Adding Captions Automatically" on page 304.

For information about working with a caption for an item that's set for text wrapping, see "Creating Floating Captions" on page 198.

Create a Table of Figures

1. Add captions to all your figures.

2. Click in the document where you want the table of figures to appear.

3. Choose Index And Tables from the Insert menu.

4. Click the Table Of Figures tab.

5. Select Figure as the caption label.

6. Select a format for the table.

7. Turn on the Show Page Numbers check box.

8. Turn on the Include Label And Number check box.

9. Click OK.

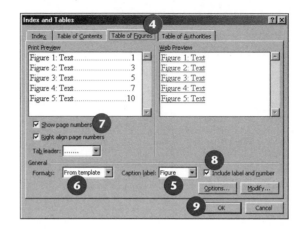

A table of figures is a table of contents.

Putting Tables into Your Document

Tables are powerful organizational and layout tools that can contain words, pictures, hyperlinks, numbers, and even other tables. If you're familiar with the old way of using tabs to align the columns in a table, forget it! What with proportional fonts and complex layouts, a tab-based table often turned into a misaligned, confusing mess. A Microsoft Word table provides a spreadsheet-like environment of columns, rows, and cells, into which you place your content. But the similarity with spreadsheets ends there—Word gives you powerful formatting choices but doesn't have the mathematical capabilities that a spreadsheet provides.

Word gives you several ways to create and manage tables. The simplest way? Let Word do it for you! Word creates a generic table, and then, after you add your information, Word can automatically format the table. If you prefer, you can create your table manually—draw it yourself, add rows and columns, drag borders to resize table elements, drag the table to a new location, and so on. This is fun when your goal is a creative design, or when you're working with a single document and consistency isn't an issue. When precision is important, you can specify the exact dimensions of rows and columns, the table's absolute position on the page, the space between the table and its accompanying text, and so on.

Creating a Table

If you think of tables merely as containers for numbers, think again. Tables are a superb way to organize almost any kind of information, and Word makes it so easy. You can actually draw your table with a little onscreen pencil. Then you put your content into the cells, adding more rows and columns if you need to, or changing their sizes to make everything fit.

	Fruit	Vegetable
Option 1	Apple	Potato
Option 2	Orange	Corn
Option 3	Pear	Eggplant

Create a Table

1. Click the Tables And Borders button on the Standard toolbar to display the Tables And Borders toolbar.

2. Click the Show/Hide ¶ button if it's not already turned on.

3. Click the Draw Table button if it's not already turned on.

4. Drag the pencil pointer to create the outline of the table, and release the mouse button.

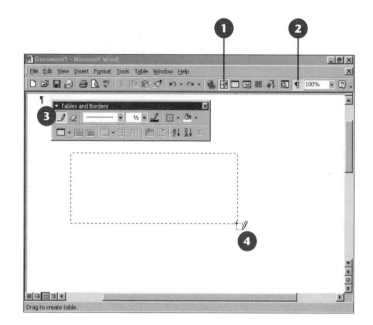

Add Columns and Rows

1. Drag the pencil pointer from the top table boundary to the bottom table boundary to create a column. Repeat to create all the columns you need.

2. Drag the pencil pointer from the left or right table boundary to the opposite table boundary to create a row. Repeat to create all the rows you need.

Draw vertical lines to create columns.

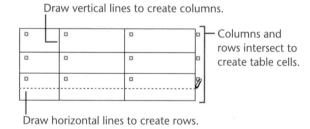

Columns and rows intersect to create table cells.

Draw horizontal lines to create rows.

TIP

Cell markers. *The little circular mark inside each table cell is the cell marker, a non-printing formatting mark that stores formatting information about the cell and is similar to a paragraph mark.*

TIP

Table tab. *To insert a tab inside a table cell, press Ctrl+Tab.*

TRY THIS

Put Tab to work. *If the table is going to have several rows, all with the same dimensions, create only the first couple of rows. You can add new rows automatically by pressing the Tab key when you're in the last (bottom right) cell of the table.*

SEE ALSO

For information about adjusting the size and appearance of table cells, see "Changing the Sizes of Columns and Rows" on page 160 and "Changing the Look of a Table" on page 162.

For information about changing the text formatting in a table, see "Changing the Look of Text in a Table" on page 164.

Add Content

1. Click the Draw Table button to turn it off.

2. Click in the first cell and insert your content.

3. Press the Tab key to move to the next cell, and add your content. Press Enter only to start a new paragraph inside a table cell. Continue using the Tab key to complete your table.

Press Tab to move to the next cell.

Press Tab to move to the first cell in the next row.

¤	Fruit¤	Vegetable¤	¤
Option·1¤	Apple¤	Potato¤	¤
Option·2¤	Orange¤	Corn¤	¤
Option·3¤	¤	¤	¤

Press Tab to create a new row.

Press the Up or Down arrow key to move to the previous or next row.

Press Shift+Tab to move to the previous cell.

Format a Table

1. Click anywhere inside the table.

2. Click the Table AutoFormat button on the Tables And Borders toolbar.

3. Select a format.

4. Turn formatting options on or off, as desired.

5. Click OK.

Select None to remove all formatting.

Preview the selected format.

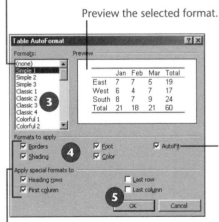

Turn on to change the column width to fit the longest text in each column. Turn off to prevent changes in column and table widths.

Turn check boxes on or off to customize the selected format.

The Anatomy of a Table

The Move box appears when the mouse pointer is positioned over the table.

Table cells in a row are merged into a single cell.

Different borders can be used to define areas.

Shading

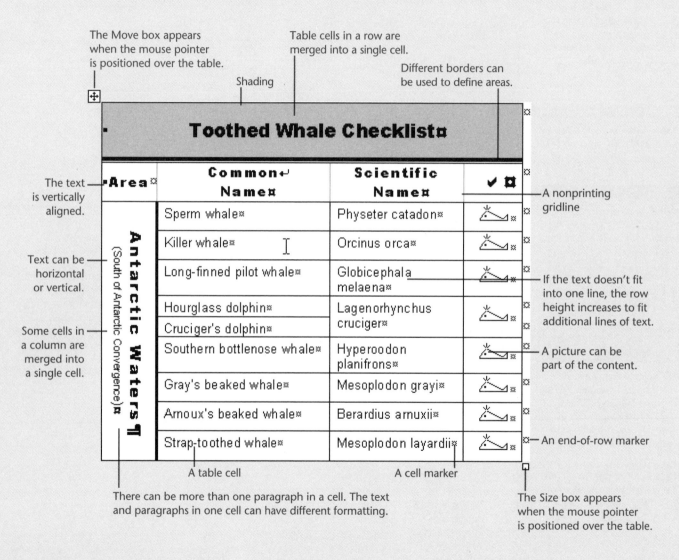

The text is vertically aligned.

Text can be horizontal or vertical.

Some cells in a column are merged into a single cell.

A nonprinting gridline

If the text doesn't fit into one line, the row height increases to fit additional lines of text.

A picture can be part of the content.

An end-of-row marker

A table cell

A cell marker

There can be more than one paragraph in a cell. The text and paragraphs in one cell can have different formatting.

The Size box appears when the mouse pointer is positioned over the table.

Toothed Whale Checklist

Area	Common Name	Scientific Name	✔ ✿
	Sperm whale	Physeter catadon	
	Killer whale	Orcinus orca	
	Long-finned pilot whale	Globicephala melaena	
	Hourglass dolphin / Cruciger's dolphin	Lagenorhynchus cruciger	
	Southern bottlenose whale	Hyperoodon planifrons	
	Gray's beaked whale	Mesoplodon grayi	
	Arnoux's beaked whale	Berardius arnuxii	
	Strap-toothed whale	Mesoplodon layardii	

Antarctic Waters (South of Antarctic Convergence)

Customizing a Table Layout

A Word table can be more than just a grid of equally sized rows and columns. If you want a table heading to span several columns, you can simply draw new cell boundaries and erase old ones. You can combine two cells into one larger one, or split one cell into two smaller ones. Word gives you a great deal of flexibility in the layout of your table.

Menu Options		Week 3
	Fruit	Vegetable
Option 1	A: Apple B: Banana	Corn
Option 2	Orange	Potato
Option 3	Pear	Eggplant

SEE ALSO

For information about creating complex table layouts by placing one table inside another and adding space between columns, see "Creating a Side-by-Side Layout" on page 190.

Divide One Cell into Two

1. Display the Tables And Borders toolbar if it's not already visible.

2. Click the Draw Table button.

3. Click a cell boundary, drag to the opposite boundary, and release the mouse button. Add as many cell boundaries as you need.

4. Click the Draw Table button to turn it off.

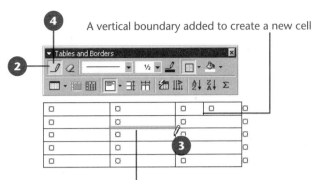

A vertical boundary added to create a new cell

A horizontal boundary added to create a new cell

Combine Two Cells into One

1. Click the Eraser button.

2. Click a cell boundary. To delete several cell boundaries, drag the Eraser pointer to include all cell boundaries. If you accidentally delete the wrong boundary, click the Undo button on the Standard toolbar.

3. Click the Eraser button to turn it off.

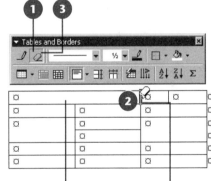

A boundary was removed to merge two cells.

A boundary becomes highlighted when you click it with the Eraser.

Changing the Sizes of Columns and Rows

You can change the width of columns and the height of rows to suit your content or design. If, when you drew your table, you wanted the rows and columns to be of equal dimensions, but they turned out to be different sizes, a click of a button will even them up for you. You can also manually adjust the dimensions of rows and columns, or of individual cells.

No.	Name	Job Title
1.	Rick	Problem-solver
2.	Roberta	Monarch of her domain
3.	Pierre	Irrigator, cultivator
4.	Baiser	Vintner

TIP

Low overhead. *If the row height isn't tall enough to fit all your text (including all paragraph formatting), the row height adjusts automatically.*

Standardize Column Width

1. Select the columns that are to be the same width.

2. Click the Distribute Columns Evenly button on the Tables And Borders toolbar.

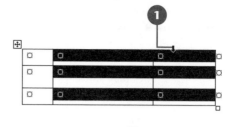

The columns are now the same width.

Standardize Row Height

1. Select the rows that are to be the same height.

2. Click the Distribute Rows Evenly button on the Tables And Borders toolbar.

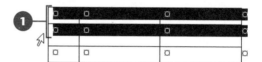

The rows are now the same height.

Adjust Column Width

1. Click anywhere in the table so that no cells are selected.

2. Move the mouse pointer over the right boundary of a column until the mouse pointer changes into the Horizontal Resize pointer.

3. Drag the boundary to the left to decrease the column width or to the right to increase the column width.

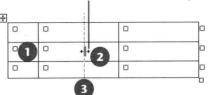

The Horizontal Resize pointer

The boundary is moved to a new location, changing the width of both columns.

Adjust Row Height

1. Move the mouse pointer over the bottom boundary of a row until the mouse pointer changes into the Vertical Resize pointer.

2. Drag the boundary up to decrease the row height or down to increase the row height. Use the measurements on the vertical ruler to make precise adjustments.

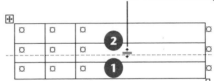

The Vertical Resize pointer

The boundary is moved to a new location, changing the height of the top row only.

Changing the Look of a Table

The easiest and quickest way to give an entire table a distinctive appearance is with the Table AutoFormat feature, but you can create your own custom design by adding borders and shading. Although Word usually applies borders to a table when it's being drawn, you can create a table without borders and then add your own elements.

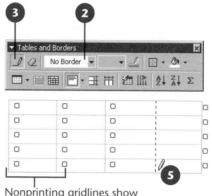

Create a Table Without Borders

1. Display the Tables And Borders toolbar if it's not already visible.

2. Select No Border.

3. Click the Draw Table button, and draw the outline of your table.

4. If you don't see any gridlines around your table's cells, choose Show Gridlines from the Table menu.

5. Finish drawing your table, and then click the Draw Table button to turn it off.

Nonprinting gridlines show the layout of the table.

Add a Border

1. Select the cells that are to have the same type of border.

2. Select a line style.

3. Select a line weight.

4. Select a line color.

5. Select a border style.

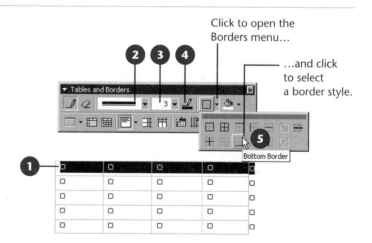

Click to open the Borders menu...

...and click to select a border style.

Add an Individual Cell Border

1. Select a new line style, weight, and color for the border.

2. Click the Draw Table button.

3. With the pencil pointer, draw along the cell boundary to add the border. Turn off the Draw Table button when you've finished.

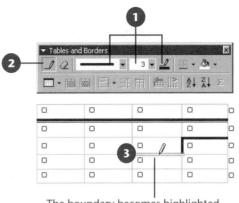

The boundary becomes highlighted when you draw along it with the Draw Table pointer.

Add Shading

1. Select the cells that are to have the same type of shading.

2. Select the shading.

3. Repeat steps 1 and 2 to add different shading to different cells.

Click to open the Shading Color menu...

...and click to select a shading color.

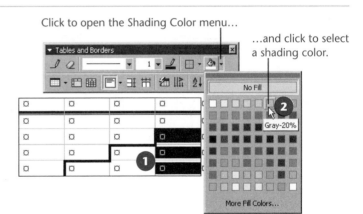

Changing the Look of Text in a Table

As you create and modify a table, you might want to adjust the look of the text. For example, you probably want your table headings to be bigger and bolder than the text in the individual cells. You might want to change the alignment of the headings or of the text in the cells. You might even want text to run vertically instead of horizontally. Here's how to do all of the above.

Change the Look

In an existing table containing text, do any of the following:

- Select the cells that are to have the same formatting, and apply a paragraph style.

- Select cells, and apply direct paragraph or text formatting.

- Click in a paragraph or select multiple paragraphs in a cell, and apply a paragraph style.

- Click in a paragraph or select multiple paragraphs in a cell, and apply direct paragraph formatting.

- Select text within a cell, and apply a character style.

- Select text within a cell, and apply direct font formatting.

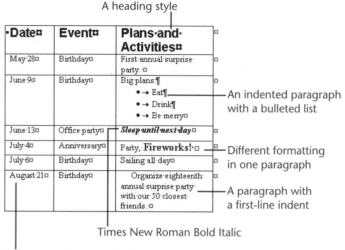

A heading style

An indented paragraph with a bulleted list

Different formatting in one paragraph

A paragraph with a first-line indent

Times New Roman Bold Italic

Times New Roman, left-aligned

SEE ALSO

For information about applying paragraph and text formatting, see "Customizing Paragraphs" on page 28.

For information about setting margins within cells and inserting space between columns, see "Creating a Side-by-Side Layout" on page 190.

For information about character styles, see "Creating an Inline Heading" on page 194.

TIP

Show, don't hide. *When you're working in a table, turn on the Show/Hide ¶ button so that you can see all the cell markers and paragraph marks. They help you to identify the different paragraphs in a cell.*

TRY THIS

All change. *To set the alignment or text direction for all the cells of the table at once, move the mouse pointer over the table until you see the little Move box at the top left of the table. Click the box to select the entire table, and then click the Alignment button or the Change Text Direction button.*

Set the Alignment

1. Display the Tables And Borders toolbar if it's not already visible.

2. Click in the cell, or select multiple cells to be changed.

3. Click the down arrow next to the Alignment button, and click the alignment you want.

4. Repeat steps 2 and 3 to adjust the alignment in other cells.

The Move box

Click to open the Alignment menu.

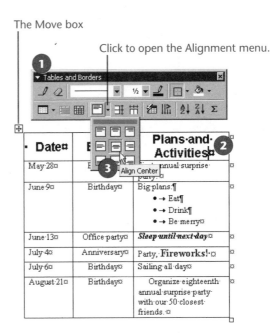

Set the Text Direction

1. Click in the cell, or select multiple cells to be changed.

2. Click the Change Text Direction button. Continue clicking the button until you see the desired text direction.

3. Use the Alignment button if necessary to adjust the horizontal and vertical alignment.

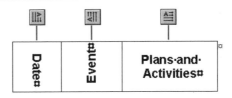

Moving a Table

If you're not happy about the position of a table, you can easily move it into a better location. When you drag a table, you can position it both horizontally and vertically on the page, just as you can position a picture on the page. When you move the table horizontally, you're also setting it to have text wrapping, so, if there's room, any text can wrap around all four sides of the table.

SEE ALSO

For information about setting text to wrap around a table, see "Wrapping Text Around a Table" on page 172.

TIP

Your motion is tabled.
If you drag a table and drop it on top of another table, the first table becomes "nested" inside the second table. If this isn't what you want, click the Undo button.

Move the Table

1. Switch to Print Layout view or Web Layout view if you aren't already in either view.

2. Hold the mouse pointer over the table until the little Move box containing a four-headed arrow appears at the top left of the table.

3. Place the mouse pointer over the Move box.

4. Drag the table to a new location.

When you move the table from here... ...to here...

Antarctica and sub-Antarctica. It spends much of its time deep below the surface, on long dives, searching for the squid on which it survives. ¶

Quick·Identification¤

Length¤	4.5-7.5 m.¤
Color¤	Brown¤
Dorsal Fin¤	Tall, robust¤
Dive Period¤	14-30 mts¤

Identification¶
A medium-size (4.5-7.5 m.) toothed whale with a single blowhole. The dorsal fin is tall, curved, and very robust, with a thick base. The color ranges from reddish-brown to brown, but in poor lighting conditions appears gray or black. There are usually numerous scratches and circular scars on the body, with some animals being extensively scarred. The bulbous head is difficult to distinguish and the beak is rarely displayed above water. ¶

Distribution¶
The Southern bottlenose whale has been observed during the summer throughout the open waters of the Antarctic, except for the southern regions of the Ross and Weddell seas. It is often seen near the edge of the pack ice, but rarely ventures far into the pack. Most of the population appears to be in the Antarctic waters during the summer. ¶
The winter range is unknown, but the animals might move ahead of the advancing ice pack during the fall and spend the winter in the pelagic regions of the mid latitudes. ¶

...the text wraps around the table.

Antarctica and sub-Antarctica. It spends much of its time deep below the surface, on long dives, searching for the squid on which it survives. ¶
Identification¶
A medium-size (4.5-7.5 m.) toothed whale with a single blowhole. The dorsal fin is tall, curved, and very robust, with a thick base. The color ranges from reddish-brown to brown, but in poor lighting conditions appears gray or black. There are usually numerous scratches and circular scars on the body, with some animals being extensively scarred. The bulbous head is difficult to distinguish and the beak is rarely displayed above water. ¶

Quick·Identification¤

Length¤	4.5-7.5 m.¤
Color¤	Brown¤
Dorsal Fin¤	Tall, robust¤
Dive Period¤	14-30 mts¤

Distribution¶
The Southern bottlenose whale has been observed during the summer throughout the open waters of the Antarctic, except for the southern regions of the Ross and Weddell seas. It is often seen near the edge of the pack ice, but rarely ventures far into the pack. Most of the population appears to be in the Antarctic waters during the summer. ¶
The winter range is unknown, but the animals might move ahead of the advancing ice pack during the fall and spend the winter in the pelagic regions of the mid latitudes. ¶
Population¶
The Southern bottlenose whale is second only to the minke whale in cetacean abundance in the Antarctic, but accurate population estimates are difficult due to the long dives of the

Positioning a Table

A table is usually positioned with the same alignment as the accompanying text. However, you might want to set a table off a bit by changing its horizontal position—indenting or centering it, for example. By using Word's alignment settings instead of moving the table manually, you'll ensure that the settings will remain in effect even if you change the margins or any other page-layout settings.

It was a dark and stormy night. The wind howled through the broken windows.

The sun shone brightly as I squinted across the water, looking for a sail on the distant horizon.

SEE ALSO

For information about setting text to wrap around a table, see "Wrapping Text Around a Table" on page 172.

Set the Alignment

1. Right-click anywhere in the table, and choose Table Properties from the shortcut menu. (If the table has been moved, and if it has also been set for text wrapping, select the entire table before you right-click it.)

2. On the Table tab, select an alignment.

3. If you want the table to be left-aligned but indented from the left margin, select the distance the table is to be indented. (Note that if you save the document as a Web page, Word will ignore this left indent.)

4. Click OK.

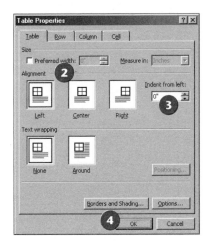

Sizing a Table

A table usually grows as you add content. When the content doesn't fit into a single line of text, the cell expands vertically to include as many lines as are necessary to accommodate all the text in that cell. You can improve the table's appearance by changing its dimensions so that the content will fit properly.

TIP

Web tables. *The width is listed as "Preferred" because, if you save the document as a Web page, the dimensions of the table might change when it's viewed in a Web browser.*

TIP

Different measurements. *To change the unit of measurement, choose Options from the Tools menu, and select a different unit on the General tab of the Options dialog box.*

Set the Table Width

1 Right-click anywhere in the table, and choose Table Properties from the shortcut menu.

2 On the Table tab, turn on the Preferred Width check box.

3 Specify the total width of the table, including all the columns.

4 Specify whether the setting is to be in units of measurement or by percentage.

5 Click OK.

Change the Table Dimensions

1 Hold the mouse pointer over the table until the Size box appears at the bottom right of the table.

2 Place the mouse pointer over the Size box.

3 Drag the box to resize the table.

All the columns will be resized proportionally to fit into this total width.

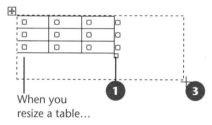

When you resize a table...

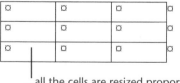

...all the cells are resized proportionally.

Creating a Large Table

Although it's fun to use the Draw Table pencil, when you need to create a really large table you undoubtedly don't want to draw dozens—or even hundreds—of rows and columns. You don't have to. If you know the dimensions you need for the table, you can use the Insert Table command to instantly create a table with the correct number of rows and columns. And if the table is so long that it spans pages, you can have the table headings repeat at the top of the table on each page.

TIP

Fit for your document. *The AutoFit options are primarily for online documents and Web pages.*

SEE ALSO

For information about using Print Preview, see "Checking the Layout" on page 58.

Create a Table

1. Point to Insert on the Table menu, and choose Table from the submenu.
2. Specify the number of rows and columns.
3. Specify whether you want the table
   - ◆ To have a fixed total width.
   - ◆ To resize automatically to fit the window.
   - ◆ To resize automatically to accommodate the contents.
4. Click OK.

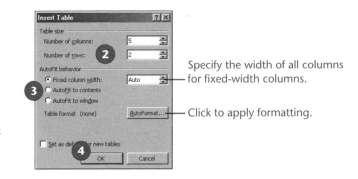

Specify the width of all columns for fixed-width columns.

Click to apply formatting.

Specify Headings

1. Select the entire top row of the table.
2. Choose Heading Rows Repeat from the Table menu.
3. Use Print Preview showing multiple pages to confirm that the headings do repeat.

Headings at the top of the table...

...are automatically repeated when the table spans two or more pages.

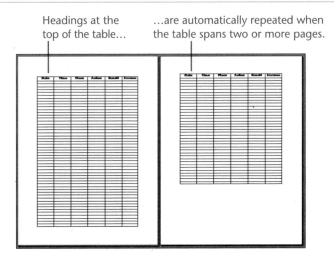

Modifying a Large Table

Word gives you a variety of ways to modify your tables. You'll find that some techniques work best for small tables and that others are geared to larger tables. When you're working on a large table, you probably want changes to happen quickly and automatically. It takes just a few clicks to add or delete rows or columns and to have new rows and columns take the same formatting as adjacent rows and columns.

> **TIP**
>
> **And your name is?** *The Insert Table button changes to become a button that denotes the last action you carried out from the list. For example, when you choose Insert Rows Above, the button becomes the Insert Rows Above button.*

Add Rows

1. Display the Tables And Borders toolbar.

2. Select cells in the same number of rows as the number of rows you want to insert.

3. Click the down arrow next to the Insert Table button, and click

    ◆ Insert Rows Above to add the rows above the selected cells.

    ◆ Insert Rows Below to add the rows below the selected cells.

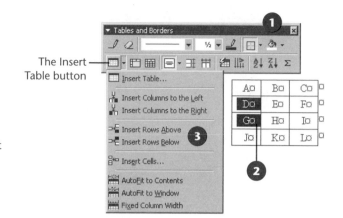

The Insert Table button

Add Columns

1. Select cells in the same number of columns as the number of columns you want to insert.

2. Click the down arrow next to the Insert Table button (or whatever this button's name has changed to), and click

    ◆ Insert Columns To The Left to add columns to the left of the selected cells.

    ◆ Insert Columns To The Right to add columns to the right of the selected cells.

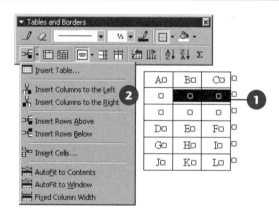

Quick select. *The Delete Rows or Delete Columns command appears only when you've selected entire rows or columns. To quickly select an entire row, move the mouse pointer over the left border of the row. The pointer changes into a dark arrow. Double-click to select the entire row.*

To select multiple rows, don't release the mouse button after you double-click. Instead, drag the pointer to include all the rows to be selected, and then release the mouse button.

To select entire columns, move the mouse pointer over the top border of the column. The pointer changes into a dark, downward-pointing arrow. Single-click to select a column, or drag to include all the columns to be selected, and then release the mouse button.

Don't break rows. *A large table that doesn't fit on a single page usually continues on the next page. To prevent the table from breaking in the middle of a row, turn off the Allow Row To Break Across Pages option on the Row tab of the Table Properties dialog box on the Table menu.*

Delete Rows

1. Select the rows to be deleted, and right-click.

2. Choose Delete Rows from the shortcut menu.

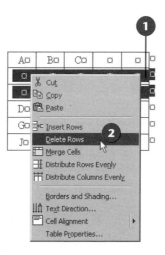

Delete Columns

1. Select the columns to be deleted, and right-click.

2. Choose Delete Columns from the shortcut menu.

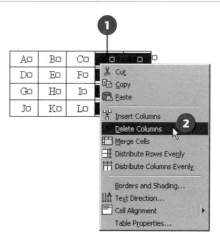

Wrapping Text Around a Table

One of the great features Word gives you is the ability to wrap text around a table. With just a few mouse clicks, you can achieve a professional-looking text wrap around two, three, or all four sides of a table. Aside from the design flexibility this feature gives you, it's also very useful for placing explanatory material directly beside the table so that it instantly catches your reader's eye.

> A medium-size (4.5-7.5 m.) toothed whale with a single blow-hole. The dorsal fin is tall, curved, and very robust, with a thick base. The color ranges from reddish-brown to brown, but in poor
>
> | QUICK FACTS | |
> | --- | --- |
> | Size | 4.5-7.5 m. |
> | Color | Brown |
> | Dive time | 14-30 mins. |
>
> lighting conditions appears gray or black. There are usually numerous scratches and circular scars on the body, with some animals being extensively scarred. The bulbous head is difficult to distinguish and the beak is rarely displayed above water.

SEE ALSO

For information about using the Move box, see "Moving a Table" on page 166.

Set the Text Wrap

1. With the mouse pointer positioned over the table, drag the Move box and move the table to where you want it in relationship to your text.

2. Double-click the Move box to display the Table Properties dialog box.

3. Under Text Wrapping, select the Around option if it's not already selected.

4. Click Positioning.

5. Change the settings to specify the distance between the table and the text on the left, right, top, and bottom of the table.

6. Click OK.

7. Click OK.

8. Use the Move box in the table to adjust the table's position in relationship to the text if necessary.

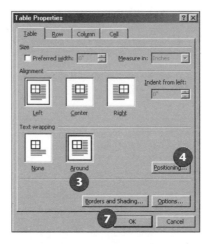

Putting Pictures into Your Document

Putting pictures into your documents is one of the most exciting and satisfying ways to use today's technology. In the not-too-distant past, combining text and graphics images—whether those images were drawings, photographs, or clip art—was an expensive and time-consuming proposition. You had to gather up all the separate pieces—your typed text and all the graphics images you were planning to use—and take them to a typographer. Type shops were the only businesses able to afford the technology that could combine text, pictures, and other elements. Now, using the power of Microsoft Word, you can create these complex documents with very little effort or time.

As you might expect, Word gives you the ability to do much more than just plop those pictures into your documents! You can modify your pictures by changing their size or cropping out the parts you don't want. For a really professional look, you can wrap text around your pictures in various configurations. With the right kind of scanner, you can scan your treasured family photographs directly into Word, and you can even apply stunning special effects with Microsoft Photo Editor. Last but not least, you can use Word's Clip Gallery to organize your ever-expanding picture files by categories and keywords so that you can find your pictures in an instant.

Inserting Clip Art

The Clip Gallery is a Microsoft Office tool that manages your art collection and makes it easy to find and insert pictures. You can scroll through different categories or conduct a search using keywords. When you add a picture to a document, the picture becomes part of the document.

TIP

Artistic character. *An inserted picture behaves just like a single character—albeit a large one—unless you change the way text wraps around it. The picture can be part of a paragraph, with text, pictures, and other content on either side of it, or it can be the only item in a paragraph.*

SEE ALSO

For information about changing the way text wraps around a picture, see "Wrapping Text Around a Picture" on page 181.

Find and Insert a Picture

1. Click in your document where you want to place the clip art.

2. Point to Picture on the Insert menu, and choose Clip Art from the submenu. Click the Pictures tab if it's not already selected.

3. Do either of the following:
   - Type a search word, and press Enter.
   - Click an appropriate category.

4. Click a picture you think you might want to use.

5. Click the Preview Clip button to view the picture. Click the button again to close the preview.

6. Repeat steps 3 through 5 until you find the picture you want.

7. Click the Insert Clip button.

8. Close the Insert ClipArt dialog box.

Enter your search text...

...or select an appropriate category.

Click to view all the categories.

Click to get pictures from Microsoft over the Internet.

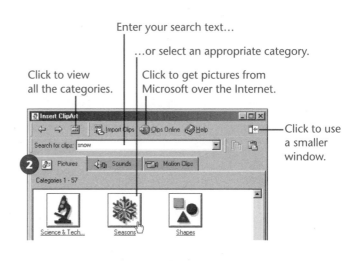

Click to use a smaller window.

Click to copy the picture to the Clipboard instead of inserting it into your document.

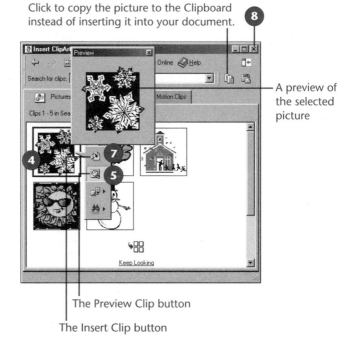

A preview of the selected picture

The Preview Clip button

The Insert Clip button

Inserting a Picture from a File

You can add different types of picture files to a single document—photographs and drawings, as well as clip art—provided you have the proper file converters for the file formats. Word comes with a variety of converters, and many graphics programs supply their own converters.

TIP

Update the link. *If a linked picture hasn't changed even though the source picture file has changed, click the picture and press the F9 key to update the LINK field.*

TIP

Get the picture. *If you see an empty box instead of a picture, choose Options from the Tools menu, and turn off the Picture Placeholders check box on the View tab.*

Insert a Picture

1 Click in your document where you want to insert the picture.

2 Point to Picture on the Insert menu, and choose From File from the submenu.

3 Navigate to the folder containing the picture, and select the picture from the list in the Insert Picture dialog box.

4 Click the down arrow next to the Insert button, and click

◆ Insert to copy the picture and store it in the Word document.

◆ Link To File to connect to the picture file and update the picture whenever the source picture file changes.

◆ Insert And Link to copy the picture, store it in the Word document, and update the picture whenever the source picture file changes.

Navigate through your folders to locate the picture you want.

Click to change your view of the file information and to see a preview of the selected picture.

Click to select the way the picture is added to the document.

Adding a Picture from a Scanner

With a TWAIN-compatible scanner, you can scan a picture directly into Word, using your scanning software. The picture becomes part of the document and isn't stored as a separate file unless you save the document as a Web page.

Get the Picture

1. Click in your document where you want to insert the picture.

2. Point to Picture on the Insert menu, and choose From Scanner Or Camera from the submenu.

3. In the Insert Picture From Scanner Or Camera dialog box, select your scanner program (if necessary), and do any of the following:

   ◆ Select a resolution (not available if your scanner doesn't support automatic scans).

   ◆ Click Insert for an automatic scan (not available if your scanner doesn't support this feature).

   ◆ Click Custom Insert to use your scanning software to make settings and scan the picture.

4. Click in the Word document to see your picture.

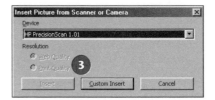

It was a dark and stormy night. A scream—or was it just a gull complaining about being forced to take flight by the storm?

Cropping a Picture

A simple way to modify a picture is to eliminate, or *crop,* the parts of it that you don't want. When you crop a picture in Word, you're cropping only the *display* of the picture, not the picture itself, so you can always restore the complete contents of the original picture if you want.

Crop a Picture

1. Click the picture to select it and show its boundaries.

2. If the Picture toolbar isn't displayed, right-click the picture, and choose Show Picture Toolbar from the shortcut menu.

3. Click the Crop button on the Picture toolbar.

4. Place the mouse pointer over a sizing handle, and drag the picture's boundary until the part of the picture you want to remove is no longer included in the boundary. Drag the sizing handle away from the picture to increase the dimensions of the picture and create white space.

5. Crop the picture using other sizing handles if necessary.

6. Click outside the picture to see the results.

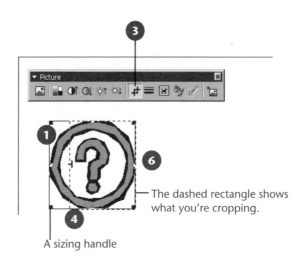

The dashed rectangle shows what you're cropping.

A sizing handle

9

Questions

By cropping a picture, you can show only the part you want.

Sizing a Picture

It's a rare occurrence when an inserted picture fits your document perfectly, so you'll often need to modify an image by sizing it. If you simply need the picture to look good, you can size it visually, tweaking it until it's just right. If the picture's size must be consistent with that of other pictures, however, or if your document must meet precise specifications, you can set the exact size of the picture.

> **TIP**
>
> **One picture, many sizes.**
> *When you size a picture, it's only the display of the picture that changes. Word retains the original picture, so you can change its dimensions repeatedly.*

Change the Size Visually

1. Click the picture to select it and show its boundaries.

2. Place the mouse pointer over a sizing handle, and drag the picture's boundary until the picture is the size you want.

3. If the size isn't quite right, do either of the following:

   ◆ Click the Undo button on the Standard toolbar to reverse the sizing changes you just made.

   ◆ Display the Picture toolbar if it's not already displayed, and click the Reset Picture button to restore the picture to its original dimensions.

Drag a corner handle to resize the vertical and horizontal dimensions proportionally.

Drag a middle handle to change the horizontal dimension.

Drag a middle handle to change the vertical dimension.

The picture isn't distorted when you drag with a corner handle.

The picture is stretched when you resize it horizontally.

The picture is elongated when you resize it vertically.

TRY THIS

Do it both ways. *Select a picture, and drag a horizontal or vertical sizing handle. Right-click the picture, choose Format Picture from the shortcut menu, and click the Size tab. Note that your changes are reflected in the Height and Width size and scaling. Turn off the Lock Aspect Ratio check box, change the size or scaling values, and click OK. Note that the picture now has the dimensions you specified in the Format Picture dialog box.*

TIP

Change the size. *When a picture is linked to a file, Word uses the Includepicture field. If, after you change its size, the picture reverts to its original dimensions, the field did not contain the Mergeformat switch necessary to retain the changed size. To fix this, delete the picture, and then reinsert it using the Picture command on the Insert menu.*

SEE ALSO

For information about linking to a picture using the Picture command, see "Inserting a Picture from a File" on page 175.

Specify the Size

1. Right-click the picture, and choose Format Picture from the shortcut menu.

2. Click the Size tab.

3. With the Lock Aspect Ratio check box turned on, do either of the following:

   ◆ Specify a new measurement for either the height or the width of the picture, and press Tab to have Word fill in the other measurement and the scaling percentage.

   ◆ Specify a scaling percentage for either the height or the width of the picture, and press Tab to have Word fill in the other scaling percentage and the dimensions for height and width.

4. Click OK.

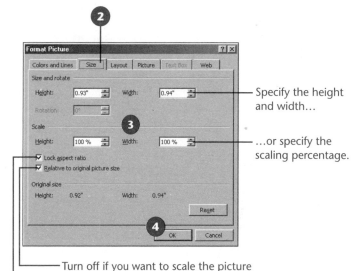

Specify the height and width...

...or specify the scaling percentage.

Turn off if you want to scale the picture relative to the currently displayed image rather than to the original picture.

Turn off if you want to distort the picture with different scaling for height and width.

Changing a Picture's Appearance

You've got the right picture, but you're not completely satisfied with the effect—perhaps the details aren't clear when the picture is printed, or the image is a bit too dark when you see it on line. Don't worry: you can modify the image, convert the picture into a completely different type of image, or just tweak it until it looks the way you want.

TIP

Ephemera. *Changes to the picture affect only the image you see. The original picture still exists, unchanged, and you can always restore it by clicking the Reset Picture button on the Picture toolbar.*

SEE ALSO

For information about adding a border to a picture, see "Placing a Border Around an Object" on page 201.

Convert the Image

1. Click the picture if it's not already selected, and display the Picture toolbar if it's not already displayed.

2. Click the Image Control button on the Picture toolbar.

3. Click the type of image you want.

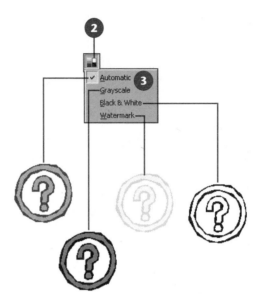

Tweak the Picture

1. Click the picture if it's not already selected.

2. Click a button on the Picture toolbar to adjust the contrast or brightness of the picture.

3. Continue clicking the buttons to add or decrease the contrast or brightness.

Decreases the contrast.   Decreases the brightness.

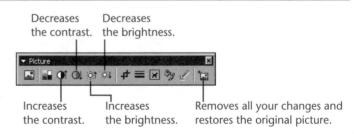

Increases the contrast.   Increases the brightness.   Removes all your changes and restores the original picture.

Wrapping Text Around a Picture

If you want to integrate a picture with the text in a document, you can *wrap* the text around the picture. Word offers several different wrapping styles, and it's fun to experiment with them and see how easily you can create a professional-looking layout for your document.

TIP

Double duty. *With Click And Type enabled, double-click at the right of a picture to set the picture for text wrapping and to start a new paragraph.*

SEE ALSO

For information about using Click And Type, see "Starting Anywhere on the Page" on page 26.

For information about fine-tuning the way text wraps around a picture, see "Wrapping Text Around an Object" on page 196.

Set the Wrap

1. Open a document that contains text and a picture, click the picture to select it, and display the Picture toolbar if it's not already displayed.

2. On the Picture toolbar, click the Text Wrapping button, and choose the text-wrapping option you want from the drop-down list:

    ◆ Square for text on all four sides

    ◆ Tight for text on four sides around an irregularly shaped picture

    ◆ Top And Bottom for text above and below the picture only

3. Drag the picture to adjust where it appears in the paragraph and how the text wraps around it.

4. If you want to set the picture so that the text doesn't wrap around it, choose Picture from the Format menu, click In Line With Text on the Layout tab, and click OK.

The Text Wrapping button

Square wrap

It was a dark and stormy night. The wind howled through the broken windows. Moldy shutters banged the dank walls. "Why relentlessly against but the shrieking wind me?" I murmured, away. "Why not!" it carried my voice or was it just a gull jeered. A scream— complaining about being forced to take flight by the storm? A hand ripping at the door's rotted timbers—or just a branch brushing against the house?

The sun shone brightly as I squinted across the water, looking for a sail on the distant horizon. I knew the ship would come, sooner or

later. They had promised to return and I trusted them—I know not why.

Top And Bottom wrap

Editing a Picture

When you modify a photograph or a drawing using the tools on the Picture toolbar, you're changing only the current view of the picture. The original picture remains unchanged. To make permanent changes to the picture, you can use Microsoft Photo Editor, a tool that comes with Office. Photo Editor also lets you add special effects that can enhance or even substantially change the picture.

TIP

Find Photo Editor. *If Microsoft Photo Editor 3.0 doesn't appear in the Picture Editor list in the Options dialog box, click the Windows Start button, and choose Photo Editor from the Microsoft Office Tools submenu.*

SEE ALSO

For information about installing Office components, see "Adding or Removing Components" on page 306.

Select the Editor

1. Choose Options from the Tools menu.

2. On the Edit tab, select Microsoft Photo Editor 3.0 Photo from the Picture Editor list.

3. Click OK.

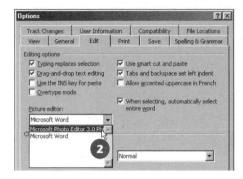

Edit the Picture

1. Right-click the picture, and choose Edit Picture from the shortcut menu.

2. Do any of the following:

   ◆ Select an area, copy it, and paste it to duplicate it.

   ◆ Use the Smudge or the Sharpen tool to change the contrast in an area.

   ◆ Click the Image Balance tool to adjust the brightness, contrast, and gamma setting for the entire picture.

   ◆ Use the Zoom Control to zoom in for detailed editing.

   ◆ Use the commands on the Image menu to crop or resize the picture.

The Sharpen tool

The Smudge tool

The Image Balance tool

The Select tool

The Zoom Control

Apply Special Effects

1 Do either of the following:

- ◆ To apply an effect to part of the picture, use the Select tool to select the area.

- ◆ To apply an effect to the entire picture, turn off the Select tool if it's turned on.

2 From the Effects menu, choose an effect.

3 Use the dialog box for the chosen effect to fine-tune the settings for the effect, and click Apply.

4 Do any of the following:

- ◆ Use any other editing tool or command to modify the picture.

- ◆ Choose Save As from the File menu to save the picture as a separate file.

- ◆ Choose Exit And Return from the File menu to return to the document and display the modified picture.

The Graphic Pen effect

The Chalk And Charcoal effect

The Emboss effect

The Notepaper effect

The Negative effect, with cut corners produced by using the Cropping tool

The Watercolor effect

The Texturizer effect, produced by using the Canvas type

The brightness and contrast adjusted, with oval cropping

Organizing Your Pictures

The more picture files you accumulate, the more difficult it can be to find the one you're looking for. The easy solution is to give your picture files a neatly organized home in the Clip Gallery, where you can categorize them by topic and keyword.

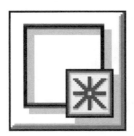

TIP

Name changes. *The Clip Gallery is an Office tool, so you can use it in your other Office programs. Its name, and even the tabs it displays, often change to reflect what you're doing and which Clip Gallery elements you're using.*

Add a Picture

1. Point to Picture on the Insert menu, and choose Clip Art from the submenu.

2. If you want to put the picture into a special category, click New Category, type a name for the category, and click OK.

3. Click Import Clips.

4. Navigate to the folder that contains the picture file.

5. Click the picture file.

6. Specify how you want to import the picture by clicking

    ◆ Copy Into Clip Gallery to add a copy of the picture file.

    ◆ Move Into Clip Gallery to add the picture and delete it from its previous location.

    ◆ Let Clip Gallery Find This Clip to record only the location of the file.

7. Click Import.

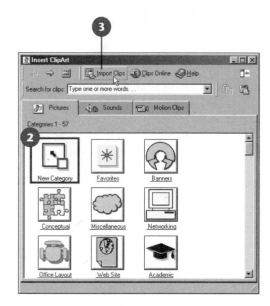

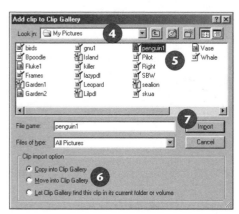

Classify the Picture

1. On the Description tab of the Clip Properties dialog box, type a description of the picture.

2. On the Categories tab, turn on the check boxes for the categories under which you want to list the picture.

3. On the Keywords tab, click the New Keyword button, type a keyword for the picture, and click OK.

4. Repeat step 3 until you've entered any other keywords you want to associate with the picture.

5. Click OK in the Clip Properties dialog box.

6. Close the Insert ClipArt dialog box when you've finished.

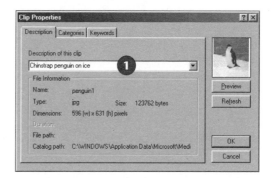

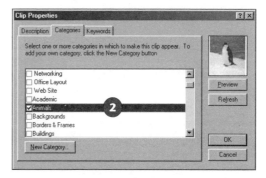

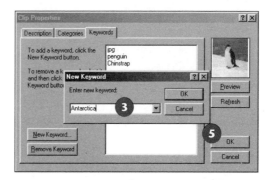

Desktop Publishing

Desktop publishing requires neither a desktop (a kitchen table or a lap will do) nor a publisher. Desktop publishing is simply a collection of tools and techniques that let you design and lay out pages so that they look the way you want.

Microsoft Word provides many of the features you'll find in most commercial desktop publishing programs, so, unless you need to do really specialized tasks, you can use Word to accomplish the most frequently used publishing techniques. For example, you can wrap text around charts or other objects; add sidebars, pull quotes, callouts, dropped capital letters, and borders; and twist text into fantastic shapes using WordArt.

You'll encounter a few new terms in this section. Some tasks involve working with *text boxes* and objects that *float* above the text. Text boxes give you the freedom to put text inside a *speech balloon* or to *flow* text between columns on different pages. An object that floats is on a different *layer* from that of other objects; you can put a floating object on top of your text or behind it to create special effects.

This section of the book shows you how to use the power of Word to enhance your own creativity. We hope it will spark your imagination and free you to come up with new ideas and new approaches in your work.

Flowing Text into Columns

You can flow text into multiple columns on a page, like the columns in a newspaper or magazine. By dividing a page into separate sections, you can even vary the number of columns in each section of the page.

SEE ALSO

For information about changing the margins and the page orientation within a document, see "Setting Up the Page Dimensions" on page 43.

For information about changing the layout of existing text, see "Using Different Layouts in One Document" on page 104.

For information about using text boxes to flow text into different locations, see "Flowing Text Among AutoShapes" on page 215 and "Flowing Text into Sidebars" on page 216.

Specify the Number of Columns

1. Without worrying about the layout just yet, add the content to your document.

2. Click the Show/Hide ¶ button on the Standard toolbar if it's not already turned on.

3. Select the text that is to be flowed into columns.

4. Click the Columns button on the Standard toolbar, select the number of columns you want, and click. Word makes the selected text into a separate section by inserting Continuous section breaks before and after the selected text.

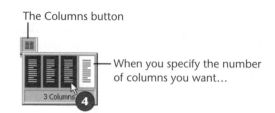

The Columns button

When you specify the number of columns you want...

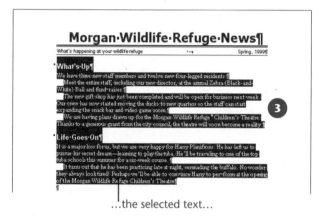

...the selected text...

...flows into those columns.

The title remains in a single column that spreads across the page.

Modify the Layout

1. Click anywhere in the section that has the columns.

2. Choose Columns from the Format menu.

3. Specify the arrangement of the columns.

4. Click OK.

Use a predesigned setup...

Turn on to include a vertical line centered between adjacent columns.

...or keep this check box unchecked...

...and design your own column arrangement.

Tweak the Layout

1. If the ruler isn't already displayed, choose Ruler from the View menu.

2. Hold down the Alt key, drag a column margin to the location where you want it, and release the Alt key. Repeat for other column margins.

3. Do either of the following to improve the text flow:

   ◆ Turn on hyphenation to smooth the ragged right edge of the text.

   ◆ Press Ctrl+Shift+Enter to create a column break and start text in the next column.

When you hold down the Alt key, the ruler indicates the column widths.

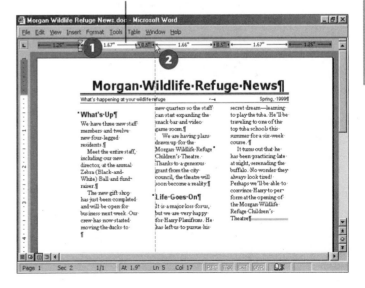

Creating a Side-by-Side Layout

A side-by-side layout is often used to present an item—a picture, a title, or a topic, for example—in one paragraph, along with a description or an explanation of the item in the adjoining paragraph. It's easy to create this type of layout using a Word table. For a more complex layout, you can even insert a table inside another table.

Create the Layout

1. Click the Insert Table button on the Standard toolbar, and drag out a one-row-by-two-column table.

2. Resize the columns to the size you need.

3. Format each cell with the appropriate paragraph style.

4. Choose Table Properties from the Table menu and, on the Table tab, click the Options button.

5. Set the margins you want inside each cell.

6. Specify whether you want spaces between the cells.

7. Click OK.

8. Enter your side-by-side paragraphs. To add another row, click in the last cell, press Tab, and enter your content. Repeat until you've inserted all the content.

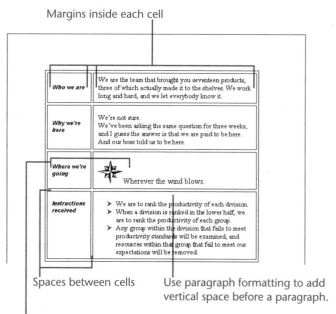

Margins inside each cell

Spaces between cells

Use paragraph formatting to add vertical space before a paragraph.

The paragraph content is always side by side, regardless of the size or type of content.

Separate tables. *Create two tables, and size one table so that it will fit inside a cell of the other table. Select the smaller table, press the F2 key, click in a cell of the larger table, and press Enter. Now move the mouse pointer over the inserted table until the Move box appears at the upper left corner. Drag the Move box and place the inserted table outside the larger table.*

For information about adding or removing borders, see "Changing the Look of a Table" on page 162.

Diagonal borders. *You can use diagonal borders to "cross out" a cell (to indicate that there's no information for that particular cell). Diagonal borders don't split or otherwise affect the properties of the cell.*

Insert a Table

1. Create and format a table with a side-by-side layout.

2. If you don't want the layout to look like a table, remove all the borders. If the gridlines aren't already displayed, choose Show Gridlines from the Table menu to see the cell boundaries while you're working on the table.

3. Click inside the cell of the table that is to contain the inserted table.

4. Click the Insert Table button on the Standard toolbar, and drag out the number of rows and columns you want in the inserted table.

5. Adjust the table borders and cell dimensions to meet your requirements.

6. Add content and formatting to the inserted table.

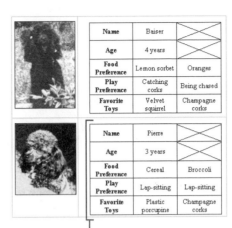

A separate table inside
a single cell of a larger table

1

Creating Margin Notes

A popular design choice for many documents is to create wide outside margins and then use them to place notes—cross-references or tips, as in this book, for example—that are separate from the flow of the document's main content.

SEE ALSO

For information about changing the width of the margins, see "Setting Up the Page Dimensions" on page 43.

For information about creating a style, see "Creating Styles from Scratch" on page 74.

TIP

One side only. *If you'll be printing on only one side of the page—that is, if the document is not set for mirror margins—create a wide left or right margin, and position the frame on the left or right side of the page.*

Create a Layout

1. Choose Page Setup from the File menu, and, on the Margins tab, set wide outside margins for the document. Click OK.

2. Press Enter to insert a new paragraph.

3. Choose Style from the Format menu, click the New button, and name the style.

4. Click the Format button, and choose Frame.

5. Under Text Wrapping, select None.

6. Under Horizontal, set Position to Outside and Relative To to Page.

7. Set the horizontal Distance From Text to the amount of space you want between the note and the main text column of the document.

8. Under Size, set the Width to Exactly, and the At setting to the width of your note.

9. Click OK. Format the paragraph and font as desired, and close the dialog boxes.

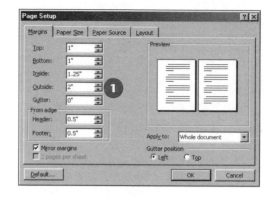

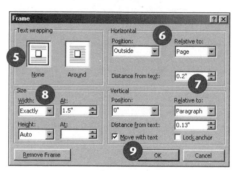

Create a Margin Note

1. Click at the beginning of the paragraph that you want to place the margin note next to.

2. Press Enter.

3. Move back to the empty paragraph and type the text of the margin note.

4. With the insertion point still in the margin note, select the margin-note style from the Style drop-down list on the Formatting toolbar.

Move a Margin Note

1. Click the margin note to select its frame.

2. Click the Cut button on the Standard toolbar.

3. Click at the beginning of the paragraph that you want to move the margin note next to.

4. Click the Paste button on the Standard toolbar.

The text you've formatted with the margin-note style appears in the outside margins of the document.

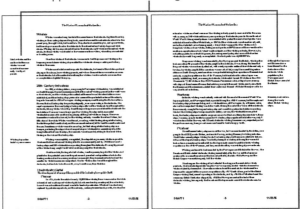

When you cut the margin note from here…

…and paste it here…

…it appears in the margin here.

Creating an Inline Heading

Many document designs use *inline headings*—that is, the first sentence (or part of the first sentence) of a paragraph is formatted as a bold or italic subheading. An inline heading is also called a *run-in* heading because, unlike more prominent headings, it doesn't have its own separate paragraph but is run in with the paragraph text. Just as you create main headings with a paragraph style, you create inline headings with a style, which is called a *character* style.

TIP

Line spacing. *Depending on your formatting choices, an inline heading can make your paragraph's line spacing inconsistent. If you want all the lines in the paragraph to have the same vertical spacing, choose Paragraph from the Format menu, and set the Line Spacing to At Least and the At value to the same size as that of the inline heading's font.*

Create a Style

1. Choose Style from the Format menu.

2. Click the New button.

3. Enter a name for the style.

4. Select Character as the style type.

5. Turn on the Add To Template check box.

6. Click Format, and design the heading.

7. Click OK.

8. Click the Close button to close the Style dialog box.

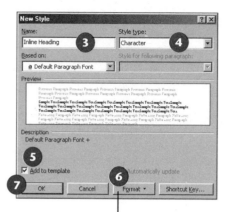

Specify font, language, border, and shading, as desired.

Create the Inline Heading

1. Start a new paragraph, using the correct paragraph style.

2. Choose an inline heading style from the Style drop-down list on the Formatting toolbar.

3. Type the heading text.

4. Press Ctrl+Spacebar to turn off the character style, and then type the remaining paragraph text.

A character style formats only the characters it's applied to, not the entire paragraph.

Life Goes On. It is a major loss for us, but we are very happy for Harry Planifrons. He has left us to pursue his secret dream—learning to play the tuba. He'll be traveling to one of the top tuba schools this summer for a six-week course.

Adjusting the Spacing Between Characters

Sometimes you'll need to squeeze more text into a line; sometimes you'll want to spread the text out to fill up a line. Perhaps you want to create a special look in a heading by condensing or expanding the text. You can achieve all these effects by adjusting the widths of characters and the spaces between words.

SEE ALSO

For information about adjusting the character spacing in WordArt, see "Creating Stylized Text" on page 218.

TIP

Watch this space. *As a side effect of your increasing or decreasing the spacing between characters, Word adjusts the spacing between words too.*

Adjust the Spacing

1. Select the text to be adjusted.

2. Choose Font from the Format menu, and click the Character Spacing tab.

3. Change the settings to adjust the spacing:

   ◆ In the Scale list box, select or type a percentage to expand or condense the width of each character.

   ◆ In the Spacing list box, select Expanded or Condensed, and, in the By text box, enter a value to expand or condense the spacing between characters.

4. To *kern*—that is, to decrease the spacing between—certain pairs of letters, turn on the Kerning For Fonts check box, and specify a minimum font size to be kerned. (Word uses its own list to determine which letter pairs, in which fonts, may be kerned.)

5. Click OK.

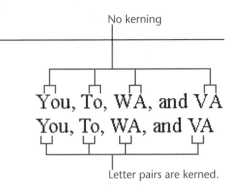

No kerning

You, To, WA, and VA
You, To, WA, and VA

Letter pairs are kerned.

This text is not adjusted.
This text is scaled to 80%.
This text is scaled to 150%.
This text is condensed by 1 pt.
This text is expanded by 1 pt.
This text is scaled to 80% and condensed by 1 pt.
This text is scaled to 80%
      and expanded by 1 pt.
This text is scaled to 150%
      and condensed by 1 pt.
This text is scaled to 150%
      and expanded by 1 pt.

Wrapping Text Around an Object

When you insert an *object* into a document—a chart or a ClipArt picture, for example—you can specify how you want the text to *wrap* around the object, or you can set the text to be displayed behind or in front of the object. You can also change the shape of the text wrap to follow the shape of the object, or set the text to wrap around only part of the object.

TIP

Use the default. *You can use the Text Wrapping button on the Picture toolbar if you prefer to use the default values for the Wrap To and Distance From Text settings.*

SEE ALSO

For information about inserting pictures, see "Inserting Clip Art" on page 174 and "Inserting a Picture from a File" on page 175.

Set the Wrap

1. In a document that already contains an inserted object, click the object to select it.

2. Choose Object (or Picture) from the Format menu, and click the Layout tab.

3. Click the Advanced button.

4. On the Text Wrapping tab of the Advanced Layout dialog box, select the type of wrap you want.

5. Specify which side or sides of the object you want the text wrap applied to.

6. Specify the minimum spacing between the object and the text.

7. Click OK, and click OK again to close the Format Object (or Picture) dialog box.

8. Drag the object (or picture) to the location you want.

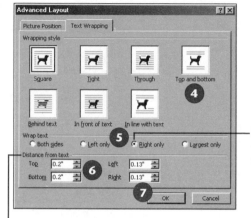

The text is set to wrap on the right side only.

Specifies the amount of white space between the object and the wrapped text.

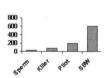

Population

The Southern bottlenose whale is second only to the minke whale in cetacean abundance in the Antarctic, but accurate population estimates are difficult due to the long dives of the animals. The best estimate for the Antarctic area (south of 60°S latitude) during the summer is about 599,000 animals. It is the most abundant odontocete in the area. Although the population estimates require some assumptions on the detectability of the species during sighting surveys, the numbers do provide a good indication of the impact of this species on the Antarctic ecosystem.

This chart indicates that there are substantially larger numbers of Southern bottlenose whales than the more frequently observed odontocete species.

Change the Wrapping Shape

1. Click the object to select it if it's not already selected.

2. Display the Picture toolbar if it's not already displayed.

3. Click the Text Wrapping button on the Picture toolbar, and choose Edit Wrap Points.

4. Change the wrapping points.

5. Click outside the object to deselect it.

Wrap Only Part of the Object

1. Click at the point where you want to stop the text wrap.

2. Choose Break from the Insert menu.

3. Select the Text Wrapping Break option, and click OK.

The wrapping line defines the outer edges of the object for text-wrapping purposes.

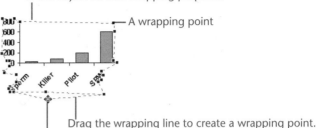

A wrapping point

Drag the wrapping line to create a wrapping point.

Drag a wrapping point to change the wrapping outline.

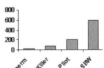

Population¶

The·Southern·bottlenose·whale·is·second·only·to·the·minke·whale·in·cetacean· abundance·in·the·Antarctic,·but·accurate·population·estimates·are·difficult·due·to· the·long·dives·of·the·animals.·The·best·estimate· for·the·Antarctic·area·(south·of·60°S·latitude)· during·the·summer·is·about·599,000·animals.·It·is· the·most·abundant·odontocete·in·the·area.¶

Although·the·population·estimates·require·some·assumptions·on·the·detectability· of·the·species·during·sighting·surveys,·the·numbers·do·provide·a·good·indication· of·the·impact·of·this·species·on·the·Antarctic·ecosystem.¶

A Text Wrapping Break ends the text wrap around the object.

Creating Floating Captions

When you've inserted an object and set its text wrapping so that you can move the object to any location on the page, the object is "floating" on a different electronic layer from that of the text. You can also create a floating caption that will stay attached to the object when you move it.

SEE ALSO

For information about creating nonfloating captions, see "Creating Captions" on page 129.

For information about text wrap, see "Wrapping Text Around an Object" on page 196.

For information about moving objects around, see "Positioning an Object on a Page" on page 204.

For information about working with text boxes, see "Flowing Text into Sidebars" on page 216.

Create a Floating Caption

① Display the Drawing toolbar if it's not already displayed.

② Click the object to select it, and specify its text wrapping if you haven't already done so.

③ Choose Caption from the Insert menu.

④ Type the caption text, and click OK.

⑤ Size and position the caption text box if necessary.

⑥ Click the Select Objects button on the Drawing toolbar.

⑦ Drag a selection rectangle to encompass the object and the caption text box.

⑧ Right-click in the selection rectangle, point to Grouping on the shortcut menu, and click Group.

⑨ Set the text wrap for the grouped object, and move it to the location you want.

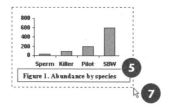

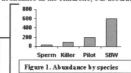

Population

The Southern bottlenose whale is second only to the minke whale in cetacean abundance in the Antarctic, but accurate population estimates are difficult due to the long dives of the animals. The best estimate for the Antarctic area (south of 60°S latitude) during the summer is about 599,000 animals. It is the most abundant odontocete in the area. Although the population estimates require some assumptions on the detectability of the species during sighting surveys, the numbers do provide a good indication of the impact of this species on the Antarctic ecosystem.

When objects are grouped, they act like a single object.

Placing a Line Border Around a Page

You can create a very nice "finished" look by placing a border around an entire page. Word provides a wide variety of easily applied, customizable line styles.

SEE ALSO

For information about placing a border around a paragraph, see "Adding a Border to a Paragraph" on page 40.

For information about placing a border around text in an online document, see "Making Text Stand Out" on page 236.

Create a Page Border

1. Choose Borders And Shading from the Format menu, and click the Page Border tab.

2. Select a setting.

3. Select a line style, color, and width.

4. Select the part of the document that will have this border.

5. Click OK.

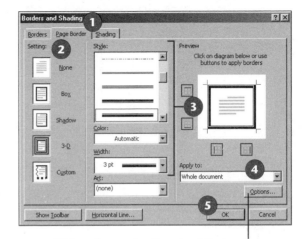

Click to change the distance of the border from the edge of the page or from the text.

Create a Custom Border

1. Choose Borders And Shading from the Format menu, and click the Page Border tab.

2. Click the Custom setting.

3. Select a line style, color, and width.

4. Click a border button.

5. Repeat steps 3 and 4 if you want to add different line styles to the other sides of the page border.

6. Click OK.

The preview shows the arrangement of the border line styles.

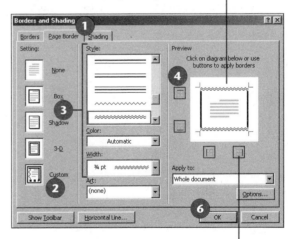

Click to add or remove a border.

Placing an Art Border Around a Page

You can go beyond line borders and add one of Word's attractive and fanciful art borders around a page. How about a border of cupcakes or ice-cream cones for a party invitation, palm trees for a travel brochure, or ladybugs for an environmental newsletter? It's hard to resist playing with the different looks you can create with this huge collection of art borders, and it's so easy!

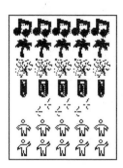

Create an Art Border

1. Choose Borders And Shading from the Format menu, and click the Page Border tab.

2. Click the Box setting.

3. Select the art you want to use.

4. Specify the size of the art.

5. Click a border button if you want to remove the border from that side. To put it back, click the button again.

6. Select the part of the document that will have the selected border.

7. Click the Options button if you want to change the distance of the border from the page edge or from the text.

8. Click OK.

The selected art forms the border.

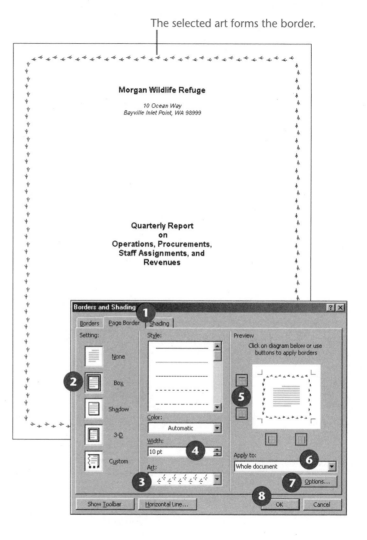

Morgan Wildlife Refuge

10 Ocean Way
Bayville Inlet Point, WA 98999

Quarterly Report
on
Operations, Procurements,
Staff Assignments, and
Revenues

Placing a Border Around an Object

To make an inserted object stand out, you can place a border around it. If the object is in line with the text, you can apply standard borders, such as those you'd apply to a paragraph. If the object is set for text wrapping and can be positioned anywhere on the page, you can add a rectangular line border that becomes part of the object.

SEE ALSO

For information about placing a border around a paragraph, see "Adding a Border to a Paragraph" on page 40.

For information about wrapping text around an object, see "Wrapping Text Around an Object" on page 196.

For information about placing a border around text in an online document, see "Making Text Stand Out" on page 236.

Place a Border Around an Inline Object

① Right-click the object to which you want to add a border, and choose Borders And Shading from the shortcut menu.

② On the Borders tab, specify the type of border you want.

③ Verify that Picture is selected in the Apply To section.

④ Click OK.

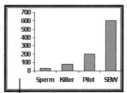

An inline object uses the same types of borders as those you'd apply to a paragraph.

Place a Border Around an Object with Text Wrapping

① Right-click the object, and choose Format Object (or Format Picture) from the shortcut menu.

② On the Color And Lines tab, select the border's line color, style, size, and weight.

③ Click OK.

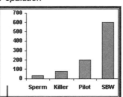

An object with text wrapping uses the object's line properties to create a rectangular border.

Creating a Drawing

For those of us who aren't great artists, Word's drawing tools provide a quick and easy way to create a variety of professional-looking drawings directly on the page. For an extremely complex drawing, you'll probably want to use a drawing program and then insert the picture, but try using Word's tools first. As artistically challenged individuals, we were really astonished at some of the lively effects we created.

TIP

Zoom in. *Use the Zoom box on the Standard toolbar if you want to see a highly detailed view of your drawing when you're working with small shapes. If you have a wheel mouse, hold down the Ctrl key and rotate the wheel to zoom in or out quickly.*

Create a Drawing

1. Display the Drawing toolbar if it's not already displayed.

2. Click AutoShapes, point to a type of AutoShape, and click the shape you want.

3. Drag the mouse to create the shape in the dimensions you want. Hold down the Shift key while dragging to draw the shape without distortion.

4. Use the adjustment handle, if present, to modify the shape.

5. Select and then format the shape using the tools on the Drawing toolbar.

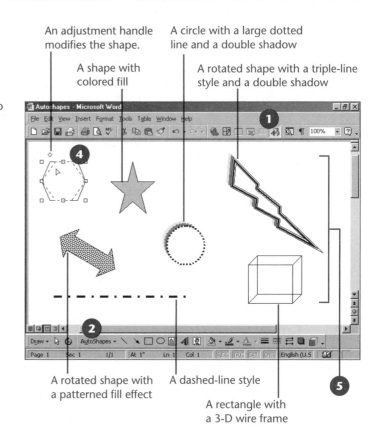

An adjustment handle modifies the shape.

A shape with colored fill

A circle with a large dotted line and a double shadow

A rotated shape with a triple-line style and a double shadow

A rotated shape with a patterned fill effect

A dashed-line style

A rectangle with a 3-D wire frame

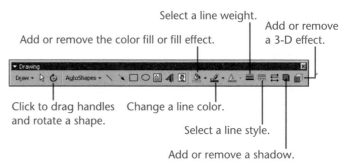

Select a line weight.

Add or remove a 3-D effect.

Add or remove the color fill or fill effect.

Click to drag handles and rotate a shape.

Change a line color.

Select a line style.

Add or remove a shadow.

TIP

Artistic combinations.
*You can combine your drawing
with other objects, such as
pictures or graphs.*

TRY THIS

Group the group. *Draw
a banner AutoShape and put
stars and other AutoShapes on
top of the banner. Group all
the AutoShapes, including the
banner. Draw the Bevel
AutoShape, and then drag the
grouped banner on top of it.
Stack the AutoShapes so that
the Bevel AutoShape is behind
the banner. Resize the Bevel
AutoShape if necessary, and
position the banner. Now select
the entire Bevel AutoShape and
the banner and group them.*

SEE ALSO

*For information about arranging
AutoShapes and other objects
relative to each other, see
"Aligning Objects" on page 206.*

*For information about adding
a picture to an AutoShape, see
"Adding a Background to an
Object" on page 210.*

*For information about includ-
ing text with AutoShapes, see
"Creating a Callout" on
page 211.*

Combine Drawings

1. Create and format additional AutoShapes.

2. Drag the objects (the drawings) to arrange them.

3. Right-click an object, choose Order from the shortcut menu, and change the stacking order of the object. Continue rearranging until the objects are in the desired sequence.

4. Click the Select Objects button on the Drawing toolbar, and drag to enclose all the objects in the selection rectangle.

5. Right-click one of the selected objects, point to Grouping on the shortcut menu, and choose Group from the submenu.

6. Drag the drawing to the location you want.

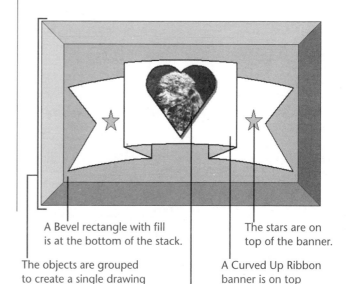

A Bevel rectangle with fill is at the bottom of the stack.

The stars are on top of the banner.

The objects are grouped to create a single drawing that can be moved as a unit.

A Curved Up Ribbon banner is on top of the rectangle.

A Heart with a picture as the fill effect is on top of the banner.

Positioning an Object on a Page

An object—whether it's a picture, an AutoShape, a graph, or any other type of object that's set for text wrapping—is associated with, or *anchored to,* the paragraph nearest where you inserted the object. It's quite simple to position objects where you want them. If the paragraph moves to a different page, any object anchored to the paragraph moves with it.

TIP

Gridlock? *If you can't move an object into the position you want, check to make sure that the object isn't set to snap to the grid.*

SEE ALSO

For information about using the grid, see "Aligning Objects" on page 206.

Move an Object into a Relative Position

1. If the object isn't set for text wrapping, use the Picture toolbar to set the text wrapping to Square, Tight, or Top And Bottom.

2. Display the Drawing toolbar if it's not already displayed.

3. Click the object to select it.

4. Click the Draw button, point to Align Or Distribute, and choose Left, Center, or Right alignment. If the commands are grayed, choose Relative To Page, and then reopen the list and choose an alignment.

5. Click the Draw button, point to Align Or Distribute, and choose Top, Middle, or Bottom alignment.

6. Click the Text Wrapping button on the Picture toolbar, and adjust the wrap as desired.

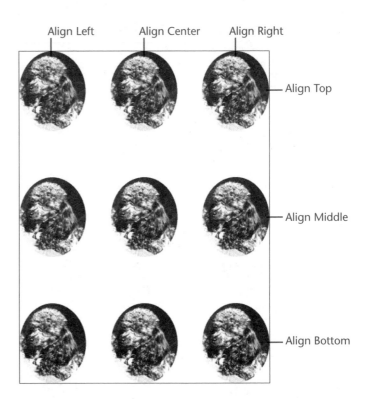

Align Left Align Center Align Right

Align Top

Align Middle

Align Bottom

TIP

Find the anchor. *Each object is anchored to a paragraph, a line, or a character. To see where an object is anchored, turn on the Show/Hide ¶ button if it's not already turned on, and click the object. You should see a little anchor where the object is anchored.*

TIP

Picas, points, and more. *To use a different unit of measurement in the current document, type a number, followed by the unit of measurement: pi for picas, pt for points, in for inches, or cm for centimeters. To change the unit of measurement permanently, choose Options from the Tools menu, click the General tab, and select the unit of measurement you want.*

TIP

It's all relative. *If you turn off the Relative To Page option (under Align Or Distribute on the Draw button's menu), you can use the alignment options to align objects relative to each other. You must have two or more objects selected before these alignment options become available.*

Fine-Tune the Object's Position

1. Right-click the object, and choose Format Picture, Format Object, or Format AutoShape from the shortcut menu.

2. On the Layout tab, click the Advanced button, and click the Picture Position tab.

3. Under Horizontal, select Absolute Position, and specify the distance you want the object to be to the left of the margin, page, column, or character.

4. Under Vertical, select Absolute Position, and specify the distance you want the object to be below the margin, page, paragraph, or line.

5. Turn the Move Object With Text check box on or off.

6. Turn the Lock Anchor check box on or off.

7. Turn the Allow Overlap check box on or off.

8. Click OK.

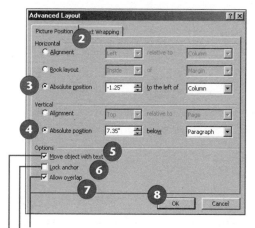

Leave on to allow objects to overlap each other.

Turn on to keep the object on the same page as the paragraph it's anchored to, even if the horizontal and vertical measurements are from the page or margin.

Leave on to keep the object in the same position relative to the paragraph or line (vertical position) or the character (horizontal position) it's anchored to.

Aligning Objects

When you insert objects—pictures, AutoShapes, or graphs, for example—that are set for text wrapping, aligning them properly on the page can sometimes be quite tricky. Word provides several tools that can help you position all the objects precisely where you want them.

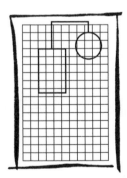

Line Up the Objects

1 Display the Drawing toolbar if it's not already displayed.

2 Click the Draw button, and choose Grid.

3 Turn on the Snap Objects To Grid check box if it's not already turned on.

4 Set the dimensions for your layout grid. Turn off the Use Margins check box if you want the grid's boundaries to be different from the document's margins.

5 Turn on the Display Gridlines On Screen check box.

6 Turn on the Vertical Every check box, and set the interval for the display of vertical and horizontal gridlines.

7 Click OK.

8 Drag the object near to where you want it to align. It will snap to the closest gridlines.

Objects align to the closest gridlines even if all gridlines are not displayed.

Objects align to the grid you specify.

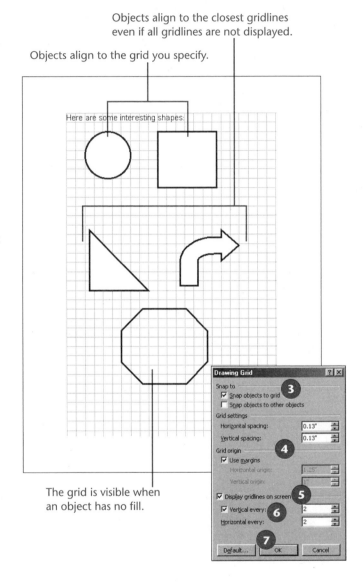

Here are some interesting shapes.

The grid is visible when an object has no fill.

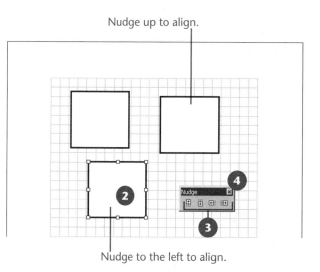

TIP

Gridlock. *When the Snap Objects To Grid check box is turned on and you create or resize an object, the object is drawn or resized by the same increment set for the grid, and it aligns to the grid. If you want to make the object a slightly different size or place it in a slightly different location, you can either change the spacing of the gridlines or turn off the Snap Objects To Grid check box.*

SEE ALSO

For information about specifying the exact position of an object, see "Positioning an Object on a Page" on page 204.

TIP

A little nudge. *When the Snap Objects To Grid check box is turned off, the Nudge buttons move the object one pixel at a time.*

Fine-Tune the Alignment

1. Click the Draw button, point to Nudge, and drag the little bar at the top of the submenu into your document to create a floating toolbar.

2. Click to select the object to be moved.

3. Click a Nudge button to move the object one gridline at a time. Continue using the Nudge buttons until you've positioned the object where you want it.

4. Select another object to move, or click the Close button on the Nudge toolbar to close it.

Connect AutoShapes

1. Click the Draw button, and choose Grid.

2. Turn on the Snap Objects To Other Objects check box, turn off the Snap Objects To Grid check box, and click OK.

3. Drag a shape near to another shape until it aligns to the border of the shape.

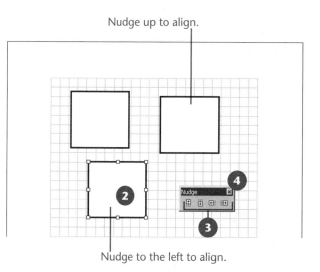

Nudge up to align.

Nudge to the left to align.

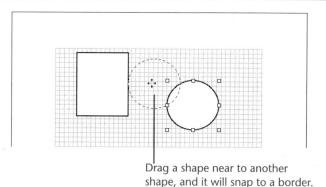

Drag a shape near to another shape, and it will snap to a border.

Creating a Watermark

Watermarks are pictures or text (such as a company logo) that sit "behind" the main text. They appear on every printed page as if they were part of the paper. In dedicated desktop publishing programs, you create a watermark by placing a graphic on a background layer. In Word, you place the graphic that you want as a watermark on the same layer as the header and footer.

SEE ALSO

For information about adding a background to an online document, see "Creating a Background" on page 226.

TIP

Lose the background.
If you're using a picture with a solid background that you want to eliminate, use the Set Transparent Color tool on the Picture toolbar.

Add a Picture

1. Choose Header And Footer from the View menu, and change the Zoom setting to Whole Page.

2. On the Header And Footer toolbar, click the Show/Hide Document Text button.

3. Choose Text Box from the Insert menu, and drag out a text box to hold your picture.

4. Point to Picture on the Insert menu, choose From File from the submenu, and insert the picture.

5. Drag the picture's sizing handles to create the watermark in the size you want. If necessary, adjust the size of the text box.

6. Drag the text box to position the picture where you want it.

7. Choose Text Box from the Format menu, and, on the Colors And Lines tab, set the Line Color to No Line. Click OK.

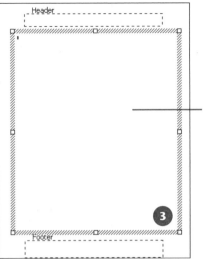

Use a text box with no border to hold and position the picture.

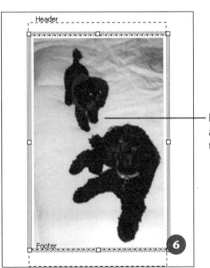

Position the text box and the picture to create the effect you want.

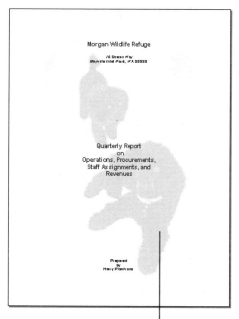

TIP

Use a template. *It's a good idea to create your watermark in a template so that you won't need to re-create it each time you want to use it.*

TRY THIS

Different watermarks.
Before you create a watermark, choose Page Setup from the File menu. On the Layout tab, turn on the check box for different odd- and even-page headers and footers, and click OK. Now create one watermark for the odd-numbered pages and another one for the even-numbered pages.

TIP

No watermark. *If you want only a single instance of a picture behind some text on a single page, format the picture's text wrapping to Behind Text.*

SEE ALSO

For information about text wrapping, see "Wrapping Text Around a Picture" on page 181 and "Wrapping Text Around an Object" on page 196.

Make It a Watermark

1. Click the picture to select it. Click the Image Control button on the Picture toolbar, and choose Watermark.

2. On the Picture toolbar, use the Brightness and Contrast buttons and the Cropping tool to adjust the image.

3. Click the Close button on the Header And Footer toolbar, and set the Zoom control to 100%.

4. Add some text to verify that the watermark is visible and that it doesn't obscure the text.

5. If necessary, choose Header And Footer from the View menu, adjust the picture, and click Close on the Header And Footer toolbar.

6. If you're going to save the document as a template, delete any text that isn't part of the watermark, and then save and close the document.

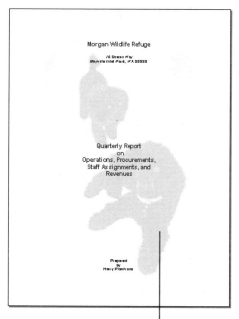

The Image Control Watermark setting makes the picture light enough not to interfere with the text.

Adding a Background to an Object

When you insert an object into a document, the object is inserted inside its own rectangle. You can see the dimensions of the rectangle by clicking the object and noting the location of the sizing handles. You can add a background color or pattern that replaces the transparent color within the rectangle that contains the object.

TIP

Transparent color. *To set a transparent color for a picture or an object, use the Set Transparent Color tool on the Picture toolbar. Note that you can't set a transparent color for every type of picture or object, so you might need to do a little experimenting.*

Add a Background

1. Right-click the object, and choose Format Object (or Format Picture) from the shortcut menu.

2. On the Colors And Lines tab, under Fill, click the down arrow next to the Color button, and do any of the following:

   ◆ Click a color to apply it as the background color.

   ◆ Click More Colors, select a different color, and click OK.

   ◆ Click Fill Effects, and select a gradient, texture, pattern, or picture.

3. If you selected a color, turn on or leave off the Semitransparent check box to control the intensity of the color.

4. Click OK.

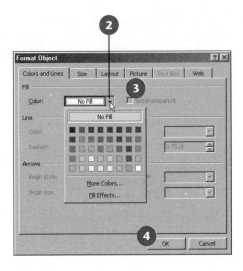

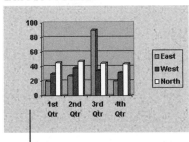

Latest results:

A textured background is added to fill in the transparent area behind the object.

Creating a Callout

A *callout* is a combination of a graphics element and a text box. Although its purpose is similar to that of a caption—to explain the content of a graphic—a callout is part of the graphic, whereas a caption is placed outside the graphic.

Create a Callout

1. Display the Drawing toolbar if it's not already displayed.

2. Click the AutoShapes button, point to Callouts, and choose the type of callout you want from the submenu.

3. Drag the mouse to draw the callout shape.

4. Type and format the text for the callout.

5. Resize the callout shape to fit the text.

Format the Callout

1. Click the callout if it's not already selected.

2. Use the tools on the Drawing toolbar to format or modify the callout.

3. Move the callout to where you want it.

4. Drag the callout line to where you want it.

5. Group the callout with its associated object.

Drag the adjustment handle to elongate or reposition the "tail" of the AutoShape.

Add shadow effects.

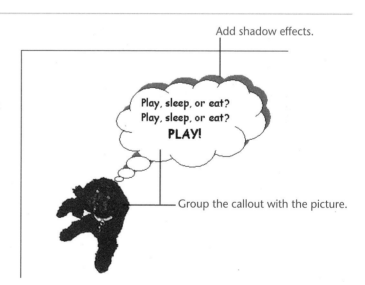

Group the callout with the picture.

Creating a Dropped Capital Letter

A *drop cap*, sometimes called a "fancy first letter," adds style and interest to a document, and attracts the reader's eye to the page. Drop caps are typically used at the beginning of chapters or sections, as in this book.

TIP

Decorate a drop cap.
A drop cap is created as a separate paragraph, using a frame, so you can add borders and shading to it as you can with any paragraph.

TRY THIS

A "drop word"? *You don't have to restrict the drop-cap effect to one solitary letter. Try selecting several letters, or even an entire word, and then apply a drop-cap style.*

Create a Drop Cap

1. Click at the right of the first letter of your paragraph.

2. Choose Drop Cap from the Format menu to display the Drop Cap dialog box.

3. Select a position for the drop cap. (Use the None position to remove an existing drop cap.)

4. Do any of the following to customize the drop cap:

   ◆ Select a different font.

   ◆ Specify a different number of lines over which you want the drop cap to extend.

   ◆ Specify an increased horizontal distance between the drop cap and the text.

5. Click OK.

A three-line drop cap in the text

It was a dark and stormy night. The wind howled through the broken windows. Moldy shutters banged relentlessly against the dank walls. "Why me?" I murmured, but the shrieking wind carried my voice away. "Why not!" it jeered. A scream—or was it just a gull complaining about being forced to take flight by the storm? A hand ripping at the door's rotted timbers—or just a branch brushing against the house?

A three-line drop cap in the margin

It was a dark and stormy night. The wind howled through the broken windows. Moldy shutters banged relentlessly against the dank walls. "Why me?" I murmured, but the shrieking wind carried my voice away. "Why not!" it jeered. A scream—or was it just a gull complaining about being forced to take flight by the storm? A hand ripping at the door's rotted timbers—or just a branch brushing against the house?

Creating a Pull Quote

A *pull quote* is a short piece of text, extracted from your document, that calls attention to the content of the page and adds visual interest. You'll want to set the pull quote off from the rest of the text by surrounding it with some white (or colored) space in the shape of your choice.

SEE ALSO

For information about placing an object relative to a paragraph or to the page, see "Positioning an Object on a Page" on page 204.

TIP

Active text boxes. *All AutoShapes contain text boxes that you can activate with the Add Text command. Text boxes are automatically activated for Callout AutoShapes.*

Draw the Area

1. Select and copy the text you want to use for the pull quote.

2. Display the Drawing toolbar if it's not already displayed, click the AutoShapes button, point to a type of AutoShape, and click the shape you want.

3. Drag the mouse to draw the approximate size and shape of the area for the pull quote.

Add the Text

1. Right-click the AutoShape, and choose Add Text from the shortcut menu.

2. Paste and format the copied text, and resize the AutoShape if necessary.

3. Choose AutoShape from the Format menu, set the text wrapping to Tight, remove or change the line border, and add shading if desired. Click OK.

4. Position the pull quote where you want it.

Use an AutoShape to define the way the text wraps around the pull quote.

It was a dark and stormy night. The wind howled through the broken windows. Moldy shutters banged relentlessly against the dank walls. I murmured, but the shrieking wind carried my voice away. "Why not!" it jeered. A scream—or just a gull complaining about being forced to take flight by the storm? A hand ripping at the door's rotted timbers—or just a branch brushing against the house?

Remove the AutoShape's line; or use a line style, color, or fill for dramatic effects.

It was a dark and stormy night. The wind howled through the broken windows. Moldy shutters banged relentlessly against the dank walls. "Why me?" the shrieking wind away. "Why not!" scream—or was it complaining about take flight by the ripping at the door's just a branch brushing against the house?

"Why me?" I murmured. "Why not!" it jeered.

I murmured, but carried my voice it jeered. A just a gull being forced to storm? A hand rotted timbers—or

Writing Text Sideways

You can write any text sideways by placing the text in a text box and then rotating the text.

TIP

Write this way! *You can also write text sideways in a table cell, and in a multitude of directions using WordArt.*

SEE ALSO

For information about using the alignment buttons on the Formatting toolbar, see "Using Standard Styles" on page 23.

For information about controlling the horizontal alignment of paragraphs, see "Indenting Paragraphs" on page 30.

For information about changing text direction in a table, see "Changing the Look of Text in a Table" on page 164.

For information about using WordArt to create text as art, see "Creating Stylized Text" on page 218.

Create a Text Box

1. Choose Text Box from the Insert menu.

2. Drag out a text box to the dimensions you want.

3. Choose Text Box from the Format menu, set the text wrap to Square, select a fill color and border lines if desired, and modify the margins inside the text box as necessary. Click OK.

4. In the text box, type or paste the text that you want to run sideways.

5. Click the Change Text Direction button on the Text Box toolbar. Click the button again if you want the text to run in a different direction.

6. Format the text, and adjust the paragraph alignment, indents, and spacing as necessary.

Use the alignment buttons on the Formatting toolbar to control the vertical alignment within the text box.

Use the paragraph spacing settings to control the horizontal alignment within the text box.

Morgan Wildlife Refuge News

Spring, 1999

What's happening at your wildlife refuge

What's Up
We have three new staff members and twelve new four-legged residents.

Meet the entire staff, including our new director, at the annual Zebra (Black-and-White) Ball and fundraiser.

The new gift shop has just been completed and will be open for business next week. Our crew has now started moving the ducks to new quarters so they can start expanding the snack bar and video game room.

We are having plans drawn up for the Morgan Wildlife Refuge Children's Theatre. Thanks to a generous grant from the city council, the theatre will soon become a reality.

Life Goes On
It is a major loss for us, but we are very happy for Harry Planifions. He has left us to pursue his secret dream—learning to play the tuba. He'll be traveling to one of the top tuba schools this summer for a six-week course.

It turns out that he has been practicing late at night, serenading the buffalo. No wonder they always look tired! Perhaps we'll be able to convince Harry to perform at the opening of the Morgan Wildlife Refuge Children's Theatre.

A New Look
We redesigned the newsletter to speak to both our young and older audience.

You'll find a list running through the entire newsletter, naming all the animals that are residents of Morgan Wildlife Preserve. See how many animals you've seen.

Newsletters are expensive, of course, so any donation you make will be greatly appreciated.

Species Facts
The inside pages include a new feature—a detailed description of one animal species.

Southern Bottlenose Whale
The Southern bottlenose whale is a common but often overlooked whale of Antarctica and sub-Antarctica. It spends much of its time deep below the surface, on long dives, searching for the squid on which it survives.

Identification
A medium-size (4.5-7.5 m.) toothed whale with a single blowhole. The dorsal fin is tall, curved, and very robust, with a thick base. The color ranges from reddish-brown to brown, but in poor lighting conditions appears gray or black. There are usually numerous scratches and circular scars on the body, with some animals being extensively scarred. The bulbous head is difficult to distinguish and the beak is rarely displayed above water.

Distribution
The Southern bottlenose whale has been observed during the summer throughout the open waters of the Antarctic, except for the southern regions of the Ross and Weddell seas. The Southern bottlenose whale has been observed during the summer throughout the open waters of the Antarctic, except for the southern regions of the Ross and Weddell seas

The text box has black fill and white text.

Flowing Text Among AutoShapes

AutoShapes can contain text, and you can flow text—or anything else that can be inserted into a text box—among the shapes to create all sorts of interesting and high-impact designs.

Add Text to a Shape

1. Display the Drawing toolbar if it's not already displayed.

2. Click the AutoShapes button, select an AutoShape, and drag the mouse to draw the AutoShape.

3. Right-click the shape, and choose Add Text from the shortcut menu.

4. Paste or type the text.

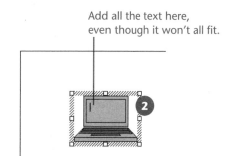

Add all the text here, even though it won't all fit.

Flow Text into Another Shape

1. Draw another AutoShape.

2. Right-click the shape, and choose Add Text from the shortcut menu.

3. Click the first shape to select it.

4. Click the Create Text Box Link button on the Text Box toolbar.

5. Click the Text Flow mouse pointer inside the second shape.

6. Continue creating AutoShapes and flowing text among them.

Text flows from the first AutoShape... ...to the next linked shape... ...and on through all the linked shapes.

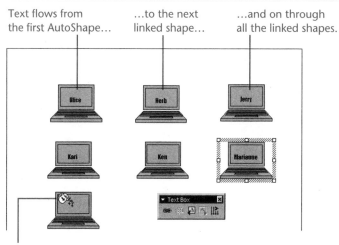

The Text Flow mouse pointer

Flowing Text into Sidebars

You can create text that flows from one location to another by placing the text in a text box and linking that text box to a second one. As you edit the text, it ebbs and flows between the text boxes. This is very useful when you're working with items such as sidebars that often continue on another page.

SEE ALSO

For information about an alternative way to create a sidebar when all the text is contained in a single sidebar, see "Creating Margin Notes" on page 192.

For information about adding text to AutoShapes, see "Flowing Text Among AutoShapes" on page 215.

For information about creating AutoText entries, see "Inserting Frequently Used Information" on page 272.

Create the Flow

1. Set up your document so that it has wide margins to hold the sidebar.

2. Choose Text Box from the Insert menu.

3. In the wide margin, drag out a text box to the dimensions you want for the sidebar.

4. With the text box selected, choose Text Box from the Format menu. Select a fill color and border lines, if desired, and modify the internal margins if necessary. Click OK.

5. Create, format, and place a second text box where you want the sidebar text to continue.

6. Select the first text box.

7. Click the Create Text Box Link button.

8. Click the Text Flow mouse pointer in the second text box.

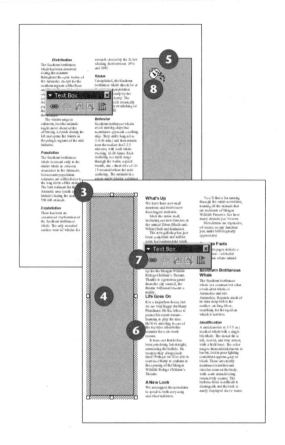

For information about setting different margins in one document, see "Using Different Layouts in One Document" on page 104.

...continues here.

TIP

Save the design. *If you're going to use the same sidebar design several times in a document, or in different documents, save the formatted text box as an AutoText entry before you place any text in it. If you're going to use the same layout again, save the document as a template.*

TIP

Select all. *To select all the text in linked text boxes, click in one text box and choose Select All from the Edit menu.*

TIP

Mirror margins. *To create a flowing sidebar on the left side of even-numbered pages and the right side of odd-numbered pages, set mirror margins for the document, and create a large inside margin. If you don't want this sidebar layout to continue throughout your document, change the margins for the rest of the document.*

SEE ALSO

Add the Content

1. In a separate document, create and format the text for the sidebar.

2. Select and copy the text.

3. Click in the first text box and paste the text.

4. Tweak the sidebars using any of the following methods:

   ◆ Add or delete text so that the content will fit in the text boxes.

   ◆ Change the formatting of selected text or paragraphs.

   ◆ Add pictures or other elements.

   ◆ Change the size of the text boxes.

   ◆ Hyphenate the text using automatic hyphenation.

Text pasted here...

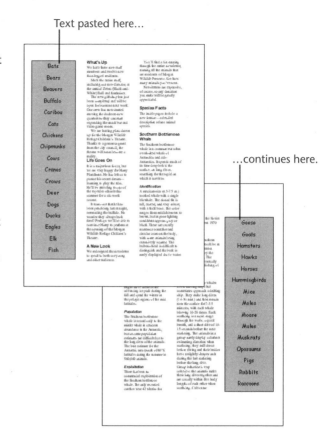

Creating Stylized Text

You can achieve some spectacular text effects by creating text as art. Word uses an accessory program called WordArt that lets you twist your text into weird and wonderful shapes and three-dimensional configurations, and then inserts the result into your document as an object. WordArt might look a bit jagged and rough on your computer screen, but the edges will smooth out when it's printed, and the results can be dazzling. Try it. But heed our warning—it's addictive!

Create Some WordArt

1. Display the Drawing toolbar if it's not already displayed.

2. Click the Insert WordArt button to display the WordArt Gallery.

3. Click a WordArt style to select it in the WordArt Gallery.

4. Click OK.

5. In the Edit WordArt Text dialog box, select a font, a font size, and any emphasis. The same formatting will apply to all the text in the WordArt.

6. Type your text. (Note that you have to press Enter to start a new line in WordArt.)

7. Click OK.

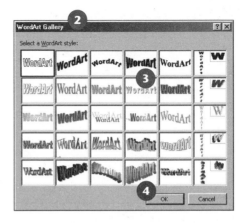

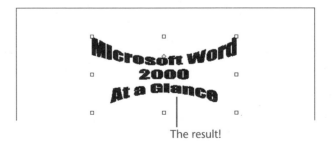

The result!

TRY THIS

Time for some fun. *Create some WordArt, and then use the WordArt toolbar to change the shape, color, and rotation. Use the 3-D button on the Drawing toolbar to apply a 3-D effect. Click 3-D Settings on the 3-D button, and use the 3-D toolbar to change the tilt, lighting, and 3-D angle. Amazing, isn't it? And so much fun!*

SEE ALSO

For information about text wrap, see "Wrapping Text Around a Picture" on page 181 and "Wrapping Text Around an Object" on page 196.

Fine-Tune the Result

1. Use the WordArt toolbar to
   - ◆ Change the text.
   - ◆ Choose another style.
   - ◆ Change the fill color or effect.
   - ◆ Change the shape.
   - ◆ Rotate text to any angle.
   - ◆ Equalize character height.
   - ◆ Change alignment.
   - ◆ Adjust character spacing.

2. Use the Drawing toolbar to
   - ◆ Add or change a shadow.
   - ◆ Apply 3-D effects.
   - ◆ Stack and group the WordArt with any other objects.

3. Place the WordArt where you want it, and set the text wrap.

Add a shadow.

Use a button shape with a different font and a 3-D effect.

Change the font and align the type using Stretch Justify.

Choose a shape, switch to vertical text, rotate it, and add a double shadow.

Printing to a Remote Printer

When you've put together a particularly creative or important document, you might need to take it to an outside source—a service bureau, for example, or a friend who has a good color printer—to get the best results. You'll need to set up your document to print on that specific printer, and then you'll print the document to a file. You can then copy the print file to the printer.

TIP

Font problems. *If you find that the wrong fonts are being printed, you can solve the problem by using only TrueType fonts and embedding them in the document (use the Save tab of the Options dialog box on the Tools menu), or by making sure that your computer has the same PostScript or printer fonts installed as the ones that are being used by the printer.*

Create a Print File

1. In Windows, install the remote printer you'll be using.

2. In Word, choose Print from the File menu, select the installed printer from the Name drop-down list, and click Close.

3. Create your document, or review the existing document for any last-minute changes.

4. Choose Print from the File menu.

5. Turn on the Print To File check box, and click OK.

6. In the Print To File dialog box, type a name for the print file, and click OK.

Print the File

1. Transfer the print file to the computer that's connected to the printer.

2. In Windows, click the Start button, point to Programs, and choose MS-DOS Prompt (or Command Prompt).

3. Use the Copy command to copy the file to the printer.

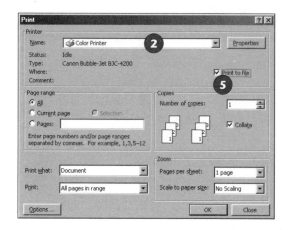

Printing Two Pages on One Sheet

If your layout requires small pages, you can print two pages on one sheet of paper. You get all the same page elements you'd get if you printed the information on separate sheets—margins, headers, page numbers, and so on—but you use half the amount of paper! Word lays out the pages assuming that you'll fold or cut the page along its center line.

TIP

Out of order! *Word prints the pages consecutively, so if you print on both sides of the paper, the pages won't be in the correct order if you bind them into a book.*

Specify the Layout

1. Choose Page Setup from the File menu.

2. On the Margins tab, turn on the 2 Pages Per Sheet check box.

3. Adjust the margins if necessary. If you're using a gutter measurement, check the preview to verify that the gutter is where you expect it to be.

4. On the Page Size tab, select the orientation you want. Again, use the preview to verify that the layout is correct.

5. Click OK.

6. Add the content, and then print the document as you would any other document.

With Landscape orientation, the first page prints next to the second page.

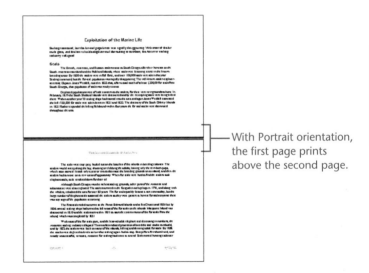

With Portrait orientation, the first page prints above the second page.

Printing Thumbnails

Thumbnails—tiny images of your pages—are usually used as a quick and handy reference to the content of a document. In commercial printing, thumbnails are used to create a *storyboard,* which the printer checks to confirm the layout and sequence of the pages.

Print the Thumbnails

1. Complete your document, proofread it, and use Print Preview with multiple pages displayed to verify that your layout is correct.

2. If you want to see a representation of the page edges (instead of content only), add a page border to the document. To display the full dimensions of the page, set the margins for the page border to zero (0).

3. Choose Print from the File menu.

4. Specify the number of pages you want to be printed on a single sheet. (The more pages you specify, the smaller each thumbnail will be. The content is usually readable when you print no more than eight thumbnails to a page.)

5. Click OK. (Be patient— thumbnails can take a while to print.)

All the information is included in the little images but can be too small to read.

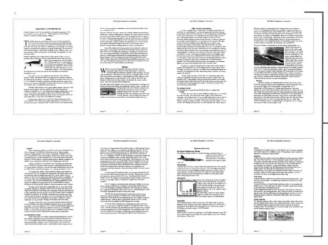

A page border provides a good representation of the page dimensions.

11

Working on a Network

Although printed documents are still an important part of most offices, many companies, from giant corporations to mom-and-pop operations, are doing more of their business on line. Working on a network reduces the clutter, expense, and time spent on paperwork, with the added benefit of saving some trees.

Microsoft Word provides an abundance of features that are designed to make your online work simple, efficient, and even enjoyable. There's a special view that scales a document to the size of your monitor for easy reading on line; you can use color schemes and special effects to add impact to your online documents and communications; and it's a snap to create active *hyperlinks,* or jumps, that move you instantly from place to place within a document or to designated spots in other documents.

Working on a network also simplifies collaboration with coworkers: you can circulate or route a document for comments or editing and then review the returned documents and accept or reject the proposed changes. We discuss one collaboration method—circulating a document on line with Word's tools and formatting available—in this section. The other way, which we discuss in the next section, is to work with Web documents so that anyone with a Web browser can review a document.

Reading a Document On Line

Most of us still feel that a printed document is easier on the eye than its screen version. However, Word's Web Layout view improves onscreen readability so much that it just might bring us closer to the day when the promise of the paperless office becomes a reality. Web Layout view makes your document look and act just like a Web page—it changes line breaks so that the document's text fits horizontally; sets the page length to one screenful; and can bring your document to life with animation, videos, sounds, brilliant colors, and jumps to other locations. However, Web Layout view has the same limitations as a Web page, so you'll find that you don't have as much control of the layout as you do in Print Layout view.

View a Document On Line

1. Click the Web Layout View button at the bottom left of the window.

2. Click the Document Map button on the Standard toolbar to display the Document Map if it's not already displayed.

3. Click the section you want to read to jump to that section.

4. Review the document.

5. Do any of the following:

   ◆ Click a plus or minus sign in the Document Map to expand or collapse the listing of topics.

   ◆ Close the Document Map to view the full width of the document.

   ◆ Click a hyperlink to jump to another location or another document.

   ◆ Edit the document or add comments.

   ◆ Use the Web toolbar to navigate to other documents or to return to the original document.

The Web toolbar

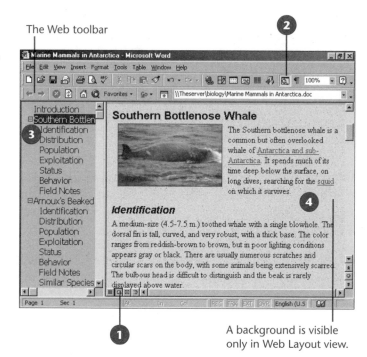

A background is visible only in Web Layout view.

Creating an Online Word Document

A Word document becomes an effective online document when you format it with elements that are designed for online use. Word provides all the features you need to create an attention-getting online document.

SEE ALSO

For information about an alternative way of jumping to information, see "Creating Cross-References" on page 118.

For information about adding a background, see "Creating a Background" on page 226.

For information about adding themes, see "Formatting an Online Document" on page 227.

For information about protecting a document, see "Limiting Access to a Document" on page 229.

For information about adding hyperlinks, see "Creating a Hyperlink to a File" on page 230 and "Creating a Hyperlink to a Specific Part of a Document" on page 232.

Create a Document

1. Switch to Web Layout view.

2. Apply a theme or add a background to the page.

3. Add your content.

4. Add special online elements:
   - ◆ Hyperlinks for jumps within the document, to other documents, or to Web pages
   - ◆ Sound or video clips
   - ◆ Pictures or other colorful items

5. If you want to protect the document so that no one can make unauthorized changes to it, choose Options from the Tools menu, and, on the Save tab, enter a password in the Password To Modify box. Click OK.

6. Save the completed document as a Word document in a shared folder, and close it.

7. Create hyperlinks to your document from other documents or from an e-mail message.

A hyperlink to another part of this document

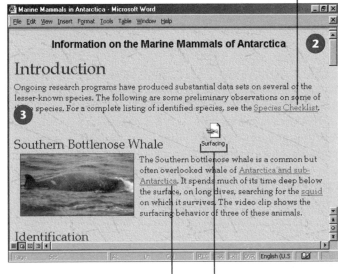

A hyperlink to another document   A video clip

Creating a Background

When you're creating a document that's going to be viewed using Web Layout view, you can add an interesting background to enhance your text: colors, gradients, patterns that come with Word, or even an existing picture.

TIP

Background effects.
The Gradient tab lets you choose a predesigned gradient background or create your own gradient. The Pattern tab lets you use a patterned background in the color of your choice. The Picture tab lets you insert a background picture that fills the entire document window.

TIP

Onscreen background.
A background is visible only in Web Layout view; it will not be printed if you print the document.

Add a Solid Background

1. In Web Layout view, point to Background on the Format menu.

2. Choose a color.

3. If you don't like any of the available colors, click More Colors, select a color, and click OK.

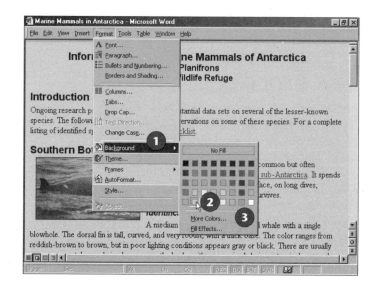

Add a More Interesting Background

1. Point to Background on the Format menu.

2. Choose Fill Effects from the submenu.

3. Click the appropriate tab, and select the type of background you want.

4. Click OK.

5. If necessary, format your text so that it's visible on top of the background.

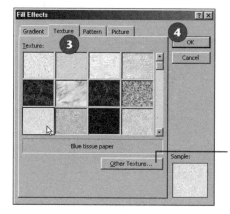

Click to use a picture file as the background texture.

Formatting an Online Document

An online document can be as simple as a text document with black text on a white background, but you can energize it with font colors, bullets, lines, and a background. Word provides many *themes*, which are coordinated sets of these elements. Try them out, and see how they transform your online documents!

SEE ALSO

For information about creating an online document, see "Creating an Online Word Document" on page 225.

TIP

Views. *All the theme elements are visible in Web Layout view. In the other views, the background is not visible, but any changes you've made to the text formatting are displayed.*

Use a Theme

1. Start a new document or open an existing one that you want to use on line.

2. Chose Theme from the Format menu.

3. Select a theme.

4. Select the options to be included in the theme:

   ◆ Vivid Colors to use more intense colors in the theme

   ◆ Active Graphics to include animated graphics, such as motion clips from the Clip Gallery— but be aware that the graphics are active only when they're viewed in a Web browser.

   ◆ Background Image to include an image as the background

5. Click OK.

Preview the theme elements.

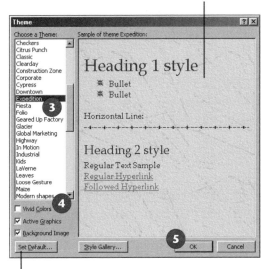

Click if you want all new documents to use this theme.

Sharing an Online Document

One of the reasons you put your documents on line might be so that other people can work on them. But what do you do when you're ready to work on a document and someone else is using it? Let Word handle it! Word can coordinate the usage of a document so that you can read the document that's currently in use and then be notified when it's available for editing.

SEE ALSO

For information about comparing two documents and incorporating changes, see "Comparing Documents" on page 250.

Open the Document

1. Open the document you want to use.

2. If Word tells you that the document is in use, click Notify to open the document as a read-only document.

3. Review the document. Any changes you make to the document appear only in your copy, not in the main document.

4. When Word notifies you that the document is available for editing, click Read-Write.

5. If you made changes to the read-only document, do either of the following:

   ◆ Click Discard to discard any changes you made and open the original document for editing.

   ◆ Click Save As to save your copy of the document with your changes, using a different filename, and then open the original document for editing.

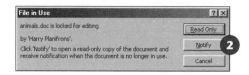

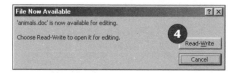

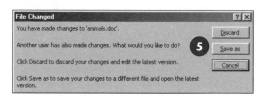

Limiting Access to a Document

If your document is posted in an area where others can access it, but you want to limit who can open it and who can make changes to it, you can use a password to control access.

TIP

Caution! *Be aware that someone who doesn't have permission to save changes to a document can still change his or her copy of the document and can then save it with a different document name.*

TIP

No entry. *Always write down your password and keep it in a safe place. If you forget the password, there is no way to open the document! If you forget the password to modify the document, you'll need to save the document with a different name.*

Set the Access

1. Choose Options from the Tools menu, and click the Save tab.

2. Do any of the following:

   ◆ Type and confirm a password to limit who can open the document.

   ◆ Type and confirm a password to limit who can save changes to the document. People without the password can open the document as a read-only document.

   ◆ Turn on the Read-Only Recommended check box to display a message box recommending that the document be opened as a read-only document each time it's opened.

3. Click OK.

4. Save the document.

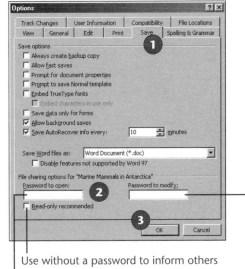

Use without a password to inform others that the document should not be modified.

Use a password to prevent unauthorized access to the document.

Use a password to prevent unauthorized changes to the document.

Creating a Hyperlink to a File

In an online document, you can create a *hyperlink* to refer to another document, and by clicking the reference you can *jump* to that document. You can also jump to different types of files— sound or video files, for example.

SEE ALSO

For information about creating jumps to specific locations in the current document or in another document, see "Creating a Hyperlink to a Specific Part of a Document" on page 232.

For information about creating hyperlinks from text, see "Converting Text into Hyperlinks" on page 234.

TIP

ScreenTips. *ScreenTips provide helpful information when you place the mouse pointer over certain screen elements.*

Create a Hyperlink

1. Type and select the text to be used for the hyperlink.

2. Save the document.

3. Click the Insert Hyperlink button on the Standard toolbar.

4. Verify that the hyperlink text is correct.

5. Select the Existing File Or Web Page option.

6. Do any of the following:

    ◆ Type the address of the Web page or the name of the file, including the entire path.

    ◆ Scroll through a list of files, Web pages, or previously inserted links, and click the file or the page you want to link to.

    ◆ Use the File button or the Web Page button to locate the file or the Web page you want to use, and click OK.

7. Click OK.

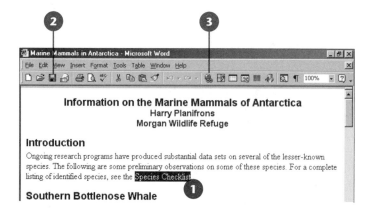

Click to type your own text for a ScreenTip that appears when the mouse pointer points to the hyperlink.

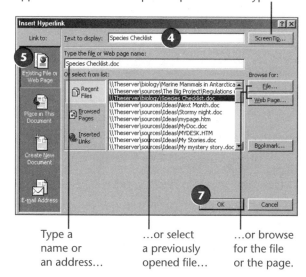

Type a name or an address...

...or select a previously opened file...

...or browse for the file or the page.

Addresses. *If you create a hyperlink to a file that's in the same folder as your main document, the address shown is relative, and only the filename is used. If the file is in a different folder, the address is absolute, and it shows the complete path as well as the filename.*

Necessary access. *When you're distributing a document that contains hyperlinks, the recipients must have access to the servers or folders where the hyperlinked material resides for the jumps to work.*

Easy changes. *To change the hyperlink text, the ScreenTip, or the destination file, select the hyperlink text and click the Insert Hyperlink button on the Standard toolbar.*

Link to a folder. *To create a hyperlink to a folder, use the right mouse button to drag the folder from Windows Explorer, drop it in the Word document, and choose Create Hyperlink Here from the shortcut menu.*

Jump Around

1. Display the Web toolbar if it's not already displayed.

2. Point to the hyperlink and use the ScreenTip to verify that this is the file you want to jump to. If the ScreenTip doesn't appear, choose Options from the Tools menu, turn on the ScreenTips check box on the View tab, and click OK.

3. Click the hyperlink.

4. Read the material.

5. Click the Back button to return to the original document.

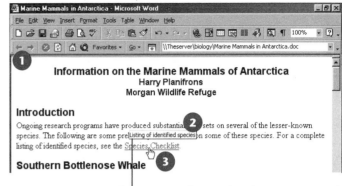

The ScreenTip shows either the text you typed for the ScreenTip or the address of the file.

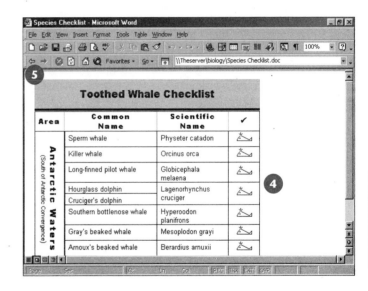

Creating a Hyperlink to a Specific Part of a Document

You don't always want to jump to the beginning of a different document. Sometimes you want to jump to a different location within the current document or to a specific location in a related document.

SEE ALSO

For information about an alternative way to jump to topics in the same document, see "Creating Cross-References" on page 118.

For information about inserting bookmarks, see "Tag a Page Range" on page 151.

For information about specifying a file as the destination of a hyperlink, see "Creating a Hyperlink to a File" on page 230.

Create a Hyperlink

1. In a document, type and select the text to be used for the hyperlink.

2. Click the Insert Hyperlink button on the Standard toolbar.

3. If you're creating a hyperlink to a different document, locate or specify the document.

4. Click Bookmark.

5. Do either of the following:
   - ◆ Select the name of the heading you want to jump to if the jump is within the same document.
   - ◆ Select the bookmark that marks the location you want to jump to.

6. Click OK.

7. Verify that the display text is correct, and add text for a ScreenTip if you want one.

8. Click OK.

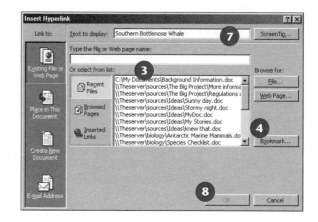

Use this item to jump back to the beginning of the document.

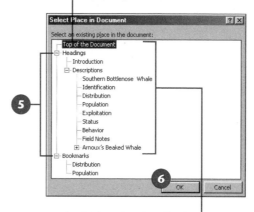

Available only when the jump is within the same document

Creating a Hyperlink to Part of an Excel Document

Microsoft Excel is often used in conjunction with Word to present technical information. You can create a hyperlink to a specific part of an Excel document to display only the information you want. If the section to be used as a hyperlink is large, copy only the first cell in the worksheet. When the hyperlink is in place, click it to jump to that part of the document.

TIP

Jump into Microsoft Office. *You can also jump to a specific location in a Word document or to a specific slide in a PowerPoint presentation.*

Create a Hyperlink

1. Open the document that contains the item you want to jump to.

2. Select the area you want to jump to.

3. Click the Copy button.

4. Switch to your Word document, and click where you want to insert the hyperlink.

5. Choose Paste As Hyperlink from the Edit menu.

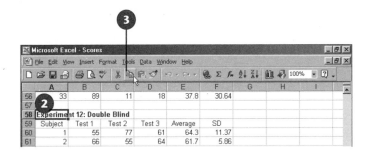

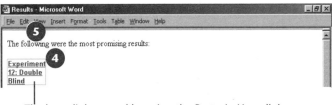

The hyperlink created by using the Paste As Hyperlink command is inserted as a table.

Change the Hyperlink Text

1. Click in the table just at the end of the hyperlink.

2. Point to Convert on the Table menu, and choose Table To Text. With Paragraph Marks selected, click OK.

3. With the hyperlink text selected, type new descriptive text for the jump.

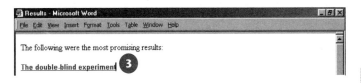

Converting Text into Hyperlinks

You can change the cryptic names, or *paths,* of network or Internet locations and e-mail addresses into easy-to-use hyperlinks, and then you can jump to a location by clicking the hyperlink. You convert text into a hyperlink using Word's AutoFormat and AutoFormat As You Type features.

TIP

Format only part of a document. *If you don't want to format the entire document, select a location before you choose AutoFormat.*

SEE ALSO

For information about changing the hyperlink text, see "Change the Hyperlink Text" on page 233.

Change Text into a Hyperlink

1. Open the document with the network or Internet location or e-mail address included as text.

2. Choose AutoFormat from the Format menu to display the AutoFormat dialog box.

3. Click the Options button.

4. Turn on the Internet And Network Paths With Hyperlinks check box if it's not already turned on.

5. Click OK.

6. Click OK.

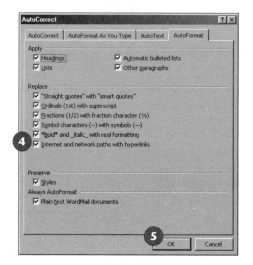

Remove a hyperlink.
To convert a hyperlink back into text, right-click the hyperlink, point to Hyperlink on the shortcut menu, and choose Remove Hyperlink from the submenu.

A new window. *To jump to a different Word document and open the document in a separate window (leaving the original document open in its own window), right-click the hyperlink, point to Hyperlink on the shortcut menu, and choose Open In New Window from the submenu.*

A new message. *Clicking an e-mail address that's formatted as a hyperlink launches a new mail message in Word.*

Type a Hyperlink

1. Choose AutoCorrect from the Tools menu, and, in the AutoCorrect dialog box, click the AutoFormat As You Type tab.

2. Turn on the Internet And Network Paths With Hyperlinks check box if it's not already turned on, and click OK.

3. Type the network path and filename, the Internet location, or the e-mail address.

4. Press the Spacebar to end the address and apply the AutoFormatting.

5. Click the link to verify that it's correct.

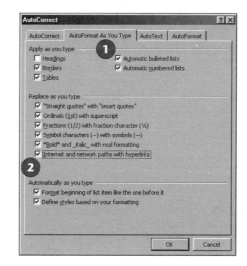

EXAMPLES OF AUTOFORMAT HYPERLINKS	
When you type this text	**Word creates this hyperlink**
http://www.microsoft.com	http://www.microsoft.com
\\Server\My folder\My Doc.doc	\\Server\My folder\My Doc.doc
DuskyC@MorganWildlife.com	DuskyC@MorganWildlife.com

Making Text Stand Out

When you're creating a document on line, you can draw your readers' attention to specific parts of the document by adding special effects to the text. Some of these effects will be printed if you decide to print the document, but text effects are designed primarily to stand out on your screen, especially when you've added a background to the document or shading to the text.

SEE ALSO

For information about adding a border to a paragraph, see "Adding a Border to a Paragraph" on page 40.

For information about adding a border to an entire page, see "Placing a Line Border Around a Page" on page 199.

For information about adding a background, see "Creating a Background" on page 226.

For information about highlighting text, see "Highlighting Text" on page 238.

Add Text Effects

1. Select the text that will have the special effect.

2. Choose Font from the Format menu, and click the Font tab.

3. Select an effect.

4. Click OK.

This text has a shadow.
This text is outlined.
This text is embossed.
This text is engraved.
This text has a shadow and is engraved.

Add Animated Effects

1. Select the text that will have the special effect.

2. Choose Font from the Format menu, and click the Text Effects tab.

3. Select an animation effect.

4. Click OK.

This text has a blinking background.
Las Vegas lights surround this text.
This text has marching ants.
This text shimmers.
This text sparkles.

Remove the effects. *As with any other font properties, you can remove any directly applied font effects and restore the paragraph's default font settings by selecting the text, holding down the Ctrl key, and pressing the Spacebar.*

Change the default font color. *The Automatic text-color setting uses the Windows setting for font color. If, in Windows, you change the font color for the Window item in the Display Properties dialog box, you'll see a different color for your text in Word and in all your other programs.*

Color for everyone. *If you use a background or shading in a document that others will view on line, consider changing the text color to a setting other than Automatic. That way, all your readers will be able to see the background and the text as you designed them, regardless of their own Windows font settings.*

Apply Text Color, Borders, or Shading

1. Display the Formatting toolbar and the Tables And Borders toolbar if they're not already displayed.

2. Select the text you want to change.

3. Do any of the following:

 ◆ On the Formatting toolbar, click the down arrow next to the Font Color button, and choose a color.

 ◆ On the Tables And Borders toolbar, select a border line style, line weight, and color, and then use the Borders button to select and apply a border.

 ◆ On the Tables And Borders toolbar, click the down arrow next to the Shading Color button, and select a shading color.

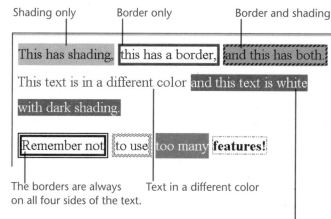

Shading only   Border only   Border and shading

This has shading, this has a border, and this has both.

This text is in a different color and this text is white with dark shading.

Remember not to use too many **features!**

The borders are always on all four sides of the text.

Text in a different color

The height of borders and shading is set by the font size and the paragraph line spacing.

Highlighting Text

When you're reviewing a document on line, you can highlight text in a variety of colors to call attention to certain information. Then, when you're looking through the document at a later date, you can use the Find command to stop at every instance of highlighted text. It's so much faster than having to scroll through the entire document searching for the material yourself.

TIP

Mouselight. *If you don't select text, clicking the Highlight button turns the mouse into a highlighter—just drag over the text to highlight it.*

TIP

Looking for the light. *To search for the next instance of highlighting after you've closed the Find And Replace dialog box, click the Find Next/Go To button at the bottom of the vertical scroll bar.*

Highlight Text

1. Select the text to be highlighted.
2. Click the down arrow next to the Highlight button to display the available colors.
3. Select a highlight color.
4. Select the next text to be highlighted.
5. Click the Highlight button to apply the same color highlight, or select a different color.

Click to remove the existing highlighting.

Find Highlighted Text

1. Choose Find from the Edit menu.
2. Click the More button if it's displayed.
3. Click the Format button, and choose Highlight.
4. Click Find Next.
5. Close the Find And Replace dialog box and review the text, or click Find Next to locate the next instance of highlighted text.

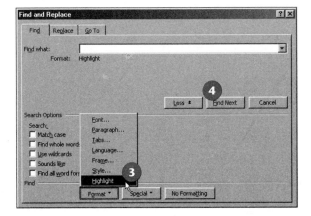

Using Word in Outlook E-Mail

Microsoft Outlook is a powerful messaging program, but it lacks the editing and formatting power of Word. You can combine the power of both programs by using Word as your editor for Outlook messages. You can also specify the format in which your messages will be sent: HTML, formatted text, or plain text.

TIP

Different windows. *When you send messages in HTML or plain text format, you compose the messages in a Word window; when you send messages in Microsoft Outlook Rich Text format, you compose the messages in an Outlook window.*

SEE ALSO

For more information about e-mail signatures and stationery, see "Sending E-Mail from Word" on page 240.

Turn on WordMail

1. In Word, set up your e-mail signature and stationery if you want to include either or both in your messages.

2. In Outlook, choose Options from the Tools menu, and click the Mail Format tab.

3. Select the file format you want to use to send messages:

   ◆ HTML to include themes, formatting, and pictures

   ◆ Microsoft Outlook Rich Text to use formatted text

   ◆ Plain Text for the greatest compatibility with other mail systems

4. Turn on the option to use Word as your e-mail editor.

5. Click OK.

6. Click the New Mail Message button on Outlook's Standard toolbar, compose your message using Word's tools, and send the message.

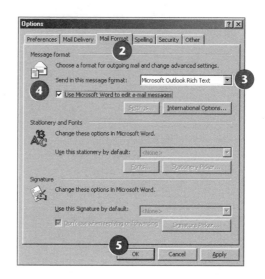

Regardless of the file format of the message, all of Word's tools are available.

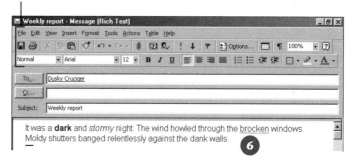

Sending E-Mail from Word

Just as you can use Word as the editor for Outlook, you can use Outlook as the messaging service for Word. You can compose your e-mail message directly in Word, using all of Word's powerful features—formatting, spelling and grammar checking, AutoText, and so on—and then send the message out in HTML format. You can even personalize your message with a colorful theme and an automatically inserted signature.

TIP

HTML messages. *A person to whom you send an HTML e-mail message needs an HTML-capable mail program such as Outlook or Outlook Express to be able read the message with its full formatting. To send the message in a different format, define the format in Outlook, and then create the message in Outlook.*

Personalize Your Message

1. In any Word document, choose Options from the Tools menu, and, on the General tab, click the E-Mail Options button.

2. On the E-Mail Signature tab, type a name to identify the signature.

3. Type and format your signature, including any additional descriptive text, a picture, or a hyperlink.

4. Click Add. Repeat steps 2 and 3 and click Add if you want alternative signatures.

5. Specify your default signatures.

6. On the Personal Stationery tab, do either of the following:

   ◆ Click the Theme button and choose a theme.

   ◆ Select fonts for new messages and for replies and forwarded messages.

7. Specify any text that you want to precede your comments.

8. Click OK; click OK again to close the Options dialog box.

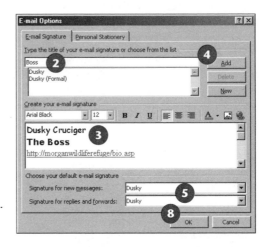

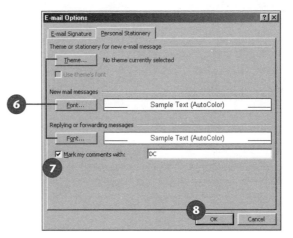

Create a Message

① Choose New from the File menu, and, on the General tab, double-click E-Mail Message.

② Click the To button. In the Select Recipients dialog box, select a name or names, click the CC or BCC button to designate other recipients, and click OK.

③ Type the subject.

④ Type the content of your message as you would in any Word document.

⑤ If you want to change your signature, right-click it, and choose a different signature from the list.

⑥ Click the Send button when the message is complete.

Click to include a file as an attachment to the message.

Click to include From or BCC lines in the address header.

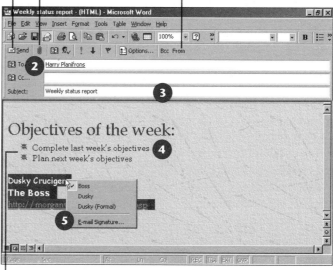

The theme you've chosen defines the background and the standard fonts.

Sending a Document as E-Mail

To send copies of a document out for others to read, you can send the document itself instead of attaching it to an e-mail message. Word works with Outlook to send the document as an HTML e-mail message, complete with all your formatting.

TIP

Two ways to send it. *Word converts a Word document into an HTML document and attaches the mail-header information to the document. To keep the document's original Word formatting, or to omit the header information, send the document as an attachment to a regular e-mail message.*

TIP

Check the formatting. *Review the document in Web Layout view to verify that the formatting you want is still there when the document is saved in HTML.*

Address Your Mail

1. Open the document if it's not already open.

2. Save the document if you've made any changes.

3. Click the E-Mail button on the Standard toolbar.

4. Click the To button, select a name or names, click the CC or BCC button to designate other recipients, and click OK.

5. Click Send A Copy.

6. Close the document.

7. When prompted to save the changes, click Yes if you want to save the e-mail addresses with the document, or click No if you don't want to save the e-mail information.

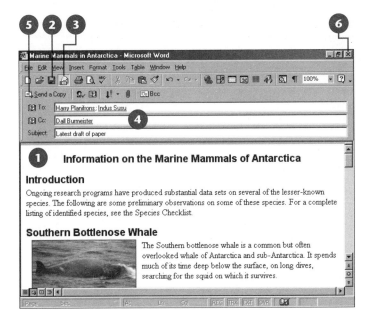

Sending a Document Out for Comments or Edits

When you send a document out to be reviewed, you can "protect" the document so that any changes will be marked or so that only comments can be added. When the document is returned, you can accept or reject the marked changes, or you can read the comments and consider the suggestions.

TIP

Passwords. *Always use a password to protect a document. If you don't, anyone can "unprotect" the document and make changes to it. But remember to write the password down and keep it in a safe place!*

SEE ALSO

For information about routing a document via e-mail, see "Routing a Document for Review" on page 244.

Prepare the Document

1. Open, or create and save, the document to be reviewed.

2. Choose Protect Document from the Tools menu.

3. Choose either of the following:
   - ◆ Tracked Changes to allow edits to be added and marked
   - ◆ Comments to allow only comments to be added

4. Enter a password, and click OK.

5. Reenter the password, and click OK.

6. Save the document.

7. Distribute the document via e-mail or post it in a shared mail or network folder.

When the Reviewing toolbar is displayed, click to quickly send the document out as an attachment to an e-mail message.

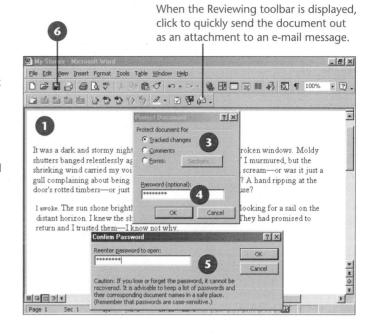

Routing
a Document
for Review

If you want a document to be reviewed by several people, you can set up a distribution list and route the document via e-mail either sequentially to each reviewer or to all the reviewers at once. When each copy of the document is returned, you can combine it with your original copy to gather all the comments in one place.

TIP

Making the rounds.
The document is routed as an attachment to an e-mail message. Most, but not all, e-mail systems support this kind of routing.

SEE ALSO

For information about protecting a document for comments or marked editing, see "Sending a Document Out for Comments or Edits" on page 243.

Distribute
the Document

1 Protect the document to allow only comments or marked editing, and save it.

2 Point to Send To on the File menu, and choose Routing Recipient from the submenu.

3 Add the recipients' names. Use the Move arrows if you want to change the order of the recipients.

4 Type a subject line.

5 Type a message to be included with the document.

6 Specify whether you want the document to be routed sequentially or sent to all reviewers at once.

7 Click Route to send the document immediately or Add Slip to send it when you close the document.

8 Save and close the document.

Click to use your Contacts list or address books...

...to add names to the routing slip.

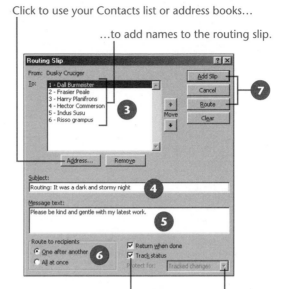

Keep turned on to receive a mail message each time the document is forwarded to the next reviewer.

Verify that the document is properly protected.

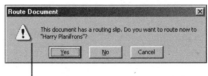

If you added a routing slip, Word asks you whether you want to route the document each time you close it.

Virus alert. *To open an attachment in a mail message, double-click the attachment, and confirm that you want to open the file. If you're uncertain about the safety of the attached file, choose to save the document on a disk, check it with a virus-checking program, and open it only when you know it's safe to do so.*

No need to merge. *If the document was routed sequentially and you made no changes to the original document while it was being routed, there's no need to merge the returned document with the original document—all the comments and changes are contained in the returned document.*

For information about reviewing comments and marked edits, see "Reviewing Reviews" on page 248.

For information about combining and comparing copies of a document that wasn't routed, see "Comparing Documents" on page 250.

Combine the Reviews

1. When the document is returned in a mail message, open the attachment to open the document in Word.

2. When Word asks you if you want to merge documents, click OK.

3. Select the original document, and click the Open button.

4. Save and close the merged document.

5. Close the returned document.

6. Repeat steps 1 through 5 for each returned review until all the reviews have been incorporated.

7. If the document is protected, choose Unprotect Document from the Tools menu. Supply the password if necessary.

8. Review the comments and any changes to the document, adding or deleting comments and accepting or rejecting changes.

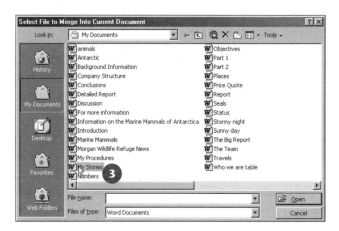

Reviewing a Document

When you're asked to review a document, the kinds of changes you can make to the document depend on whether the document was protected by the original sender and, if so, what level of protection was specified. If you're not allowed to make any changes to the document, the editing tools and menu commands are disabled.

SEE ALSO

For information about circulating a document with a routing slip via e-mail, see "Routing a Document for Review" on page 244.

Add Comments

1. Open the document if it's not already open.

2. Display the Reviewing toolbar.

3. Select the text you want to comment on.

4. Click the Insert Comment button. Word highlights the selected text, adds a comment marker, and opens the Comments area.

5. Type your comment.

6. Click Close.

7. Do any of the following:

   ◆ Repeat steps 2 through 5 to add new comments.

   ◆ Click a comment, and click the Edit Comment button to change the comment.

   ◆ Click a comment, and click the Delete Comment button to remove the comment.

The Edit Comment button   The Delete Comment button

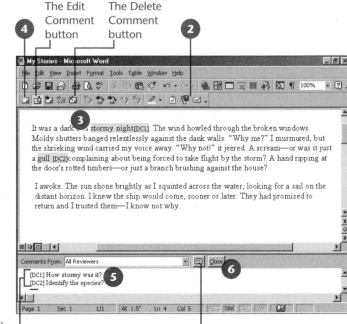

Comments are preceded by the initials of the reviewer and are numbered sequentially. (The initials are based on the User Information in the Options dialog box.)

Click if you want to record and insert a sound comment instead of a text comment.

Make Changes

1. If the document allows editing, edit the text as you would edit any document. Note the following:

   ◆ Additions appear in color and are underlined.

   ◆ Deleted text remains visible but appears in color and with a strikethrough font.

   ◆ Any line that contains a change displays a vertical line marker at the side of the page.

   ◆ If you delete one of your own additions, the text disappears instead of being marked as deleted.

2. Save the document when you've finished.

3. If the document was routed to you, click Next Routing Recipient to forward the document. If the document was sent as an e-mail attachment but was not routed, create a new e-mail message, and attach the modified document.

A marker indicating changes   Text you deleted   Text you added

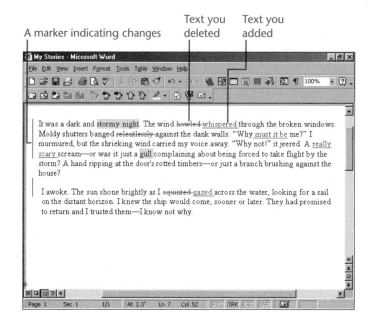

Reviewing Reviews

When a document that you sent out for review has been returned to you, you can easily review the comments and changes that have been added by the reviewers. As you review, you can add new comments or delete inappropriate ones, and you can accept or reject the changes that were made by the reviewers.

SEE ALSO

For information about routing a document and incorporating multiple reviews into a single document, see "Routing a Document for Review" on page 244.

Review the Document

1 Open the document and display the Reviewing toolbar.

2 If the document is protected, choose Unprotect Document from the Tools menu. Supply the password if necessary.

3 Do any of the following:

◆ Click Next Comment to locate and review a comment.

◆ Place the mouse pointer on a comment and review the comment.

◆ Use the buttons on the toolbar to insert a new comment or to edit or delete a selected comment.

◆ Click Next Change to locate an edit.

◆ Place the mouse pointer on an edit to see who made it.

◆ Use the Accept Change or Reject Change button to accept or reject a selected edit.

4 Repeat step 3 to review the entire document.

5 Save the document.

The Previous Comment button

The Next Comment button

The Previous Change button

The Next Change button

The Accept Change button

The Reject Change button

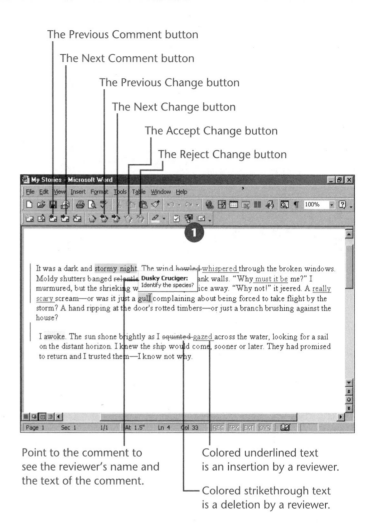

Point to the comment to see the reviewer's name and the text of the comment.

Colored underlined text is an insertion by a reviewer.

Colored strikethrough text is a deletion by a reviewer.

Combining Reviews

After you've sent a document out to several reviewers and each reviewer has returned a separate copy of the document that contains marked changes or comments, you can combine, or merge, all the documents into a single document.

SEE ALSO

For information about combining documents that were routed to reviewers, see "Routing a Document for Review" on page 244.

TIP

Combined comments. *When you merge a document that contains comments with the current document, the comments are included in the merged document but the highlighting that indicated the presence of a comment is lost. To see the markers for the comments, turn on the Show/Hide ¶ button on the Standard toolbar.*

Combine the Documents

1. Open the original document.

2. Choose Merge Documents from the Tools menu.

3. In the Select File To Merge Into Current Document dialog box, select the revised document, and click Open.

4. Repeat steps 2 and 3 for all the reviewed documents you want to combine.

5. If the document is protected, choose Unprotect Document from the Tools menu. Supply the password if necessary.

6. Review the comments and changes, adding or deleting comments and accepting or rejecting changes.

7. Save the document.

The original document

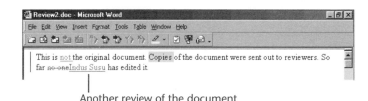

A review of the document

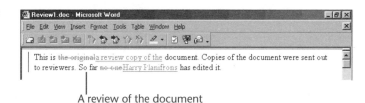

Another review of the document

When the documents are merged, all the changes and comments are contained in one document.

Comparing Documents

When you edit or rewrite a document, you don't always track and mark the changes. Sometimes you wish you had! However, if you saved the original document and the revised document with different filenames or in different locations and you want to take a look at the edits, you can compare the revised document with the original, and you can have all the changes marked for your review.

TIP

Review the changes. *If a document has tracked changes in it, review the changes and accept or reject them before comparing documents. To combine documents with tracked changes or comments, use the Merge Documents command on the Tools menu.*

Compare the Documents

1. Open the revised document and display the Reviewing toolbar.

2. On the Tools menu, point to Track Changes, and choose Compare Documents from the submenu.

3. In the Select File To Compare With Current Document dialog box, select the original document, and click Open.

4. Click the Next Change button to locate a change in the document.

5. Do either of the following:

    ◆ Click Accept Change to use the change from the revised document.

    ◆ Click Reject Change to use the text from the original document.

6. Repeat steps 4 and 5 to review the entire document.

7. Save the document. Use a different filename if you want to preserve the revisions for future review.

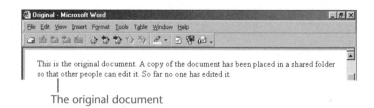

The original document

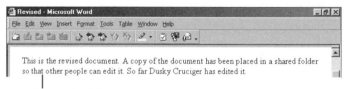

The revised document

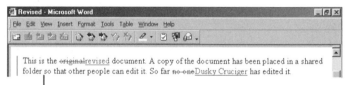

When the documents are compared, the changes are marked.

12

Working on the Web

Whether you call it the Internet, the intranet, or the Web, and whether you use it for business, homework, research, communicating, or shopping, the Web is probably already a part of your life. With that insight in mind, one of the goals of Microsoft Word's designers was to enable you to move between the Web and your own computer in an almost effortless fashion. For example, you'll see how simple it is to create *hyperlinks* in new or existing documents that quickly take you or your readers to related information on the Web. If you want to conduct meetings on the Web, Microsoft NetMeeting lets you and your colleagues confer on line and even collaborate in a nicely democratic fashion on the writing and editing of documents.

Along with a basic discussion about HTML (no, you *don't* have to learn it), this section shows you how to create, edit, and publish your own Web page. If you want to turn an existing document into a Web page, you can do that too. Word also gives you the ability to add comments (if they're requested) to someone else's Web page.

If you haven't already, you'll want to read the previous section, "Working on a Network," in conjunction with this section. The information in both sections is closely related and is useful whether you're working on a network or on the Web.

Jumping to a Web Site

You can place *hyperlinks*, or jumps, in your document that will take your online reader directly to specific Web pages. The reader must have a connection to the Web (the Internet *or* a company intranet) and a Web browser.

SEE ALSO

For information about creating ScreenTips and about creating a hyperlink to another document, see "Creating a Hyperlink to a File" on page 230.

For information about creating hyperlinks within a document, see "Creating a Hyperlink to a Specific Part of a Document" on page 232.

Create a Hyperlink

1. Click in your document where you want the hyperlink to appear.

2. Click the Insert Hyperlink button on the Standard toolbar.

3. Type the text that will appear as the hyperlink in your document. Add text for a ScreenTip if you want one.

4. With Existing File Or Web Page selected in the Link To area, click Browsed Pages.

5. From the list, select the page you want your hyperlink to jump to.

6. If the page isn't listed, click Web Page, navigate to the Web page you want, return to the Insert Hyperlink dialog box, and select the page from the Browsed Pages list.

7. Click OK.

Click to add a ScreenTip.

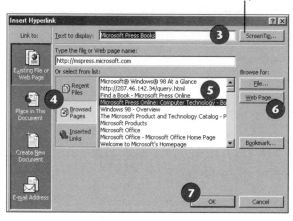

Downloading a Document from the Internet

One of the earliest, and probably still the most frequently used, ways to download a document from the Internet is with the FTP (File Transfer Protocol) method. FTP sites—special locations that are designed specifically for the transfer of files— can be a bit difficult to use. However, if you need to download documents from a site whose FTP address you've been given, you can access the site and download the documents directly into Word without having to deal with the arcane commands that are often required when you're downloading directly from an FTP site.

Define a Location

1. Choose Open from the File menu.

2. Open the Look In box, and select Add/Modify FTP Locations.

3. Type the name of the FTP site.

4. Choose to log on as an anonymous or a specific user. (Complete the user name and password areas if you're required to log on as a specific user.)

5. Click OK.

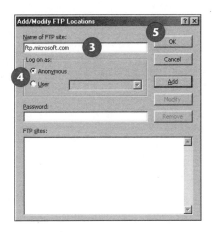

Download the Document

1. In the Open dialog box, double-click the site.

2. Specify the type of file.

3. Navigate to find the document, and then double-click it.

4. Wait for the document to download.

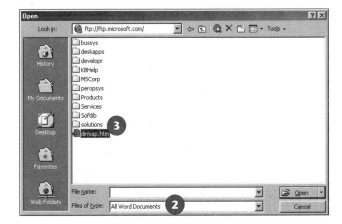

Conferring on the Web

With Microsoft NetMeeting, you can use the Internet or your company's intranet to confer with your colleagues about a document. Once the connection has been established and one person shares a document, all the meeting's participants can see the document and can even take turns editing the content.

TIP

Set it up. *The first time you use NetMeeting, you'll need to step through some rather extensive setup procedures. After the initial setup, you can start a meeting with just a click of the mouse.*

TIP

No Word. *As long as Net-Meeting is set up and running on all the computers that are participating in the conference, meeting participants can collaborate even if Word isn't installed on their machines.*

Display the Document

1 Notify all participants about the meeting, and have them start NetMeeting if it's not already running.

2 Open the document you want to display, point to Online Collaboration on the Tools menu, and choose Meet Now from the submenu.

3 Connect to the meeting participants using any of the following:

- ◆ An Internet locator service
- ◆ An address book
- ◆ The Most Recently Called List
- ◆ A computer name or network address on an intranet (click the Advanced button to enter information)

4 When the meeting members are connected, edit material, highlight text, scroll through the document, and otherwise share the material with others.

The shared document is viewed by all the meeting participants.

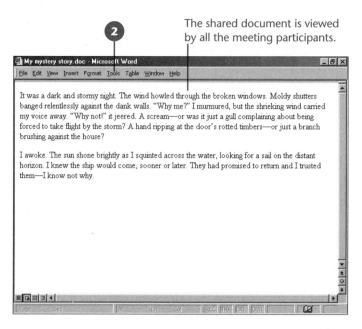

The person who started the meeting "owns" the document.

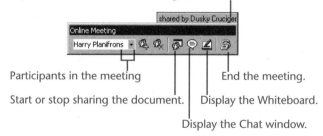

Participants in the meeting

Start or stop sharing the document.

End the meeting.

Display the Whiteboard.

Display the Chat window.

Schedule your time. *The Schedule Meeting command on the Online Collaboration submenu of the Tools menu lets you schedule a meeting using Microsoft Outlook. You can even set NetMeeting to start automatically just before the meeting.*

Tyrannical control. *Share your document, and let others edit it. Now press the Esc key to stop sharing the document, and click the Undo button to delete the edits. (But don't let this power go to your head. We don't advocate tyrannical behavior!)*

Use the icon. *To change the settings or use any additional features of NetMeeting, double-click the NetMeeting icon in the System Tray part of the Windows taskbar (near the clock).*

Do more. *You can also use Net-Meeting to display video from one computer, or to transfer files between computers.*

Share the Editing

1. Use the Whiteboard, Chat, and voice features of NetMeeting to discuss the document.

2. Click the Allow Others To Edit button. If a message is displayed, read it, and click OK.

3. Have someone double-click in the document to take control of the editing. Edits by the meeting participants will be displayed on all the computers.

4. Click in the document to regain control.

5. Click the Stop Others From Editing button to maintain full control of the document.

6. Click the End Meeting button to terminate the NetMeeting.

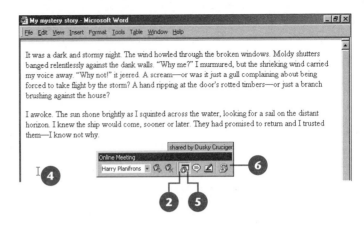

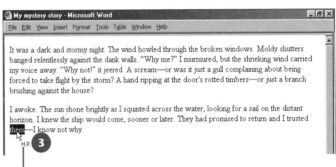

The mouse pointer displays the initials of the person who is editing the document.

HTML, Word, and the Web

Isn't it always the case? As soon as you finally get things figured out, someone somewhere changes everything! Of course, the dizzying pace of change results in better computers and improved software, and this certainly holds true for Microsoft Word. Although the integration of Web features makes working in Word a bit more complex, these features make document sharing easier and online collaborating more powerful than ever. The graphics below show a few of the changes that can occur when you convert a Word document into a Web page.

The original Word document

The header information

The title bar displays the filename.

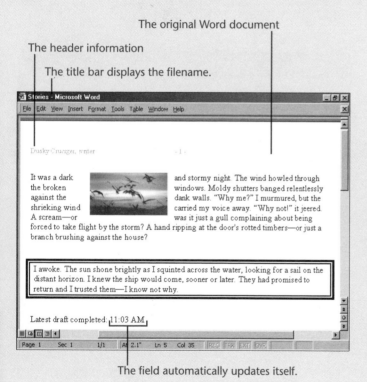

The field automatically updates itself.

The document as a Web page in Internet Explorer

The header information isn't displayed.

The title bar displays the title of the page instead of the filename.

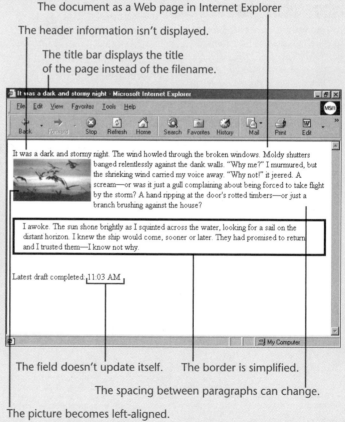

The field doesn't update itself.   The border is simplified.

The spacing between paragraphs can change.

The picture becomes left-aligned.

HTML and Word

Word normally uses its own format to store the text, formatting, hidden text, fields, pictures, and other elements you've put into your document. Word's format is what's used when you save a document as a Word document, creating a file with the familiar *.doc* extension. When you save a Word document as a Web page, you're converting the document from its basic Word format into the HTML format. HTML (Hypertext Markup Language) is the language of the Web, and it can be read by just about any computer that has a Web browser or other HTML reader. This universality, however, comes with a cost: the loss of many of Word's features. For example, your fonts, paragraphs, and color settings are only suggestions to a Web browser, so the results might not be precisely what you had in mind. On the other hand, some items, such as animated graphics, work better in a Web page than in a Word document, so you'll need to experiment to see what you like. Fortunately, you can preview a Web page without ever putting it up on the Web, and you can even convert a Web page back into a Word document.

The Best of Both Worlds

When you create a Web page in Word, any features you use that aren't supported by HTML will not appear in your Web page. But—and Word is very tricky here— all that extra information remains hidden in the Web page. So, if you then open the Web page in Word, the hidden information is retrieved, and all the original features reappear. This gives you the best of both the HTML and Word worlds, and lets you update your Web page simply and conveniently. If you allow other people to access your Web page, they can make changes using Word or any HTML editor, and you can bring the document back into Word later to fine-tune the formatting and editing.

More Web Power

Microsoft Office 2000 provides tools—the Microsoft Office Server Extensions—that enhance the power of the Web. When the administrator of a Web server installs these tools on the server, Word's ability to communicate with the server is greatly increased. This makes it easier for you to install a Web page on the server *and* provides enough power for you to conduct newsgroup-like discussions right in a Web page. You can even subscribe to a page and be notified when the page has changed. However, because this is a brand-new technology, it's likely that some Web servers won't have the server extensions installed yet. What can you can do? Complain to the Web server's management! Even without the Office Server Extensions, though, you'll find that Web pages are powerful tools for sharing information with others.

Creating a Web Page

Word provides a number of Web page templates, as well as a wizard to walk you through the creation of a custom Web page. Each template provides the basic layout for a Web page, with placeholder text and hyperlinks that you can replace or modify as you create your own Web page. The Web Page Wizard is designed to set up your whole site—the location, the navigation frames, and all the pages in the site, including any that you want to create using the templates.

Use a Template

① Choose New from the File menu.

② Click the Web Pages tab of the New dialog box, and double-click the Web Page template you want to use.

③ Modify the content by doing any of the following:

◆ Select the placeholder text, delete it, and insert your own text.

◆ Copy and paste items to create additional elements.

◆ Delete elements you don't need.

◆ Right-click a hyperlink, point to Hyperlink on the shortcut menu, and choose Edit Hyperlink to modify the hyperlink text, a ScreenTip, or the destination.

◆ Apply a theme or background.

④ Save your document frequently as you work.

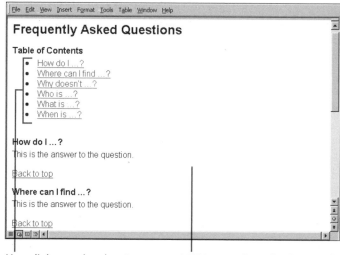

Hyperlinks are already set up to jump to headings.

A Web page from the Frequently Asked Questions template

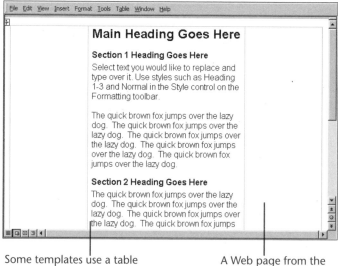

Some templates use a table to control the layout.

A Web page from the Simple Layout template

TIP

Office Server Extensions.
If your Web server has installed the Microsoft Office Server Extensions, you can save the Web pages you've created with the wizard directly to the Web server.

SEE ALSO

For information about modifying a Web page, see "Formatting a Web Page" on page 261 and "Adding Web Elements" on page 262.

For information about working with frames, see "Dividing Up the Page" on page 264 and "Adding a Web Page Table of Contents on page 266.

For information about placing your Web pages on a Web server, see "Publishing a Web Page" on page 268.

Use the Web Page Wizard

1. Choose New from the File menu.

2. Click the Web Pages tab of the New dialog box, and double-click the Web Page Wizard.

3. Step through the wizard, specifying the following design elements of the Web site:

   ◆ The name and location of the site

   ◆ The type of navigation frame or other navigation method

   ◆ The pages (blank, from a template, or existing) that are included and the order in which they're listed

   ◆ Any theme used in formatting

4. Click Finish, and wait while Word creates and saves the pages and frames.

5. Edit and then save the pages to create your Web site.

Use the hyperlinks to jump to the other pages that are part of this Web site.

An existing Web page added to the site   The main Web page

Blank pages added to the site

A page based on a template added to the site

A navigation frame

Converting a Document into a Web Page

If you need to give your colleagues greater access to your work, you can easily convert an existing Word document into a Web page. As a Web page, your Word document can be posted on the Internet or on a company intranet and can be read by anyone with a Web browser, or it can be opened in Word.

SEE ALSO

For information about using the Web Page Wizard to create a Web page, see "Creating a Web Page" on page 258.

TIP

Word does the work. *When Word saves a document as a Web page, it automatically creates a subfolder, if necessary, to hold the support files for the Web page.*

Create the Web Page

1. In your Word document, switch to Web Layout view, and review the document. Make any changes needed to improve the layout, and save the file as a Word document.

2. Choose Save As Web Page from the File menu.

3. In the Save As dialog box, specify the location, the filename, and—if you want—a different page title for the Web page. Click Save.

4. If Word tells you that certain items will be lost, read the instructions, and click

   ◆ Continue to create a Web page with the listed features eliminated.

   ◆ Cancel to return to and modify the Word document before again converting the document into a Web page.

5. Choose Web Page Preview from the File menu to see your Web page as others will see it. Close the browser when you've finished.

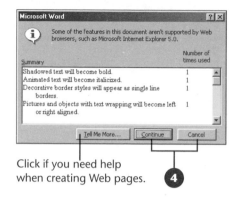

Click if you need help when creating Web pages. **4**

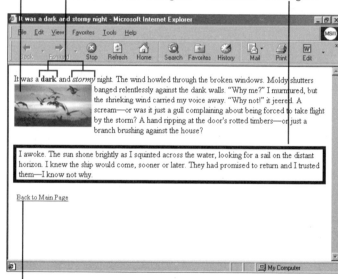

The picture alignment is changed.

The text effects are changed.   The border is changed.

Include a hyperlink to navigate back to your main page.

Formatting a Web Page

Web pages have specific formatting requirements, and Word provides you with all the tools you need to create professional-looking Web pages. When you add special elements, all the additional items—pictures, for example—are stored in a subfolder that Word creates for the Web page.

SEE ALSO

For information about using backgrounds, see "Creating a Background" on page 226.

For information about themes, see "Formatting an Online Document" on page 227.

Add Formatting

1. With your Web page open, choose any of the following from the Format menu:

    ◆ Themes to apply a preset theme

    ◆ Background to apply a color, pattern, texture, or picture as a background

    ◆ Borders And Shading, and then click the Horizontal Line button to apply a horizontal-line graphics element across the page

    ◆ Bullets And Numbering, and then click the Picture button on the Bulleted tab to apply a picture as a bullet in a list

2. Save the document as a Web page.

3. Choose Web Page Preview from the File menu to see your Web page as others will see it. Close the browser when you've finished.

A left-aligned picture with text wrapping

The Expedition theme

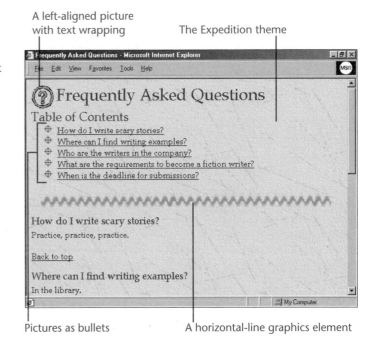

Pictures as bullets

A horizontal-line graphics element

Adding Web Elements

Once you've created a basic Web page, you can add special elements to give it that extra something that turns an ordinary document into a memorable one. Remember, though, that too many special elements can be distracting rather than helpful. You *can* have too much of a good thing!

SEE ALSO

For information about using tables to lay out a page, see "Creating a Side-by-Side Layout" on page 190.

For information about including frames in a Web page, see "Dividing Up the Page" on page 264.

Add a Movie Clip

1. Display the Web Tools toolbar, click where you want to place the movie clip, and then click the Movie button on the Web Tools toolbar.

2. Select a movie file from the list, or use the Browse button to locate the file you want.

3. Select an image to be displayed if the movie can't be played.

4. Specify the text to be displayed in browsers that can't play the movie or display the image.

5. Specify when and how often the movie plays.

6. Click OK.

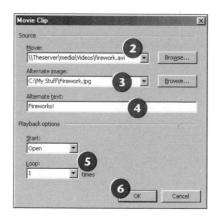

Add a Background Sound

1. Click the Sound button on the Web Tools toolbar.

2. Select a sound file from the list, or use the Browse button to locate the file.

3. Specify how often the sound plays.

4. Click OK.

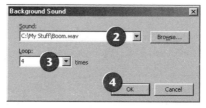

Add some text. *Alternative text is displayed while a Web page is being loaded, and it's also displayed in browsers that don't support the type of item you've inserted. It's good practice to include alternative text for all objects, including pictures. To add alternative text to a picture, choose Picture from the Format menu, and use the Web tab of the Format Picture dialog box.*

Be kind to your readers. *Pictures, sounds, movies, and other similar elements are usually large files that can take substantial time to download. To speed up the time it takes to download your Web page, limit the number of graphics and multimedia elements.*

Make changes. *To change the settings, double-click the scrolling text, and then make your changes in the Scrolling Text dialog box that appears.*

Add Scrolling Text

1. Click where you want the scrolling text.

2. Click the Scrolling Text button on the Web Tools toolbar.

3. Specify the behavior, background color, direction, and number of loops for the scrolling text.

4. Set the scrolling speed.

5. Type your text.

6. Click OK.

7. Click the scrolling text to select it, and apply the font and size you want.

8. Save your Web page.

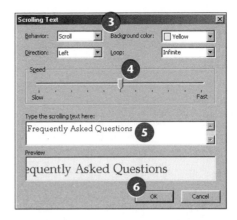

A Web page with a movie clip...   ...and scrolling text

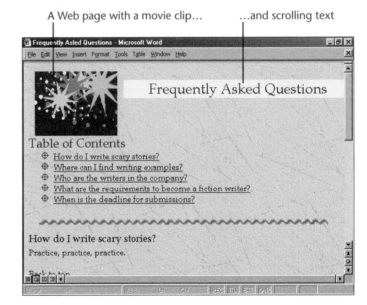

Dividing Up the Page

Web pages are often divided up, with some sections that can be scrolled and others that remain stationary. You can create this kind of layout by dividing a Web page into separate sections, using *frames*. A Web page can contain several frames, with each frame containing its own document.

Add a Frame

1. Create, save as Web pages, and close the various documents you want to add to the main Web page.

2. Open the main Web page and display the Frames toolbar.

3. Click the type of frame you want to insert.

4. Drag the border of the frame to size the frame.

5. Add more frames as needed.

Add a Document

1. Right-click in the new frame, and choose Frame Properties from the shortcut menu.

2. On the Frame tab, specify which file is to be used in the frame, and type a name for the frame.

3. On the Borders tab, specify whether you want a border between frames, and, if so, the border's size and color.

4. Click OK, and save the new Web page.

The original Web page   A new blank frame

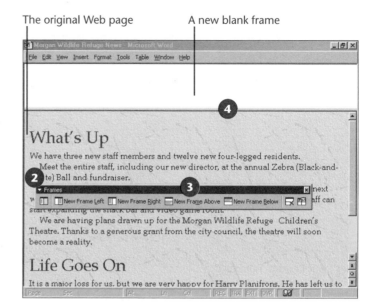

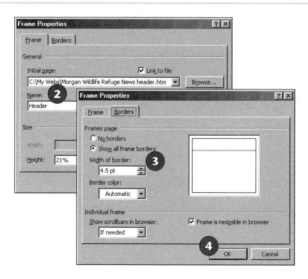

SEE ALSO

For information about adding a Web page table of contents in a separate frame, see "Adding a Web Page Table of Contents" on page 266.

TIP

Browsers and frames. *Most, but not all, Web browsers support the viewing of frames. If your document must be compatible with all existing Web browsers, use links to take your readers to separate pages instead of to frames.*

TIP

Name the frame. *When you add content to a blank frame, Word automatically names and saves the Web page file when you save the entire frame document. To name the document yourself, right-click in the frame, and choose Save Current Frame As from the shortcut menu.*

TIP

Word documents and frames. *Frames aren't for Web pages only. You can use Word documents as the contents of frames, and you can save an entire frame document as a Word document.*

Add a Hyperlink

1. In your document, select the text you want to use for the hyperlink.

2. Right-click the text, and choose Hyperlink from the shortcut menu.

3. Locate and select the Web page file that you want displayed. Use the File or the Web Page button to locate Web pages that aren't in the Recent Files or Browsed Pages lists.

4. Click the frame in which you want the Web page file to appear.

5. Verify that the correct frame is specified.

6. Click OK.

The hyperlink text

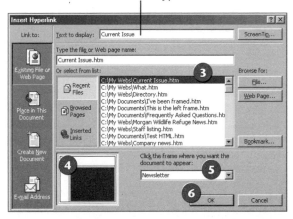

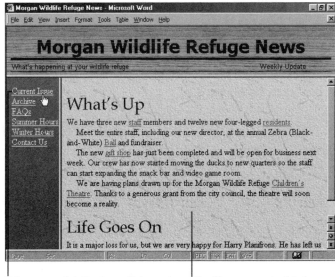

When you click the hyperlink... ...the file appears in this frame.

Adding a Web Page Table of Contents

In long Web pages, it's a good idea to create a separate table-of-contents area that contains hyperlinks to specific areas of the main document. Word does this by creating a new frame document, with your original document in one frame and the table of contents in another frame.

SEE ALSO

For information about creating a table of contents and formatting it with heading styles, see "Creating a Table of Contents" on page 108.

For information about character styles, see "Creating an Inline Heading" on page 194.

For information about working with frames, see "Dividing Up the Page" on page 264.

Add a Frame

1. Set up your Web page, using heading styles to format the items you want included in the table of contents. Save the Web page.

2. Point to Frames on the Format menu, and choose Table Of Contents In Frame from the submenu. Word creates a new document with two frames—one for the document and another for the table of contents.

3. Apply formatting to the table-of-contents frame. To change the font, change the Hyperlink and Followed Hyperlink character styles.

4. Drag the frame border to create the frame size you want.

5. Save the new Web page.

6. Choose Web Page Preview from the File menu, review the page, and close the Web browser.

When you click a hyperlink...

...you can jump directly to a specific section of the Web page.

The table-of-contents frame

The original document

Editing a Posted Web Page

To make changes to a Web page that was created in Word and posted on a Web site, you open the page and edit it in Word. If the Web server has Office Server Extensions installed, and you have the necessary permissions, you can save and post the edited page back to the Web site. You can also save the edited page as a new Word or Web document on your computer or server.

TIP

Copy it. *You can select and copy Web page content and paste it into Word. All the Web page elements, including any pictures supported by Word, will be copied.*

SEE ALSO

For information about conversions between Web pages and Word documents, and for information about Office Server Extensions, see "HTML, Word, and the Web" on pages 256–257.

Edit the Page

1. Open the Web page in Internet Explorer.

2. Click the Edit button on the Standard Buttons toolbar.

3. Switch to the Word window in which the document opens.

4. Edit the document.

5. Do any of the following:

   ◆ Click the Save button on the Standard toolbar to save your changes and replace the existing Web page.

   ◆ Choose Save As Web Page from the File menu, and save to the Web server to create a new Web page.

   ◆ Choose Save As Web Page from the File menu, and save to a folder on your computer to save the document as a local Web page.

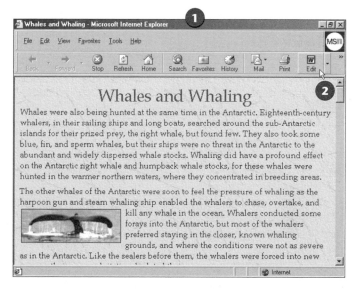

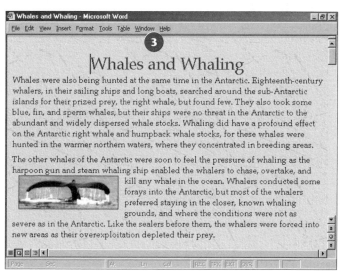

Publishing a Web Page

The good news is that it's easy to create a Web page. The not-so-good news is that your Web page might generate various complaints from readers. If your Web page will be posted on a small local intranet, all you need to do is create the page or pages and save the Web site to the proper location. However, if your Web page will be posted on the Internet or on a large corporate intranet, you'll probably want to do some last-minute tweaking of some of the settings to optimize the page for your intended audience. Then you'll be ready to post the page and any associated files on a Web server.

TIP

Get the details. *Web sites are usually strictly structured, so you'll need to know how and where to post your Web pages. Get the details before setting up your Web site.*

Make Your Settings

1. With your Web page open, choose Options from the Tools menu, and, on the General tab, click the Web Options button.

2. On the General tab, select the primary target browser for the page.

3. On the Pictures tab, select the primary screen size.

4. On the Fonts tab, select the character set and the default proportional and fixed-width fonts.

5. Make changes on the Files and Encoding tabs if you receive reports from readers about problems they've encountered when reading or editing your page.

6. Click OK.

7. Save all changes and settings to the document as a Web page.

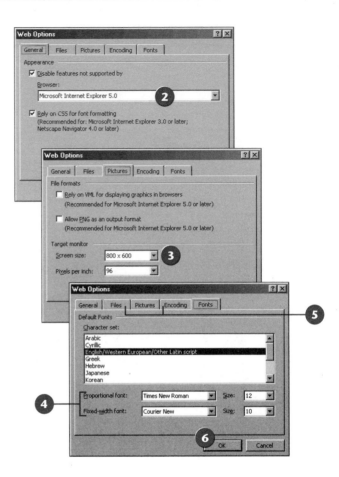

Post to a Server with Office Server Extensions

1. Choose Save As Web Page from the File menu.

2. Click the Web Folders button.

3. Select the specific Web folder. Navigate to the folder that is to contain the Web page.

4. Click Save.

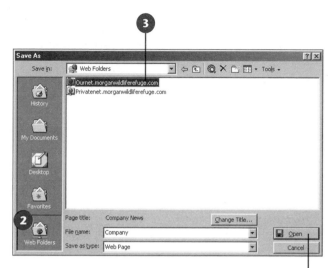

The Open button becomes the Save button when you open a valid Web folder.

Post to Other Web Servers

1. Close your document in Word.

2. In Windows Explorer, create a new folder.

3. Copy the Web page and its supporting folder into the new folder.

4. Contact your system administrator or service provider for information about transferring the entire folder to the server.

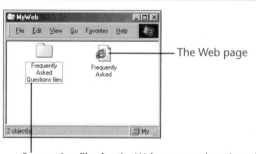

The Web page

Supporting files for the Web page are kept in a single folder.

Commenting on a Web Page

Wouldn't it be great if you could post a Web page and have your colleagues comment directly on the page? Well, some of us might have mixed feelings about that idea! However, used properly, it can be an efficient way for a number of people to collaborate on a document. If the Web page is posted on a server that has Office Server Extensions installed, you can add your own comments or read other people's comments.

> **TIP**
>
> **Web browsers.** *You can add comments to a Web page directly from some Web browsers.*

Discuss a Document

① With the Web page open in Word, point to Online Collaboration on the Tools menu, and choose Web Discussions from the submenu.

② Do any of the following:

- ◆ Click in a paragraph, and click the Insert Discussion In The Document button to add a comment to that paragraph.

- ◆ Click the Insert Discussion About The Document button to add a general comment about the document.

- ◆ Double-click a Discussion icon to display existing comments.

- ◆ Click the icon next to a comment, and choose Reply from the shortcut menu to reply to an existing comment.

③ Close the document when you've finished.

A Discussion icon indicates that there is a discussion associated with the paragraph.

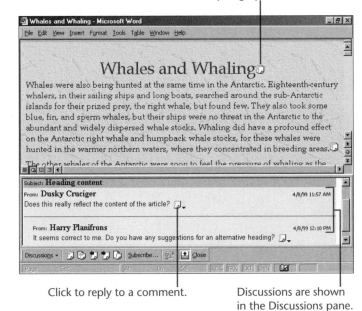

Click to reply to a comment.

Discussions are shown in the Discussions pane.

Click to automatically receive an e-mail notification when any changes are made.

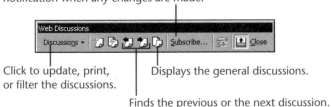

Click to update, print, or filter the discussions.

Displays the general discussions.

Finds the previous or the next discussion.

Automating Your Work

Early in this book, we talked about using Microsoft Word as a *thought processor*. Although Word can't do any original thinking for you, you can set certain features so that Word will execute on its own the actions it knows you want done.

For example, with Word's AutoText and AutoComplete features, all you have to do is type a few letters of a long scientific name or a word whose spelling always trips you up, and Word automatically inserts the entire correctly spelled word or phrase for you.

Word's mail merge feature is a marvelous time-saver when you need to send the same information to a few individuals or to a large group of people. You provide a main document and a *data source,* and Word combines, or *merges,* the information into a new, personalized document. You can create form letters, envelopes, mailing labels, awards, and so on, as well as incorporate data from Microsoft Excel and Access into mail merged documents.

With some brief but clear explanations about a complex subject—*fields*—you'll be able to use their power to further automate your work. For example, you'll be able to place a dictionary-like range of topics in a running head, insert customized messages into mail merged documents for individuals who meet certain criteria, and keep comprehensive records about your documents.

Inserting Frequently Used Information

If you type the same words or phrases repeatedly, you can save yourself a lot of time (especially if you use long technical terms or difficult names) by saving those words or phrases as *AutoText*. You assign the AutoText a short name—a nickname of sorts, with at least four letters—and when you type the nickname, or just the first few letters of it, Word's *AutoComplete* feature inserts the word or phrase into your document. And AutoText isn't limited to text; the information can be anything you can put into a document—pictures, tables, even fields. Word comes already equipped with numerous AutoText entries for some of the most common types of information.

Store the Information

1. In your document, select all the information to be included in the entry.

2. Point to AutoText on the Insert menu, and choose New from the submenu.

3. Accept the suggested name or type a new name for the entry, and click OK. (The name must contain at least four characters for the Auto-Complete feature to work.)

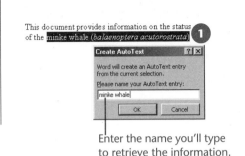

Enter the name you'll type to retrieve the information.

Insert the Information

1. Start typing the AutoText name.

2. When the AutoComplete tip appears with the AutoText entry, press Enter.

3. If the AutoComplete tip doesn't appear, choose AutoCorrect from the Tools menu, turn on the Show AutoComplete Tip For AutoText And Dates check box on the AutoText tab of the dialog box, and repeat steps 1 and 2.

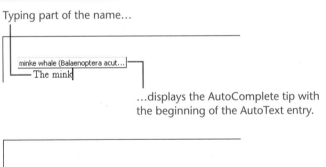

Typing part of the name...

...displays the AutoComplete tip with the beginning of the AutoText entry.

Word inserts the complete AutoText entry.

Find and Insert Information

1. Point to AutoText on the Insert menu.

2. Point to the appropriate category on the submenu.

3. Choose the AutoText name from the submenu.

4. Do either of the following to insert AutoText in special circumstances:

   ◆ Display and use the AutoText toolbar to quickly insert multiple AutoText entries.

   ◆ Point to AutoText on the Insert menu, choose AutoText from the submenu, select an AutoText entry, and click Insert to insert the AutoText into a running head.

Click to display the AutoText tab of the AutoCorrect dialog box to delete an AutoText entry or to change which open template is used.

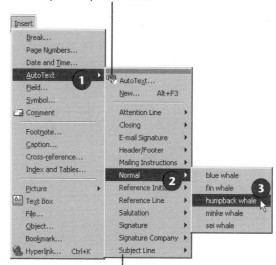

Most AutoText entries are built in, created as you complete a wizard, or created when you store information such as your name or e-mail signature.

Creating Form Letters

When you want to create personalized, computer-generated form letters, you need two items: your *main document,* which is the letter that each person on your list will receive, and a *data source,* which is a list of the names and addresses of the people to whom you're sending your letter. You'll use the information in that data source for the inside address and salutation on each letter, and for the address on the envelopes or mailing labels.

Start a Form Letter

1. Create and save a letter containing the information that will be the same in all letters. This is your main document.

2. Choose Mail Merge from the Tools menu.

3. Click the Create button.

4. Choose Form Letters.

5. Click the Active Window button.

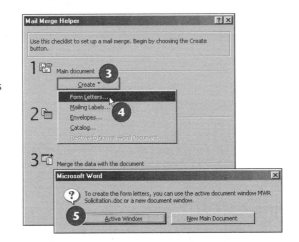

Get the Data

1. Click Get Data.

2. Choose a data source:

   ◆ Create Data Source to enter the data (names and addresses, for example)

   ◆ Open Data Source to use existing data

   ◆ Use Address Book to use data from an address book

   ◆ Header Options to use separate documents for the data and the data header

3. Click Edit Main Document.

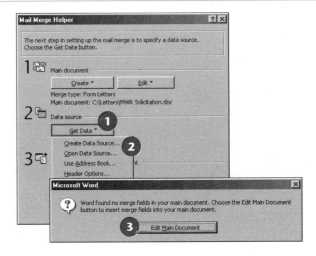

Shady fields. *To keep track of all the inserted fields, choose Options from the Tools menu, click the View tab, and select Always from the Field Shading list. The shading will help you identify the fields but won't show in the merged documents.*

For information about checking the accuracy of mail merged documents, see "Reviewing Mail Merged Documents" on page 276.

For information about creating a data source for a form letter, see "Creating a Data Source" on page 284.

For information about specifying which records are to be used in the merge, see "Selecting Records to Merge" on page 290 and "Merging Conditionally" on page 292.

Specify the Merged Data

1. Click where you want to add information from your data source.

2. Click the Insert Merge Field button, and select the type of data to be included.

3. Repeat steps 1 and 2 until all the merged data is specified.

Merge fields specify which data is inserted and where it's placed.

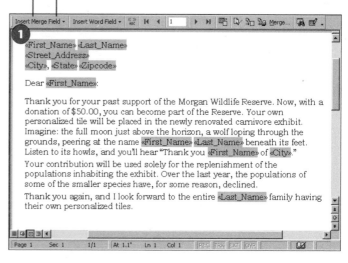

Create the Letters

1. Look over the document and correct any errors.

2. Click the Merge button on the Mail Merge toolbar.

3. Specify where the merge will be output to, which records will be used, and how blank data fields are to be handled.

4. Click Merge.

Select to merge to a printer, a new document, or an e-mail message.

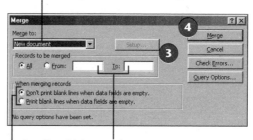

Specify which records to merge if you're not merging all records.

Control how the merge handles blank lines.

Reviewing Mail Merged Documents

What could be worse than printing or e-mailing a big batch of mail merged documents and then discovering an error in the setup or in your text? Before you execute a whole mail merge, you should always test your setup, print or e-mail a couple of samples, and inspect the results. It's well worth the extra few minutes, and can save you time, money, frustration, and embarrassment.

TIP

Mail yourself. *If you're testing a mail merge that will be output to e-mail, insert your own e-mail address into your data document and use that address to conduct your first e-mail test of the merge.*

Inspect the Merge

1. Create the main document, and attach your data source.

2. Click the View Merged Data button, and review the merged document.

3. Click the Next Record button, and review the merged document.

4. Repeat step 3 for a series of records.

You can see your merged data instead of the merge fields.

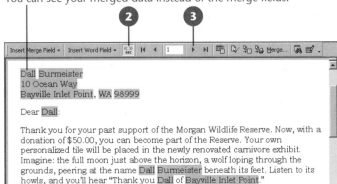

Simulate the Merge

1. Click the Merge button on the Mail Merge toolbar.

2. Make your settings.

3. Click the Check Errors button.

4. Select the option to simulate the merge.

5. Click OK.

6. Read any error messages, and correct your main document as necessary.

7. Repeat steps 1 through 6 until you've corrected all errors.

8. Close the Mail Merge Helper dialog box.

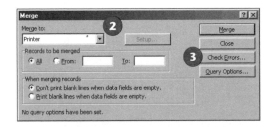

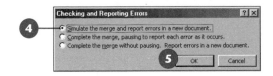

Test the Merge

1. Click the Merge button on the Mail Merge toolbar.

2. Enter a range that includes at least two records, using data records from the middle of your data set.

3. Select the target (printer, document, or e-mail message) that you'll use in the final merge.

4. Click Merge.

5. Proofread the merged document, make any corrections to the main document or the data source, and save the document.

6. Continue merging and reviewing the sample documents, and correcting the main document and the data source, until the sample merged documents are error-free.

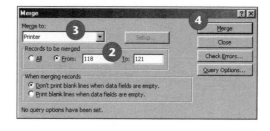

In this merged sample, the data source used two different fields for the street address, but, because the main document had only one field for the street address, that address is incomplete.

Indus Susu
Suite 10001
Bayville Inlet Point, WA 98999

Dear Indus:

Thank you for your past support of the Morgan Wildlife Reserve. Now, with a donation of $50.00, you can become part of the Reserve. Your own personalized tile will be placed in the newly renovated carnivore exhibit. Imagine: the full moon just above the horizon, a wolf loping through the grounds, peering at the name Indus Susu beneath its feet. Listen to its howls, and you'll hear "Thank you Indus of Bayville Inlet Point."

Addressing Mailing Labels

When you mail information to many people, it's often more practical or more economical (or both) to attach mailing labels than to use envelopes. Word can use your data source to create those labels for you.

TIP

Lone label. *To create a single mailing label, use the Envelopes And Labels command on the Tools menu.*

SEE ALSO

For information about selecting a data source, see "Creating Form Letters" on page 274.

Set Up the Labels

1. Start and save a new blank document.

2. Choose Mail Merge from the Tools menu.

3. Click the Create button, and choose Mailing Labels. Click the Active Window button when Word asks you which document window to use.

4. Click the Get Data button, and choose your data source. Click the Set Up Main Document button when prompted.

5. Select a label type and location.

6. Click OK.

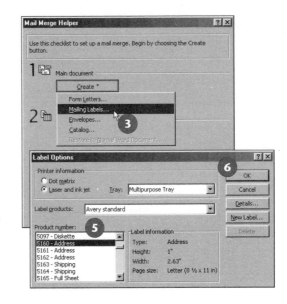

Insert the Address

1. Click Insert Merge Field, and click the data field you want to include.

2. Add any spaces or punctuation, and press Enter to start new lines as necessary.

3. Repeat steps 1 and 2 until you've completed the label information.

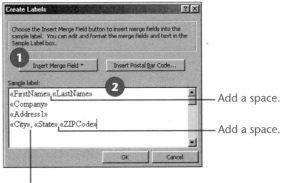

Add a space.

Add a space.

Add a comma and a space.

Add a Postal Bar Code

1. Click the Insert Postal Bar Code button in the Create Labels dialog box.

2. Specify the fields that contain the ZIP code and the street address.

3. Click OK.

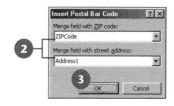

Create the Labels

1. Proofread the address, and correct any errors.

2. Click OK in the Create Labels dialog box.

3. Click Close in the Mail Merge Helper dialog box.

4. Review the layout of the main document.

5. Click either the Merge To New Document or Merge To Printer button on the Mail Merge toolbar to merge all the records, or the Merge button to merge selected records.

The Merge button

The Merge To Printer button

The Merge To New Document button

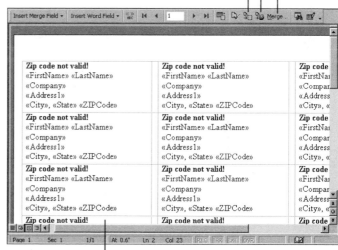

Word uses a table to lay out the labels.

Addressing Envelopes from a Mailing List

If your printer can print envelopes, you can quickly address a stack of envelopes based on a list of names and addresses.

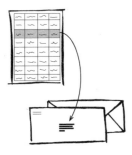

Set Up the Envelopes

1. Start and save a new blank document.

2. Choose Mail Merge from the Tools menu.

3. Click the Create button, and choose Envelopes.

4. Click the Active Window button when Word asks you which document window to use.

5. Click the Get Data button, and choose your data source.

6. When prompted, click the Set Up Main Document button.

7. On the Envelope Options tab of the Envelope Options dialog box, select the envelope size and the fonts you want to use.

8. If necessary, click the Printing Options tab, and change the way the envelopes are to be fed into the printer.

9. Click OK.

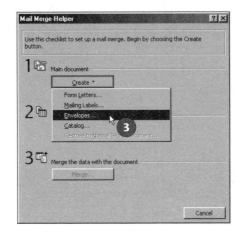

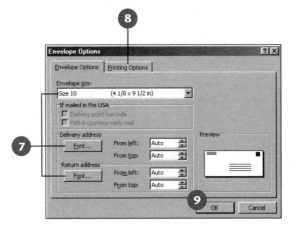

SEE ALSO

For information about creating envelopes one at a time and about changing settings in the Envelope Options dialog box, see "Addressing an Envelope" on page 82.

For information about the main document and the data source, see "Creating Form Letters" on page 274.

For information about checking the accuracy of mail merged documents, see "Reviewing Mail Merged Documents" on page 276.

For information about postal bar codes, see "Add a Postal Bar Code" on page 279.

For information about specifying which records are to be used in the merge, see "Selecting Records to Merge" on page 290 and "Merging Conditionally" on page 292.

TIP

Change of address. *If a return address isn't shown in the main document (or if the one that's shown is incorrect), choose Options from the Tools menu, and complete or correct the information on the User Information tab. If you're using envelopes with a preprinted return address, delete the return address from the main document.*

Set Up the Main Document

1. In the Envelope Address dialog box, use the items from the Insert Merge Field button to complete the address.

2. Add a postal bar code if desired. Click OK to close the Insert Postal Bar Code dialog box.

3. Proofread the address, and correct any errors.

4. Click OK.

Create the Envelopes

1. Click Close in the Mail Merge Helper dialog box.

2. Review the layout of the main document.

3. Save the document.

4. Click either the Merge To New Document or Merge To Printer button on the Mail Merge toolbar to merge all records, or the Merge button to merge selected records.

Click, and choose a data field...

...to insert the merge field here.

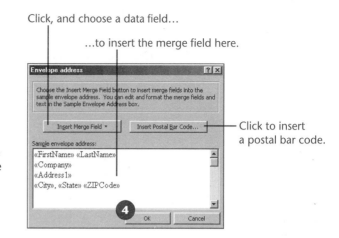

Click to insert a postal bar code.

The Merge button

The Merge To Printer button

The Merge To New Document button

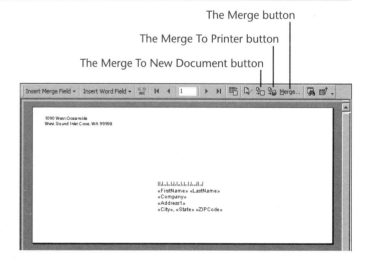

Creating Awards

Everyone deserves an award once in a while, whether it's for a crowning accomplishment or just for fun. You can use Word to create a basic award document, with blank places for the recipient's name and the achievement that is being recognized. If several people are being honored for different reasons, you can create a list of names and awards, and Word will insert them into the award document for you.

Create the Data

① Start a new blank document, and create a table with two columns and two rows.

② Type a title for each column in the top row.

③ Type the name of the recipient and the name of the award.

④ Press Tab to start a new row, and type the next recipient's name and award. Repeat until you've listed all the recipients and their awards, and then save and close the document.

The column label, or title, becomes the Merge Field name.

Employee	Award
Harry Planifrons	Perfect Attendance
Dusky Cruciger	Writing the Longest Report
Dall Burmeister	Having the Cleanest Office
Indus Susu	Creating the Best Excuse
Dall Burmeister	Making the Best Coffee
Mary Planifrons	Being a Nice Boss
Frasier Peale	Working Weekends

Create an Award Certificate

① Start a new blank document, and use Word's tools to create a handsome certificate.

② Insert and format a blank paragraph for the recipient's name.

③ Insert and format a blank paragraph for the award.

④ Save the document.

TIP

Use tables. *Tables are great tools for specialized layouts. The table at the bottom of the award allows precise placement of text and lines.*

TIP

Definition. *To Word, a catalog-type document is any document that doesn't fit the criteria for form letters, mailing labels, or envelopes. It's usually a generic sort of document with few specialized features, such as the award described here.*

SEE ALSO

For information about placing a border around a document, see "Placing a Line Border Around a Page" on page 199 and "Placing an Art Border Around a Page" on page 200.

For information about creating dramatic headings, see "Creating Stylized Text" on page 218.

For information about specifying which records are to be used in the merge, see "Selecting Records to Merge" on page 290 and "Merging Conditionally" on page 292.

Set Up the Documents

1. Choose Mail Merge from the Tools menu.

2. Click the Create button, and choose Catalog. Click the Active Window button when Word asks you which document window to use.

3. Click Get Data, choose Open Data Source, and open the data document you created.

4. When prompted, click the Edit Main Document button.

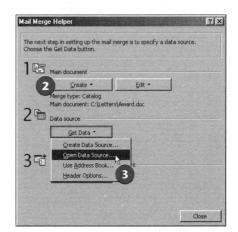

Create the Awards

1. Click in the document where the recipient's name will be placed.

2. Click Insert Merge Field, and choose the recipients-column title.

3. Click in the document where the award title will be placed.

4. Click Insert Merge Field, and choose the awards-column title.

5. Click the Merge To Printer button.

6. Hand out the awards!

Creating a Data Source

When you're creating mail merged documents, you need two things: a *main document* and a *data source*. If the data you want to use isn't already organized in an easily accessible form, you can create a data-source document and enter your data there.

SEE ALSO

For information about quickly creating a small data source, see "Creating Awards" on page 282.

For information about using data from Microsoft Excel, see "Incorporating Excel Data" on page 288.

For information about using data from Microsoft Access, see "Incorporating Access Data" on page 289.

Create a Data Source

1. Open the document you're using as your main document.

2. Choose Mail Merge from the Tools menu, and click the Create button in the Mail Merge Helper dialog box to choose the type of document you want. Use the active window for your main document.

3. Click the Get Data button, and choose Create Data Source.

4. Modify the proposed list of fields:

   ◆ Select a field, and click Remove Field Name to delete the field.

   ◆ Type a new field name, and click Add Field Name to add a new field.

   ◆ Select a field, and click a Move arrow to change the order of the field in the list.

5. Click OK.

6. Save the document.

Type a new field name, and click Add Field Name to add the new field to the list.

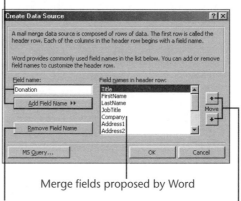

Merge fields proposed by Word

Select a field name, and click to delete the field.

Select a field name, and click to move the field up or down in the list.

Anatomy of a data-source document. *After you've created a data-source document and completed your main document, save and close both documents. Then click the Open button on the Standard toolbar, and open the data-source document. Note that the document is a standard Word table, with the names of the fields in the top row and the data you entered in the rows below. Close the document without making any changes.*

For information about changing the structure of an existing data-source document, see "Modifying a Data-Source Document" on page 287.

Enter the Data

① When Word informs you that the document contains no data records, click the Edit Data Source button.

② Enter the data for the first line.

③ Press the Tab key to move to the next line.

④ Continue typing data and pressing the Tab key to complete the record.

⑤ Click Add New after completing each record.

⑥ Continue adding and completing records until you've completed the last record.

⑦ Click OK.

⑧ Complete the main document.

⑨ Save and close the main document. When prompted, save the data-source document.

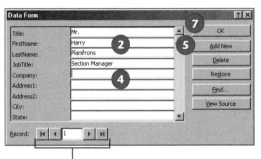

Click to browse through existing records.

Editing Data

If, when you're conducting a mail merge, you find that the data for one or more records in your data-source document is incorrect or needs to be updated, you can edit the data. You can also add new records and delete old ones.

TIP

Nonresident data. *If your data resides in another program, such as an address book or an Access database, close the main document, edit and save the data in its own program, and then reopen the main document to get the updated information.*

SEE ALSO

For information about adding or deleting data records, see "Modifying a Data-Source Document" on the facing page.

Find a Record

1. If it isn't already open, open the main document for which the data source was created.

2. Click the Edit Data Source button.

3. Click the Find button.

4. Type the information you're looking for.

5. Select the field in which it occurs.

6. Click the Find First button. If the found record isn't the one you want, click the Find Next button. Repeat until you've found the record.

7. Click Close.

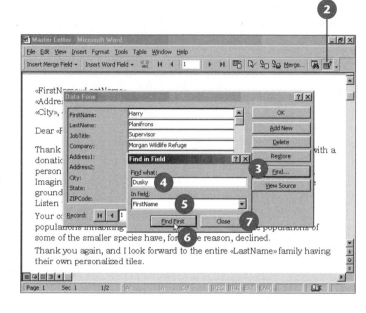

Edit a Record

1. Do any of the following:
   - Edit the text in any of the fields.
   - Add new records.
   - Delete records.

2. Click OK when you've finished.

Add, delete, or edit the text in any field.

Click to start a new record.

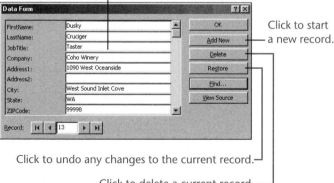

Click to undo any changes to the current record.

Click to delete a current record.

Modifying a Data-Source Document

If you're conducting a mail merge and you're using a Word data-source document, you can change the number of fields or the names of the fields in the data-source document by editing the data-source document directly. Because the data source is a table, it's a simple matter to add or delete columns when you want to add or delete fields of data.

TIP

Use the gridlines. *The data-source document contains all the information in a single table. Turn on the gridlines from the Table menu if they're not displayed so that you can see the boundaries of each data field.*

SEE ALSO

For information about creating a data-source document in Word, see "Creating a Data Source" on page 284.

Edit the Data-Source Document

1. If it isn't already open, open the main document for which the data source was created.

2. Click the Edit Data Source button.

3. In the Data Form dialog box, click the View Source button.

4. Modify the fields and records:

   ◆ Delete a column to remove a data field.

   ◆ Add a column and fill it with data to add a data field.

   ◆ Change data-field names by changing the text in the first row.

   ◆ Sort the records in alphanumeric order.

5. Save the document.

6. Click the Mail Merge Main Document button.

7. If you changed any field names, be sure to change the merge fields in the main document.

Click in the table, and then click the button to sort the records.

Edit the name to change the field name.

Delete a column to remove a field.

Click to return to the main document.

Add a column to add a new field.

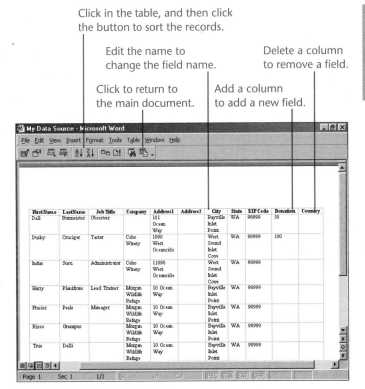

Incorporating Excel Data

Sometimes the data for a mail merge is contained in a source other than a Word document. If the information you want to use is contained in a Microsoft Excel worksheet, you can use the Excel workbook as your data source. That way, if the data in the Excel workbook is updated, your next mail merge will contain the new information.

SEE ALSO

For information about creating a Word document as a data source, see "Creating a Data Source" on page 284.

For information about using data from an Access database, see "Incorporating Access Data" on the facing page.

Prepare the Data

1. Open the workbook in Excel.

2. Organize the worksheet data so that each row is a data record and each column is a data field.

3. Save and close the worksheet.

Verify that the top row of the data contains the field name for each column.

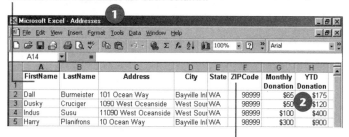

To use only part of the worksheet, select and name a range. The field names must be in the top row of the named range.

Get the Data

1. In Word, choose Mail Merge from the Tools menu, and create a main document.

2. Click the Get Data button, and choose Open Data Source.

3. Select MS Excel Worksheets.

4. Double-click the worksheet to open it.

5. Select a named range or the entire worksheet.

6. Click OK.

7. Edit the main document, and use the Insert Merge Field button to insert the data fields.

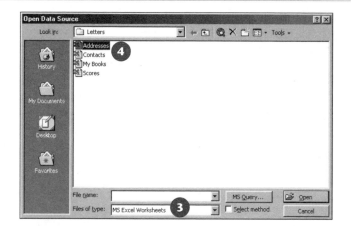

Incorporating Access Data

If you want to create mail merged documents using data that's contained in a Microsoft Access database, you can use a table from the database as your data source, or you can customize the data by using a query and then use the query as the data source.

Get the Data

1. In Word, use Mail Merge to create a main document.

2. Click the Get Data button, and choose Open Data Source.

3. Select MS Access Databases.

4. Double-click the database.

5. Select the table or query that contains the data.

6. Click OK.

7. Edit the main document, and use the Merge Field button to insert the data fields.

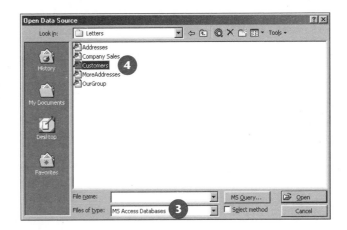

Selecting Records to Merge

When you're conducting a mail merge, you might want to use only the records in your data source that match certain criteria—addressing envelopes to clients who live in a specific postal-code area, for example, or sending letters to only the most generous donors. You can specify which records are used by testing the data in a field against data that you specify.

TIP

Query Access. *If you're using data from a Microsoft Access database, you can use a query in Access to extract the records you want. The filtering process is more powerful and flexible than Word's query options.*

SEE ALSO

For information about sorting the records in a data-source document, see "Modifying a Data-Source Document" on page 287.

Limit the Records

1. Choose Mail Merge from the Tools menu.

2. Step through the Mail Merge Helper to prepare your main document for merging.

3. Click the Merge button on the Mail Merge toolbar.

4. Specify the range of records to be merged.

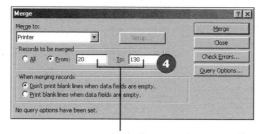

Only the records you specify will be merged.

Specify a Test

1. Click the Query Options button in the Merge dialog box.

2. Select the field to be tested.

3. Select the type of comparison.

4. Type the data you want to test against. Leave blank if Comparison is set to Is Blank or Is Not Blank.

Only records showing a monthly donation of $100 or more will be merged.

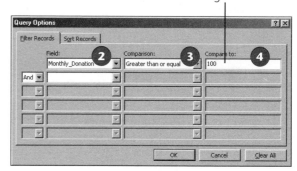

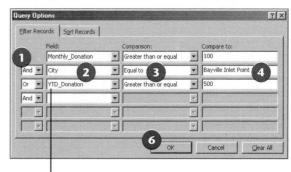

Add Tests

1. Specify the relationship between the two tests.

2. Select the field to be tested.

3. Select the type of comparison.

4. Type the data you want to test against. Leave blank if Comparison is set to Is Blank or Is Not Blank.

5. Repeat steps 1 through 4 to add tests until you've defined all the data records to be used.

6. Click OK.

7. Test your queries by merging only a few records to a document. If the queries produce the expected results, execute the full merge.

Merged documents will be generated for anyone in Bayville Inlet Point who contributed $100 or more per month and for anyone, anywhere, who contributed $500 or more this year.

Merging Conditionally

When you conduct a mail merge, you can change the text of a merged document based on conditions in your data source. For example, you can insert one message for the most generous donors, and a different one for contributors of smaller amounts of money, provided your data source contains a column that lists individual donations.

TIP

Caution! *Conditional tests can be tricky. Always review the document and its results before you conduct the full merge.*

SEE ALSO

For information about testing your setup before you print an entire mail merge, see "Reviewing Mail Merged Documents" on page 276.

Create the Test

1. Choose Mail Merge from the Tools menu, and use the Mail Merge Helper to create a main document and connect to your data source. Add to your main document the merge fields you want Word to complete for you.

2. Click in the document where you want to insert the conditional text.

3. Click the Insert Word Field button, and choose If...Then...Else from the drop-down menu.

4. Create the test.

5. Type the text to be inserted if the test result is true.

6. Type the text to be inserted if the test result is false.

7. Click OK.

8. Click the Merge button on the Mail Merge tool-bar and create your documents.

Select the field name that contains the data to be tested. Select the type of comparison.

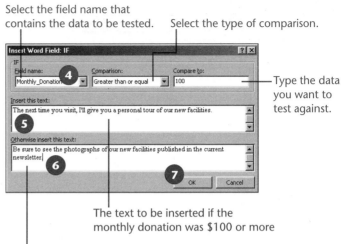

Type the data you want to test against.

The text to be inserted if the monthly donation was $100 or more

The text to be inserted if the monthly donation was less than $100

Wandering and Wondering Through Word's Fields

The term *field* can be confusing: it has different meanings depending on how it's used.

◆ A field in Word is usually a placeholder—often containing a bit of programming code—for information that gets updated automatically, such as a date or a page number.

◆ A merge field is another type of field—also a placeholder—which is used exclusively to get information from a data source.

◆ A data field is a single item in a data record.

The Anatomy of a Field

Most of the time, you're not aware of the fields that might exist in your document. You generally see the *results* of fields: the current date, perhaps, or the summing of a table. If, however, your document is suddenly transformed into a chaotic riddle of strange characters, you're seeing the other side of fields: their *code*.

Field characters enclose a field. These are special characters that Word inserts—they're not the { and } characters on your keyboard.

{ FILLIN "Enter your closing." \d "Have a pleasant day." }

Field name   Field instructions

The Anatomy of a Merge Field

A merge field is used only during a mail merge, in which you combine, or merge, a main document with a data source. Merge fields are usually visible in your main document before it's printed. If you show the full field codes for these fields, you'll see that the merge field is a special form of a field: the MERGEFIELD field.

Merge-field characters enclose the merge field.

«MonthlyDonation» — The merge-field name is the name of the data field.

{ MERGEFIELD MonthlyDonation } — A merge field is just a special type of field.

The Anatomy of a Data Field

Database programs also use the term *field,* but a data field is completely different from a field in Word. A data field is a specific item in a *data record.* A data record is one complete set of information contained in the data source. If your data source contains names, addresses, and donations, a single data record is the name, address, and donation information for an individual, and a single field in that data record is one component of the address: the city or the ZIP or postal code, for example.

The first row lists the name of each data field.   A column is one data field.

First	Last	Address	City	State	ZIP	Monthly Donation	YTD Donation
Harry	Planifrons	3 Kerguelen Place	Crozet Basin	WA	98999	65	175
Dall	Burmeister	10 Ocean Way	Bayville Inlet Point	WA	98999	50	120

A row is one data record.   A cell is a data field for a specific record.

Personalizing Merged Documents

When you're conducting a mail merge, you might want to insert different personalized messages into just a few of the documents. You can do this by having Word first fill in all the fields that are the same in all the documents and then pause to ask you for the personalized information.

Set Up the Field

1. Choose Mail Merge from the Tools menu, and use the Mail Merge Helper to create a main document and connect to your data source. Add the merge fields to the main document you want Word to complete for you.

2. Click in the document where you want to place the personalized information.

3. Click the Insert Word Field button, and choose Fill-In from the drop-down menu.

4. Type the prompt you want to see when Word asks for the personalized message.

5. Type the text of the default personalized message.

6. Click OK.

7. Click Cancel if Word immediately asks for the personalized message.

8. Save the main document.

Turn on if you want to fill in the information only once, after which Word will insert the message into every document.

Personalize the Message

1. Click the Merge button.

2. Set up your merge by designating the destination, which records are to be included, and any query options.

3. Click the Merge button in the Merge dialog box to start the merging process.

4. When the dialog box with your prompt appears, do either of the following:

   ◆ Click OK to accept the proposed message.

   ◆ Type a different personalized message, and click OK.

5. Unless you selected the option to fill in the information only once, continue responding to the prompt until you've completed the mail merge.

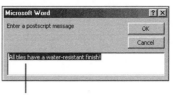

Word proposes the default text.

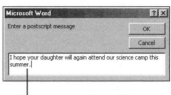

Type new text for a different personalized message.

Harry Planifrons
Lead Trainer
Morgan Wildlife Refuge

PS: I hope your daughter will again attend our science camp this summer.

The message appears in the merged document.

Inserting Changing Information

To include in a document some information that might change—the number of words, for example, or the number of the current section of the document—you can insert a field. Word often inserts fields automatically, but you have more choices and more options to customize the way a field works when you insert it directly. You can even place one field inside another to create complex nested fields.

TIP

Updates. *Fields are usually updated when you open a document and when you print it.*

TIP

Field functions. *To see more information about the function of a field, or to verify the syntax, click in the field code and press the F1 key for help.*

Insert a Field

1. Click in the document where you want the field to appear, and choose Field from the Insert menu.

2. Select a category, or select All to browse through all the field names.

3. Select a field name.

4. Add any text you want to the field.

5. Click the Options button.

6. Select any option you want.

7. Click the Add To Field button. Select and insert additional options from any other tabs that are displayed in the Field Options dialog box.

8. Add any text that is required for each option.

9. Click OK in the Field Options dialog box, and then click OK in the Field dialog box.

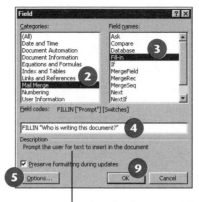

Describes the function of the selected field.

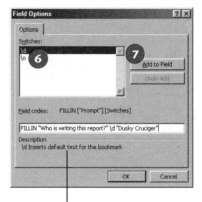

Describes the function of the selected option.

TIP

What's a switch? *A switch is part of the programming code that Word uses to determine which options are to be used.*

TIP

Fill-in fields. *Nested Fill-In fields are usually used in templates. When you use the Fill-In field for document-information fields such as Author, Subject, Title, or User Information, the information is placed in the document and in the document's Properties dialog box.*

SEE ALSO

For information about the types of fields Word uses, and about fields in general, see "Wandering and Wondering Through Word's Fields" on page 293.

For information about accessing and using the properties of a document, see "Keeping Track of Document Information" on page 300.

Nest Fields

1. Choose Options from the Tools menu, turn on the Field Codes check box on the View tab, and click OK.

2. Use the Field command on the Insert menu to insert the first field.

3. Click in the field where you want the nested field to be located.

4. Use the Field command again to insert the nested field.

5. Select both fields, right-click in the selection, and choose Toggle Field Codes from the shortcut menu.

6. Press the F9 key to update the fields.

7. Review the latest results.

8. If the results are as expected, turn off the Field Codes check box on the View tab. If the results are incorrect, select and delete the nested field, and repeat steps 3 through 7.

My Report

 { AUTHOR * MERGEFORMAT }

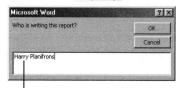 **My Report**

{ AUTHOR { FILLIN "Who is writing this report?"\d "Dusky Cruciger" } * MERGEFORMAT }

The Fill-In field is nested inside the Author field.

My Report

Dusky Cruciger

The result from the Fill-In dialog box will be used to update the Author field.

Displaying the Range of Topics on a Page

In a long document, it can be very useful to have the range of topics on a page shown in the running head for quick scanning, just as a dictionary's headers show the range of entries from first to last word on each page. You use a paragraph or character style to identify the items that are topics, insert a couple of fields in the header, and let Word do the rest.

TIP

Which style? *Use a paragraph style when the entry is a heading paragraph. Use a character style when the entry is part of a paragraph.*

TIP

Which option? *Use the other options—the \n, \r, and \w switches—to reference paragraph numbers instead of the text of the paragraph.*

Show the Range

1. In your document, assign a specific style (paragraph or character) to the topics that you want to list.

2. Choose Header And Footer from the View menu, and click where you want the range to be inserted.

3. Choose Field from the Insert menu.

4. Select the StyleRef field, and click the Options button.

5. On the Styles tab, select the style of the topic, and click the Add To Field button.

6. Click OK twice to insert the field.

7. Click where you want the last topic to be inserted.

8. Repeat steps 3 through 6.

9. On the Field Specific Switches tab, select the \l switch, click Add To Field, and click OK twice to insert the field.

This field displays the text of the first paragraph on the page with the Heading 2 style.

This field displays the text of the last paragraph on the page with the Heading 2 Style.

Header
{ STYLEREF "Heading 2" * MERGEFORMAT } to { STYLEREF "Heading 2" \l * MERGEFORMAT }

The first Heading 2 style paragraph

The last Heading 2 style paragraph

Identification to Behavior

Identification
A medium-sized (4.5-7.5 m.) toothed whale with a single blowhole. The blow, which is low and wispy, is often visible in the Antarctic but normally not in warmer waters. The blow is similar in size, shape, and duration to the blows of minke and killer whales. There are numerous rapid surfacings in the same area, followed by a long dive. The dorsal fin is tall, curved, and very robust, with a thick base. The color ranges from reddish-brown to brown, but in poor lighting conditions appears gray or black. There are usually numerous scratches and circular scars on the body, with some animals being extensively scarred. Scratches often occur in pairs, presumably caused by the paired teeth of other southern bottlenose whales. The bulbous head is difficult to distinguish, and the beak is rarely displayed above water.

Distribution
Southern bottlenose whales have been observed during the summer throughout the open waters of the Antarctic except for the southern regions of the Ross and Weddell Seas. They are often seen near the edge of the pack ice but rarely venture far into the pack. They sometimes aggregate in areas where there is substantial sea-floor contour, but not in areas where sperm whales aggregate. Southern bottlenose whales range far to the north, with observations off the coasts of Australia and New Zealand. Most of the population appears to be in the Antarctic waters during the summer. The winter range is unknown, but they may move ahead of the advancing ice pack during the fall and spend the winter in the pelagic regions of the mid latitudes.

Population
The Southern bottlenose whale may be second only to the minke whale in cetacean abundance in the Antarctic, but accurate population estimates are difficult because of the long dives of the animals. The best estimate for the Antarctic area (south of 60°S latitude) during the summer is 80,000–320,000 animals.

Exploitation
There has been no commercial exploitation of Southern bottlenose whales. The only recorded catches were 42 whales for research studies by the Soviet whaling fleet between 1970 and 1982.

Status
Unexploited, the Southern bottlenose whale should be at its maximum population level, limited only by the availability of prey. The population could eventually be affected by overfishing of squid and krill.

Behavior
Southern bottlenose whales often avoid moving ships but will sometimes approach a drifting ship. They make long dives (14–30 mts.) and then remain near the surface for 2-3.5 minutes, with each whale blowing 10–20 times. Each surfacing consists of a rapid surge through the water and a quick breath, followed by a short dive of 10-15 seconds before the next surfacing. The animals in a group rarely display a distinct swimming direction when surfacing; instead, they mill about before diving. The whale's body has a slightly sharper arch during the last surfacing before the long dive.

-2-

Inserting Document Information

Word keeps track of all sorts of information about a document: its file size, the person who last worked on it, the number of words or pages it contains, keywords, and so on. If you want, you can insert some or all of this information into your document. All you have to do is tell Word which information you want to include.

TIP

Keeping track. *Although Word keeps track of many items automatically, it doesn't keep track of every item in the Property list. You'll need to enter some of these items yourself if you want to keep track of them.*

SEE ALSO

For information about entering document properties, see "Keeping Track of Document Information" on page 300.

Insert the Information

1. Click in the document where you want the information to be inserted.

2. Choose Field from the Insert menu to display the Field dialog box.

3. Select Document Information.

4. Select the field that provides the information you want to include.

5. Click the Options button.

6. Select the option you want.

7. Click the Add To Field button.

8. Click OK twice to insert the field.

9. To update the field manually, right-click the field, and choose Update Field from the shortcut menu.

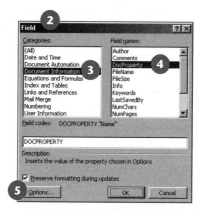

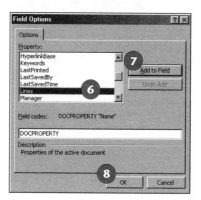

Keeping Track of Document Information

Word keeps track of a lot of information about your document. When you add your own information, you have an even more comprehensive record of a document and its history. You can then print this information for review and tracking purposes.

SEE ALSO

For information about automatically updating the Summary fields when you start a document, see "Nest Fields" on page 297.

TIP

Print the properties. *To print the properties whenever the document is printed, choose Options from the Tools menu, click the Print tab, and turn on the Document Properties check box.*

Check the Document Information

1 Save your document. (Some statistics are updated only when the document is saved.)

2 Choose Properties from the File menu.

3 Click the Summary tab.

4 Modify any incorrect information or add any missing information.

5 Click the Statistics tab, and review the document statistics. (The statistics are automatically generated by Word, and you can't modify any of these values.)

6 Click the General tab, and review the file information. (You can't modify any of these values.)

7 Click OK.

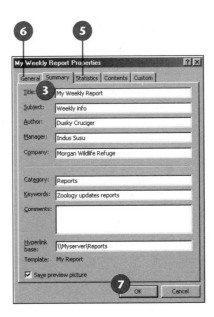

Using a template? *If a template has any of the Summary fields or Custom properties filled in, those properties will be included in the properties of any document based on that template.*

Check your properties. *Click the Open button on the Standard toolbar, and, in the Open dialog box, select Properties from the Views button. Select a document to see its properties. Click Cancel when you've finished. Now use Windows Explorer to locate a Word document. Right-click the document, and choose Properties from the shortcut menu. Note that all the same property information is displayed.*

Search for properties. *To find and open a document based on one of its properties, select Find from the Tools button in the Open dialog box. Specify the type of property and its value, specify a location, and click Find Now. Documents with matching properties will be listed in the Open dialog box.*

Include Additional Properties

① Click the Custom tab.

② Do either of the following:

  ◆ Type a new property name in the Name box.

  ◆ Select a property name from the Name list.

③ Select the type of data to be used for that property.

④ Type the value, or content, of the property.

⑤ Click Add.

⑥ Repeat steps 2 through 5 for any additional properties. Click OK, and save the document.

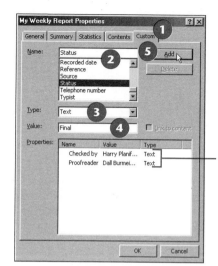

The completed properties

Print the Information

① Choose Print from the File menu to display the Print dialog box.

② In the Print What list, choose Document Properties.

③ Click OK.

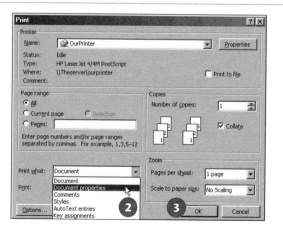

Controlling Automatic Changes

Automatic text formatting, automatic insertion of long words or complete phrases, and automatic correction of common misspellings or transpositions are wonderful time-savers—provided they work the way you want them to. To make these tools do your bidding, you have to tell Word what (and what not) to do.

TRY THIS

AutoFormat As You Type magic! *Make sure that all the options on the AutoFormat As You Type tab are turned on. Type * Fruit. Apples and Oranges. Press Enter, and type Grain. Wheat and Rye. Press Enter, turn off the Bullets button on the Formatting toolbar, type ---- and press Enter. Then type +----+----+ and press Enter. Now try to figure out which AutoFormat As You Type feature caused which effect!*

Set AutoFormat Options

1 Choose AutoCorrect from the Tools menu, and click the AutoFormat As You Type tab.

2 Turn options on or off to include or exclude formatting features.

Replaces characters with special characters, and applies character formatting.

Creates special formats.

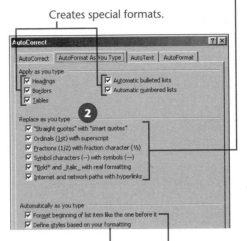

Creates new paragraph styles based on any special formatting you apply.

Automatically repeats any special character formatting applied to the beginning of a list item.

Control AutoComplete Tips

1 Click the AutoText tab.

2 Turn on the Show AutoComplete Tip For AutoText And Dates check box if you want to see AutoComplete tips on the screen, or turn it off to disable the AutoComplete feature.

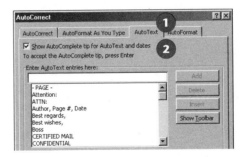

TRY THIS

AutoCorrect magic! *Make sure that all the options on the AutoCorrect tab are turned on. Type the following: THis is due tuesday. will it be done? :-). Try to figure out which AutoCorrect feature caused which change!*

SEE ALSO

For more information about AutoCorrect, AutoFormat, and the spelling- and grammar-checking features, see "Behind-the-Scenes Magic" on page 27.

For information about automatic spelling and grammar checking and automatic spelling correction, see "Turning On the Proofing Tools" on page 46.

For information about the AutoText feature, see "Inserting Frequently Used Information" on page 272.

Set AutoCorrect Options

① Click the AutoCorrect tab.

② Turn check boxes on or off to include or exclude the AutoCorrect features.

③ Turn on the Replace Text As You Type check box to have Word automatically replace a symbol or an incorrectly spelled word in the left column of the list with another symbol or the correctly spelled word in the right column. Turn off the check box if you want Word to ignore the list.

④ Do either of the following to modify the text that is replaced as you type:

◆ Create a new entry by typing the item to be replaced, typing the replacement text, and then clicking Add.

◆ Delete an existing entry by clicking the entry in the list and then clicking Delete.

⑤ Click OK when you've finished.

Click to add or delete exceptions to Word's automatic correction of two initial capital letters or the capitalization of the first letter after the apparent end of a sentence.

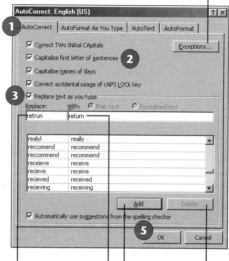

Type the text you usually type incorrectly...

Click to add a new entry...

...or click to remove a selected entry from the list.

...and type the correct replacement text.

Adding Captions Automatically

If you want to add captions to graphics elements in your documents—pictures, tables, or charts, for example— Word can do most of the work for you. All you have to do is specify which items are to be captioned. When you add the items to the document, the captions and their sequential caption numbers are inserted automatically. You can then add descriptive text if necessary.

SEE ALSO

For information about adding captions manually, see "Creating Captions" on page 129.

TIP

Don't try this. *You can't use the AutoCaption feature with any elements that have text wrapping.*

Turn on the AutoCaption Feature

1. Choose Caption from the Insert menu.

2. Click the AutoCaption button in the Caption dialog box.

3. Turn on the check box for the type of element to which you want to add a caption.

4. Select a label for the caption. If the appropriate label isn't listed, click New Label, type the label you want, and click OK.

5. Select the location you want for the caption.

6. Repeat steps 3 through 5 for any other elements that you want to be automatically captioned.

7. Click OK.

8. In your document, insert the item that will have an automatic caption.

9. Add text to the caption if necessary.

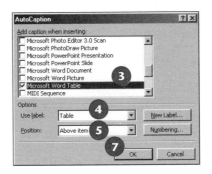

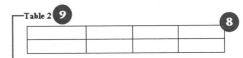

Table 1: Comparison of costs.

	Unit 1	Unit 2	Unit 3
Part 1102	$13.50	$17.75	$19.90
Part 1103	$16.50	$16.65	$22.10
Part 1104	$18.32	$20.12	$25.21
Part 1105	$20.07	$21.01	$32.50

With the AutoCaption feature set to Table, Word inserts a caption and a sequential number each time you insert a table.

Customizing Word

Throughout this book we've talked about customizing Microsoft Word's tools and features to streamline your work and meet your specific needs—creating custom dictionaries for specialized terms, adding AutoText and AutoCorrect entries to minimize errors, customizing templates to save time, and so on.

Now we'll talk about customizing Word itself—changing the program's environment and specifying exactly how *you* want various elements to be displayed, stored, or accessed. For example, you can create your own commands, rename existing menus and commands, move menus into different positions, add your own tabs to the New dialog box, and add tools to or delete them from toolbars. You can speed up Word's performance, and, if the program is performing poorly, you can run diagnostic programs to fix it. Of course, you can work productively in Word without ever changing anything, but if there are aspects of the program you wish you could change, it's good to know that you probably can.

One caution: if your computer is part of a network on which company system policies are being used, check with the system administrator before you attempt to make any changes. System policies usually set what you can and can't customize, and you can avoid considerable frustration by being forewarned.

Adding or Removing Components

Word contains such a multitude of components that you probably haven't needed or wanted to install all of them on your computer. You can install additional components on an as-needed basis or remove components that you never use so as to save some hard disk space.

TIP

First-use installation. *If a component is set to be installed on first use, Word automatically installs it when you need it, provided you have access to the Office or Word CD or the network installation files.*

TIP

Find the tools. *You can find some of the Office tools that are shared with Word by clicking the Start button, pointing to Programs, and then pointing to Office Tools.*

Add or Remove Components

1. With all your Office applications closed, do either of the following:
   - Insert the Office or Word CD into your CD drive.
   - Choose Add/Remove Programs from the Windows Control Panel, select your Office program from the list, and click the Add/Remove button.

2. Click the Add Or Remove Features button.

3. Click the plus signs to expand the outline of the components until you find the item you want to add or remove.

4. Click the down arrow to display the installation choices, and select an installation choice.

5. Repeat steps 3 and 4 for any other components you want to change.

6. Click Update Now.

7. Start Word, and verify that the component or components have been installed or uninstalled.

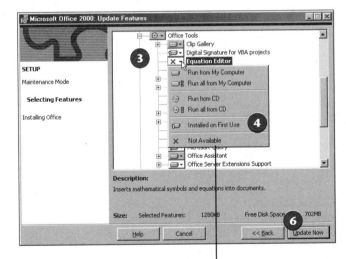

Select to remove an installed item.

Changing Where Word Stores Files

If you don't like the locations where Word accesses tools and information and stores documents, you can change those locations and create the organization that works best for you.

Warning! *If you're working on a network that's set up for "roaming," where your profile is used regardless of which computer you're using, do not change file locations without first consulting the system administrator.*

Change the format.
To change the file format that's used when you save a document, specify a different format on the Save tab of the Options dialog box.

Change the File Location

1. Choose Options from the Tools menu, and click the File Locations tab of the Options dialog box.

2. Select the item whose location you want to change.

3. Click the Modify button.

4. Locate and click the folder that you're designating as the new location.

5. Click OK.

6. Repeat steps 2 through 5 to change any other file locations.

7. Click OK.

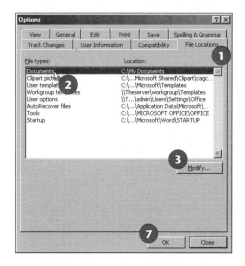

Organizing Your Templates

When you choose New from the File menu, you can see that Word has organized its templates according to their type. As you'd expect, letters and faxes are located on the Letters & Faxes tab, Web pages are on the Web Pages tab, and so on. However, your customized templates get lumped together on the General tab. If you're not satisfied with this arrangement, you can reorganize the templates under any categories you prefer.

TIP

Find your templates. *To locate your templates, right-click a template in the New dialog box, choose Properties from the shortcut menu, and click the General tab.*

Add Folders

1. Using Windows, locate the folder that contains your templates.

2. In that folder, create folders with the names of the categories under which you want to classify the templates:

   - Use the same name as an existing tab in the New dialog box to have the templates in that folder appear on the existing tab.

   - Use a unique name to create a new tab and have the templates in that folder appear on that tab.

3. Drag your templates into the appropriate folder(s). Note that a new folder will create a tab in the New dialog box only if there is a template in the new folder.

4. In Word, choose New from the File menu.

5. Verify that the templates are on the correct tabs.

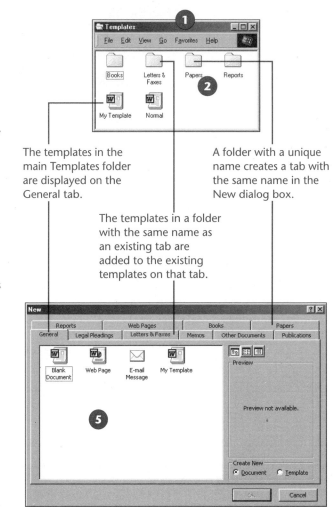

The templates in the main Templates folder are displayed on the General tab.

A folder with a unique name creates a tab with the same name in the New dialog box.

The templates in a folder with the same name as an existing tab are added to the existing templates on that tab.

Controlling the Office Assistant

Some people love their Office Assistant—that little animated character who hangs around on your Desktop waiting to give you advice and answer your questions—and others can't *stand* it. Depending on how you feel about the Assistant, you can change the way it works, choose your favorite among different Assistants, or banish it forever if it drives you crazy.

TIP

Bye-bye. *To remove the Assistant temporarily, right-click it, and choose Hide from the shortcut menu. If you do this several times in different sessions, Word will ask you if you want to turn off the Office Assistant permanently.*

Set the Options

1. If the Office Assistant isn't displayed, choose Show The Office Assistant from the Help menu.

2. Right-click the Assistant, and choose Options from the shortcut menu.

3. Turn check boxes on or off to specify the way you want the Assistant to work.

4. Click OK.

5. Try using the Assistant to see whether you like the settings.

Select an Assistant

1. Right-click the Assistant, and choose Choose Assistant from the shortcut menu.

2. Review the different Assistants by clicking the Next and Back buttons.

3. When you see the Assistant you want, click OK.

4. If prompted, insert the Office or Word CD.

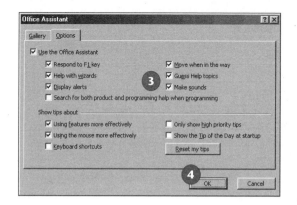

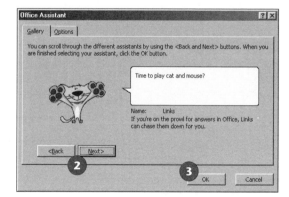

Managing Toolbars

Word provides such a multitude of toolbars that you'll probably find it necessary to do some toolbar management. For example, you might want to move a toolbar into a different location, or expand a toolbar that's sharing a line with another toolbar so that you can see all the buttons, or make yet another toolbar into a little window that sits, or "floats," conveniently on top of your document.

> **TIP**
>
> **Ahoy!** *A toolbar is either "docked" or "floating." A docked toolbar resides at one of the four sides of your Word window. A floating toolbar floats over your text in a little window of its own.*

Move a Docked Toolbar

① Point to a blank part of the toolbar or to the raised bar on the toolbar.

② Drag the toolbar into any of the following locations:

- ◆ Above or below another docked toolbar to stack the toolbars

- ◆ On the same line as another toolbar to have both toolbars share the same line

- ◆ At any side of the Word window to dock the toolbar at that side

- ◆ In the document area to change the toolbar into a floating toolbar

Resize a Docked Toolbar

If the toolbar shares a line with another toolbar, either

- ◆ Double-click the raised bar to expand the toolbar as much as possible.

- ◆ Drag the raised bar to expand or compress the toolbar.

The Standard and Formatting toolbars sharing one line

The Picture toolbar dragged to one side of the window

The Web toolbar stacked below other toolbars

A floating toolbar

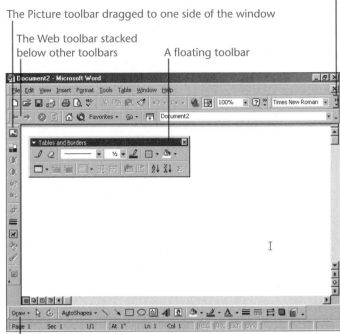

The Drawing toolbar at the bottom of the window

When one toolbar is resized...

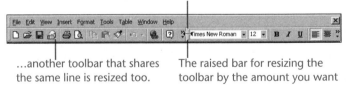

...another toolbar that shares the same line is resized too.

The raised bar for resizing the toolbar by the amount you want

SEE ALSO

For information about creating your own toolbars, see "Quickly Applying Standardized Formatting" on page 88.

For information about modifying the default setup so that the Standard and Formatting toolbars don't share the same line, see "Changing the Way Word Displays Toolbars" on page 315.

For information about reorganizing the buttons on toolbars, see "Customizing Toolbars" on page 318.

TIP

My, how you've changed!
The look of a toolbar might change when you move its position. When you move the Formatting toolbar from the top of your window to the side, for example, the Style drop-down list box changes into a button that opens the Style dialog box. Use this feature to further customize the window for the way you like to work.

Resize a Floating Toolbar

1. Point to one of the toolbar's borders.

2. Drag the border. The toolbar is resized by increments that are set by the sizes of the toolbar buttons. When the toolbar is the desired size and shape, release the mouse button.

The mouse pointer changes into the Resize pointer when it's positioned over the toolbar's border.

Move a Floating Toolbar

1. Do any of the following to move the toolbar:

   ◆ Point to the toolbar's title bar, and drag the toolbar into a new location.

   ◆ Drag the toolbar to one of the sides of the window to change the toolbar into a docked toolbar.

   ◆ Double-click the toolbar's title bar to dock the toolbar at its previous docked position.

Creating Your Own Commands

If you often find yourself executing the same series of actions over and over again, you can simplify your work and save a lot of time by recording that series of actions to create a *macro*. For example, to replace the same set of terms in different documents, or to apply special formatting to certain words, you need to record the series of actions only once, using the Find and Replace commands. With the macro stored on a menu or toolbar, you can then run the whole series as if it were a single Word command.

Set Up a Macro

1 Click in the document where you want to execute the first of the repetitive actions.

2 Point to Macro on the Tools menu, and choose Record New Macro from the submenu.

3 Type a name for the macro.

4 Specify where the macro will be stored:

- ◆ In the Normal.dot template so that it's available to all documents

- ◆ In the current document so that it's available only in this document

- ◆ In the template the document is based on so that it's available to all documents based on that template

5 Type a description so that you'll know what the macro does.

6 Click OK.

The macro name must begin with a letter and can contain as many as 80 characters (but spaces and symbols aren't allowed).

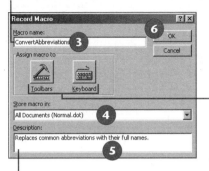

You can assign the macro to a toolbar button or key combination when you record it, but you might want to wait to assign it until after you've tested it and it has proven its worth.

Your description will appear in the Macro dialog box to remind you of the macro's function.

SEE ALSO

For information about using macros in different templates, see "Copying Between Templates" on page 73.

For information about assigning a macro to a menu, a key combination, or a toolbar, see "Adding Commands to Your Menus" on page 316.

TIP

Macro shmacro! *The word "macro" often fills people with terror—they think macros are only for "techies." Not true! All you do is record the actions you already know how to do. If you make a mistake, you can start over. If you don't believe us, try the "Try This" below.*

TRY THIS

Record a macro. *In a document, select a short piece of text. Start recording a macro named "PrintSelection." Choose Print from the File menu, select the Selection option under Page Range in the Print dialog box, and click OK. Now stop the recording. When you add the macro to the File menu or to the Standard toolbar, you can print whatever you select in any document without having to open the Print dialog box. Easy, isn't it?*

Record Your Actions

1. Execute the series of actions you want to record as a macro, using your keyboard to select text and move the insertion point.

2. If you want to execute any actions in Word without recording them as part of the macro, click Pause Recording. Click Resume Recorder to resume recording your actions.

3. When you've recorded all the actions that compose the macro, click Stop Recording.

4. Point to Macro on the Tools menu, and choose Macros from the submenu.

5. Select the macro you just recorded, and click Run.

6. If the macro performs correctly, assign it to a menu, a keyboard shortcut, or a toolbar. If it doesn't perform as expected, rerecord it using the same name.

The Recorder mouse pointer reminds you that you're recording all actions.

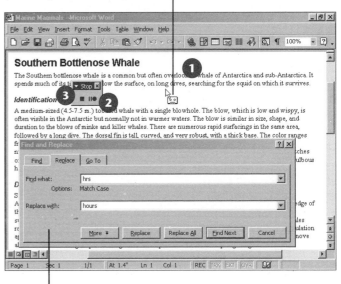

Any commands you execute and all settings in dialog boxes are recorded.

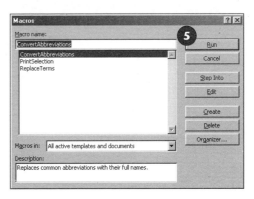

Changing the Way Word Displays Menus

Word tries to simplify your work by displaying only the most frequently used commands on a menu when you open it. As you use Word, the menus continue to adapt to your usage, placing *your* most frequently used commands on each menu. If you don't like the way the menus have adapted or if you don't want the menus to limit the commands that are displayed, you can change the way this feature works.

SEE ALSO

For information about Word's adaptive menus, see "Word's Dynamic Menus and Toolbars" on page 42.

Set Your Options

1. Choose Customize from the Tools menu.

2. On the Options tab of the Customize dialog box, do any of the following:

   ◆ Turn off the Menus Show Recently Used Commands First check box to have Word always display all the commands on every menu.

   ◆ Click the Reset My Usage Data button to have Word display the default menu items and restart adapting to your usage.

   ◆ From the Menu Animations list, specify the way you want the menus to behave when you open and close them.

3. Click Close.

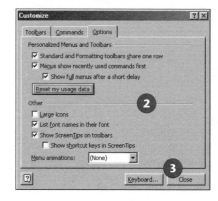

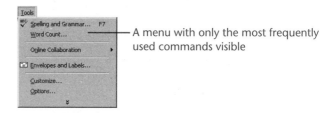

A menu with only the most frequently used commands visible

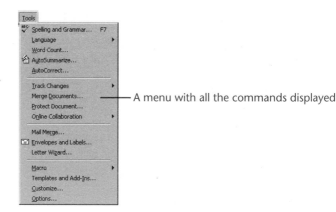

A menu with all the commands displayed

Changing the Way Word Displays Toolbars

Word conserves window space by placing the Standard and Formatting toolbars on the same line and then, based on the way you work, adapting which toolbar buttons are displayed. If you prefer easy access to all the buttons at the cost of some window space, you can tell Word to put these two toolbars on separate lines. You can also enlarge the icons on the buttons so that they're easier to see, and you can display or hide the ScreenTips that identify each button.

TIP

Change places. *When you drag the Standard or Formatting toolbar into a different position, the option that causes these two toolbars to share a line is automatically turned off.*

Set Your Options

1. Choose Customize from the Tools menu.

2. On the Options tab of the Customize dialog box, do any of the following:

   ◆ Turn off the Standard And Formatting Toolbars Share One Row check box to have the toolbars appear on separate lines.

   ◆ Turn on the Large Icons check box to increase the size of the icons on the toolbar buttons.

   ◆ Turn on or off the Show ScreenTips On Toolbars check box to show or hide the tips that identify the toolbar buttons.

   ◆ Turn on the Show Shortcut Keys In ScreenTips check box to have the ScreenTips display any keyboard shortcut keys that you can use instead of clicking a toolbar button.

3. Click Close.

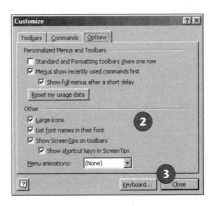

The Standard and Formatting toolbars on separate lines

Large icons on the toolbar buttons

A ScreenTip displaying shortcut keys

Adding Commands to Your Menus

Word displays the most frequently used commands on its menus, but you can place additional commands on any menu to simplify your work. Also, if you create your own commands by recording macros, you can place the macros, with appropriate descriptive names, on a menu.

Add a Command

1. Choose Customize from the Tools menu, and click the Commands tab.

2. Select a category to find the command.

3. Drag the command to the menu you want it on, wait for the menu to open, and place the command where you want it to appear.

4. Click the menu name to close the menu.

Drag from here...

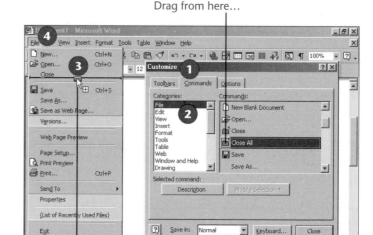

...to here.

Move a Menu or a Command

1. Click the menu name on the menu bar, and do any of the following:

   ◆ Drag a menu to a new location on the menu bar or on a toolbar.

   ◆ Drag a command to a new location on a menu or on a toolbar.

   ◆ Drag a menu or a command to a blank area of the document window to delete the menu or the command.

Some menus have been moved.

Drag a command to change its location.

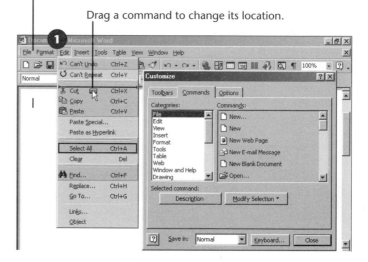

SEE ALSO

For information about assigning an item to a key combination or a toolbar, see "Quickly Applying Standardized Formatting" on page 88 and "Customizing Toolbars" on page 318.

For information about creating a macro, see "Creating Your Own Commands" on page 312.

TRY THIS

What's on the menu?
Choose Customize from the Tools menu, and, on the Commands tab, select New Menu. Drag the New Menu item from the Commands list onto the menu bar. Right-click the menu name and rename it. Now select different categories in the Customize dialog box and drag items onto the new menu.

Add a Macro

1. Select Macros in the Categories list.

2. Select the macro to be added.

3. Drag the macro to the menu you want it on, wait for the menu to open, and place the button where you want it to appear.

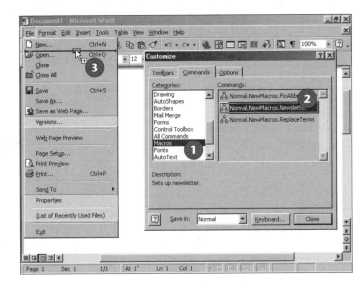

Rename a Menu or a Menu Item

1. Right-click the command or the macro name on the menu, or the menu name on the menu bar.

2. Change the text in the Name box.

3. Click outside the menu to close it.

4. Click Close to close the Customize dialog box.

Use spaces to separate words, and add an ampersand (&) before the letter you want to use as the access key (the underlined letter in a command).

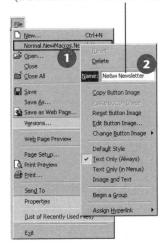

Customizing Toolbars

As you work with different types of materials, you might find yourself wishing that some of Word's toolbars could be arranged more conveniently for your purposes. Well, guess what? They can be! You can change which tools are displayed, move the tools into different places on a toolbar, and even move tools from one toolbar to another.

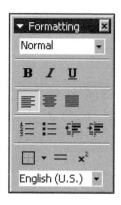

Add or Remove Buttons

1. Click the down arrow at the end of a docked toolbar or in front of the toolbar name in a floating toolbar.

2. Point to Add Or Remove Buttons to open the list of buttons.

3. Do either of the following:

   ◆ Click a checked button to remove that button from the toolbar.

   ◆ Click an unchecked button to add it to the toolbar.

4. Repeat step 3 to select the buttons you want displayed.

5. Click in your document to close the list of buttons.

Checked items appear on the toolbar.

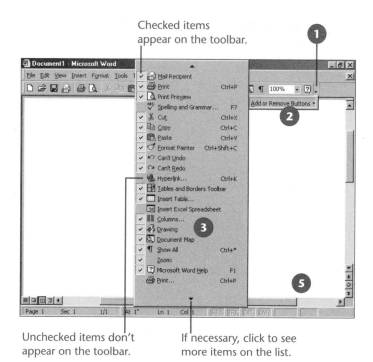

Unchecked items don't appear on the toolbar.

If necessary, click to see more items on the list.

For information about creating a new toolbar and adding different types of commands, see "Quickly Applying Standardized Formatting" on page 88.

TIP

Copy or delete a button. *Hold down the Ctrl key if you want to copy a button rather than move it. Drag a button off the toolbar to delete it.*

TIP

Reset a toolbar. *To return a toolbar to its original configuration, select the toolbar on the Toolbars tab of the Customize dialog box, and click Reset.*

Move a Button or a List Box

1. Point to a button or a list box that you want to move.

2. Hold down the Alt key and drag it to a new location on the same toolbar or on a different one.

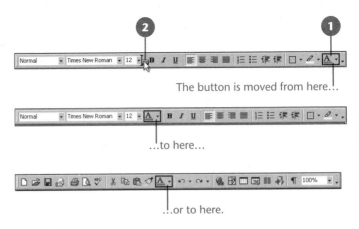

The button is moved from here...

...to here...

...or to here.

Modify a Button

1. Choose Customize from the Tools menu.

2. Right-click the button.

3. Use the commands on the shortcut menu to change the button.

4. Repeat steps 2 and 3 to change any other buttons.

5. Click Close in the Customize dialog box.

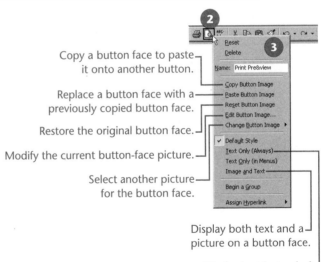

Copy a button face to paste it onto another button.

Replace a button face with a previously copied button face.

Restore the original button face.

Modify the current button-face picture.

Select another picture for the button face.

Display both text and a picture on a button face.

Display text instead of a button-face picture.

Speeding Up Word

Word's many amazing features can gobble up an amount of your computer's resources that's equally amazing. Unless your computer has a huge memory and a fast processor, you could spend a lot of time waiting...and waiting...and waiting. It's not really Word's fault—you're just putting more demands on it than your computer system can handle. You can make Word work faster by turning off some of its features. You won't be losing much; you can often run a background feature by itself or find a different way to get the same result.

Limit Your View
Word works hard to show you exactly how your docu-ment will appear, either in print or on line. To speed up your work, work in Normal view—don't worry about the layout just yet. Limit the items that are displayed in your document—for example, in the Options dialog box, turn on the Picture Placeholders option to show empty boxes instead of actual images, and turn off the Ani-mated Text option. In the Customize dialog box, turn off the List Font Names In Their Font option, and select None in the Menu Animations list.

Limit the Background Operations
If you've waited for Word to catch up with you as it checks your spelling and grammar, and if you've ever listened to it grinding away while it saves a document, it's time to suspend some of the background operations. In the Options dialog box, turn off the Background Repagination, Check Spelling As You Type, Check Grammar As You Type, and Allow Background Saves options. If you're using automatic hyphenation, turn it off. If the Office Assistant is hanging around, turn off some of its options or give it the day off. If you have a query, press the F1 key, and the Assistant will reappear.

Check the Document
After you've completed your document, you can start proofreading it using one feature at a time. With the insertion point at the beginning of the document, press the F7 key to check the spelling and grammar. Switch to Print Layout or Web Layout view and inspect the layout, including fonts and page breaks. If you want, turn automatic hyphenation back on. As a final check, turn off the Picture Placeholders option and turn on the Animated Text option.

Tweak Your System
Word often works faster when you make Windows more efficient. There are numerous places you can opti-mize performance, but you'll probably gain the most by making sure you have adequate free space on your hard disk. Word uses any extra space for temporary files; Windows uses the space to create "virtual memory." If necessary (and if possible), remove any Office features you don't use. Make sure that Word and the features you use the most are on your hard disk and don't need to be run from a CD or over a network.

For optimal performance, you'll need to keep Word, Office, and Windows up to date. Most versions of Windows have frequent updates and service packs that improve performance and fix any little bugs that might pop up. Word and Office also have occasional updates, patches, and service packs.

Repairing Word

This has probably *never* happened to you, and you might be shocked to hear it, but the terrible truth is that sometimes things actually go wrong on computers! In the unlikely event that Word or Office suddenly stops working properly, and if you suspect that some files might be damaged, you can automatically reinstall all the necessary files so that any corrupted files will be replaced.

TIP

Back up! *Always back up your files before you attempt to do any troubleshooting.*

SEE ALSO

For information about using the installation program, see "Adding or Removing Components" on page 306.

Detect and Fix Errors

1. Close all the open programs (except Word) on your computer.

2. In Word, save and close any open documents.

3. Choose Detect And Repair from the Help menu.

4. Click the Start button, and follow the instructions that appear. You'll need your Office or Word CD or your network connection to the setup files, and eventually you'll be told to close Word.

5. After the files have been fixed, run Word, and try to duplicate the problem you encountered.

6. If the problem persists, use the installation program to remove Office. Then restart the computer and reinstall Office.

7. If the problem still persists, seek professional technical help.

Word automatically starts the Repair Office part of the Microsoft Office Setup Maintenance Mode and reinstalls all the Word or Office files required for your current setup.

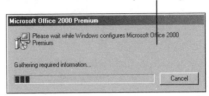

Getting More Stuff

What if you can't find the information you need in this book? And what if the Office Assistant is of no assistance? And what if you don't know how to tweak your system with the latest fixes, patches, and add-ons? Don't despair. With Internet access, you have a wealth of information, including all the latest news about Word, ways to solve problems, and links to all the new and improved software for Word.

Get Help from Microsoft

1. Connect to the Internet if you're not already connected.

2. Choose Office On The Web from the Help menu.

3. If you aren't already registered with Office Update, complete the registration information.

4. Use the navigation bar to go to the topic you want information about. Because Web pages are constantly being changed and updated, what you see might not exactly match what's shown on this page.

5. Click the links for more information, downloads, or other updates.

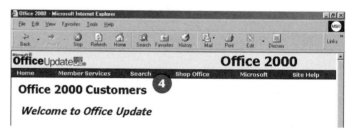

Index

Italicized page numbers refer you to information you'll find in a Tip or a "Try This" entry.

Jerry Joyce has had a long-standing relationship with Microsoft: he was the technical editor on numerous books published by Microsoft Press, and he has written manuals, help files, and specifications for various Microsoft products. As a programmer, he has tried to make using a computer as simple as using any household appliance, but he has yet to succeed. Jerry's alter ego is that of a marine biologist; he has conducted research from the Arctic to the Antarctic and has published extensively on marine-mammal and fisheries issues. As an antidote to staring at his computer screen, he enjoys traveling, birding, boating, and wandering about beaches, wetlands, and mountains.

Marianne Moon has worked in the publishing world for many years as proofreader, editor, and writer—sometimes all three simultaneously. She has been editing and proofreading Microsoft Press books since 1984 and has written and edited documentation for Microsoft products such as Microsoft Works, Flight Simulator, Space Simulator, Golf, Publisher, the Microsoft Mouse, and Greetings Workshop. In another life, she was chief cook and bottlewasher for her own catering service and wrote cooking columns for several newspapers. When she's not chained to her computer, she likes gardening, cooking, traveling, writing poetry, and knitting sweaters for tiny dogs.

Marianne and **Jerry** own and operate **Moon Joyce Resources,** a small consulting company. They are coauthors of *Microsoft Word 97 At a Glance, Microsoft Windows 95 At a Glance, Microsoft Windows NT Workstation 4.0 At a Glance,* and *Microsoft Windows 98 At a Glance.* They've had an 18-year working relationship and have been married for 8 years. If you have questions or comments about any of their books, you can reach them at moonjoyceresourc@hotmail.com.

The manuscript for this book was prepared and submitted to Microsoft Press in electronic form. Text files were prepared using Microsoft Word 97. Pages were composed using QuarkXPress 3.32 for the Power Macintosh, with text in ITC Stone Serif and ITC Stone Sans and display type in ITC Stone Sans Semibold. Composed pages were delivered to the printer as electronic prepress files.

Cover Design and Illustration
Tim Girvin Design

Interior Graphic Artist
WebFoot Productions

Interior Illustrators
s.bishop.design
Judith Joyce

Typographer
Kari Fera

Proofreader
Alice Copp Smith

Indexer
Moon Joyce Resources